YOU WILL KNOW MY NAME

CAROLYNN G. A. BROOKS

Copyright © 2016

All rights reserved. Except as permitted under the
US Copyright Act of 1976, no part of this publication may
be reproduced, distributed, or transmitted in any form or by
any means, or stored in a database or retrieval system,
without the prior written permission of the publisher.

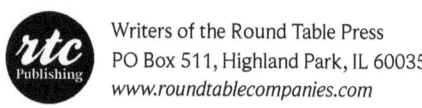

Writers of the Round Table Press
PO Box 511, Highland Park, IL 60035
www.roundtablecompanies.com

publisher: *Corey Michael Blake*
president: *Kristin Westberg*
project management: *Leeann Sanders*
executive editor: *Sarah Morrison*
editorial support: *Maureen Batty*
proofreading: *Adam Lawrence*
facts keeper: *Mike Winicour*
creative director: *Sunny DiMartino*
last looks: *Christian Panneck*

Printed in the United States of America

First Edition: September 2016
10 9 8 7 6 5 4 3 2 1

Library of Congress Cataloging-in-Publication Data
Brooks, Carolynn G. A.
You will know my name / Carolynn G. A. Brooks.—1st ed. p. cm.
ISBN Paperback: 978-1-939418-85-2
ISBN Digital: 978-1-939418-86-9
Library of Congress Control Number: 2016951002

RTC Publishing is an imprint of Writers of the Round Table, Inc.
Writers of the Round Table Press and the RTC Publishing logo
are trademarks of Writers of the Round Table, Inc.

*Scripture quotations marked KJV are taken from
the Holy Bible, King James Version, Public Domain.*

*Scripture quotations marked NIV are taken from
the Holy Bible, New International Version®, NIV®
Copyright © 1973, 1978, 1984, 2011 by Biblica, Inc.®
Used by permission. All rights reserved worldwide.*

I dedicate this book to my Creator,
   the author and perfector of my faith.

   Thank you for trusting me with this amazing assignment called life.

CONTENTS

Acknowledgments ix

Introduction xiii

prologue
SECRETS IN A BOX 1

chapters

A MYSTERIOUS MOTHER	5	**BREAKING FREE**	133
A CONFUSING START	14	**POWER**	143
IT TAKES A VILLAGE	24	**A PRAYER**	160
WHAT THAT CHILD NEEDS	37	**OUR HOUSE**	179
FINDING MY VOICE	49	**DÉJÀ VU**	193
ANSWERING THE CALL	58	**WATER IN THE DESERT**	213
AN EDUCATION	73	**AT LAST**	232
CHANGING COURSE	84	**SOMETHING WORTH FIGHTING FOR**	255
TO HAVE AND TO HOLD	96	**SHIFTING SANDS**	276
NEW LIFE	107	**VALEDICTION**	295
THOSE WHO HELP THEMSELVES	123		

Epilogue 307

ACKNOWLEDGMENTS

"What would you be willing to attempt for God if you knew you couldn't fail?" My answer every time is, "Walk boldly by faith."

Writing this book has been a challenging nine-year journey that I might not have embarked on if I had known what it would take to get to this point. Once God planted the seed and told me, "First write the book," I promised Him I wouldn't stop until the assignment was completed. And then I prayed for the wisdom, capability, and resources to bring this assignment to completion.

I want to thank the most important people who have contributed to the life that I'm sharing with you: my birth mother, who gave me life; Aunt Kathleen and Aunt Etta, who stood in the gap; and Aunt Tutta, my intercessor and the one who gave my spirit wings. I want to thank all my Dixon, Illinois heroes who were a part of the village that guided my life, helped develop my self-image, saw the gifts God had placed in me, and encouraged my potential. To my three sons, Preston, Canthon, and Clinton, who have always been my reason for living and pushing through perceived limitations. And to my husband, Jimmie, who has always trusted the paths God has put me on and encouraged me to step out boldly in faith. He forfeited so many weekends that had me locked away writing instead of cooking or doing something fun with him. He went with me wherever my research took me and never doubted the outcome. Best of all, he's always allowed me to be me.

I want to recognize and thank the three spiritual leaders and mentors who are responsible for my spiritual awakening, rebirth, and evolution: Rev. Rudolph Shoultz (Second Baptist Church, Dixon, IL); Rev. Louis E. Malone (St. Luke's Missionary Baptist Church, Rockford, IL); and Pastor Bill Winston (Living Word Christian Center, Chicago, IL). It is their voices and teachings that have given me the foundation I need to "walk boldly by faith," always willing to attempt great things for God and expecting great things from God, who is my source, my only source.

I want to acknowledge and thank my cousin Evelyn Williams-Glisson, who saved me thousands of dollars on counseling as she shared the good, the bad, and the messiest times of my life. She never said, "Your time is up," but was always available and spent hours on the telephone listening to me cry, celebrating my victories, and loving me in spite of my failures. And to my special friend Bonita Bryant: I want to thank you for always speaking this book and its message into being. You have been a godsend.

From the beginning when I took my first step of faith and began writing this book, there have been so many who encouraged me and participated by reading it, editing it, and giving their advice and invaluable suggestions. I am grateful to Corey Blake, founder and CEO of Round Table Companies, for helping me bring this vision to reality and assigning writer and senior editor Sarah Morrison to the project of critiquing, editing, and polishing the manuscript. Thank you, Sarah, for pushing me through to complete the assignment God gave me to do.

It is those who suffer the most who yield the most. And it is through pain that God gets the most out of us, for His glory and for the blessing of others. Our life is very mysterious. In fact, it would be totally unexplainable unless we believed that God was preparing us for events and ministries that lie unseen beyond the veil of the eternal world— where spirits like tempered steel will be required for special service.

—L.B. Cowman, *Streams in the Desert*

INTRODUCTION

Someone once told me, "Girl, you've got it good. I wish I was you."

I had to laugh and tell her, "My journey wasn't meant for you. In fact, my journey might have killed you."

I've had success in my life, rising to the executive ranks of the business world to the position of vice president, chief diversity officer at a Fortune 500 retailer. But as I emphasize in my diversity work, it's impossible to understand someone without taking the time to learn who they are and what they've been through.

In spring of 2007, I heard God speaking to my inner being, telling me, "Write your story." I felt the familiar spark of excitement that lets me know the Holy Spirit is directing me. Recognizing this, I was determined to be as obedient as a well-trained puppy and to move as boldly as a lion to complete the assignment I'd received in my spirit.

Yet I wasn't sure how to tell my story. I spent months trying to find someone who could help me—ghostwriters, editors, and more—but none of these options felt right. I also struggled with doubt, asking myself over and over, *Why would someone want to read my story?* The beginning of my life was unique, but many others have had more unorthodox life beginnings and faced greater adversity. Many people's stories are more captivating and profound than mine.

Then, on Monday, September 3, 2007, God abruptly awakened me at four a.m. from a sound sleep. He told me, "Start writing the book." I argued out loud with Him, saying, "I don't have the first idea how to write a book." After half an hour of tossing and turning, I threw back the covers, sat on the edge of the bed, and broke into laughter, shaking my head. I knew I had to do as the Author of my life commanded in Jeremiah 30:2 (KJV): "Write thee all the words that I have spoken unto thee in a book." I would put my trust in His plans, believing He would guide me in this assignment.

The book you're about to read is an authentic, vulnerable account of my trials, triumphs, and spiritual transformations. I was created to live my life to demonstrate the power embedded in all of us, the power to push through limitations—whether real or perceived—and show the world the glory of God.

This book is about my journey to put together the puzzle pieces of my complicated and mysterious past—puzzle pieces I found in a box, tucked away and forgotten. It's about how I used my own words of power to overcome debilitating words of destruction and evolved my self-image, overcoming traumatic events and abusive situations. My story hinges on faith, perseverance, and bold determination to defeat the weapons designed to destroy me and keep me from my destiny: unwarranted hatred and hostility, sexual abuse, racism, workplace sexual harassment, financial ruin, and even more. If my faith had been in man, I would have given up by now.

Most of us like to make plans for our lives, and I'm someone who has always had a plan—along with a back-up plan. As you walk beside me through my past, you'll see how my life seemed to get twisted out of order, taking me in *very* different directions than I'd planned. You'll come along with me through abandonment, pain, and rejection on my way to faith, forgiveness, and love.

I want to take you with me on my path to spiritual empowerment. We all need to make difficult decisions in our lives, and you'll share in the decisions I made using the information available to me at the time.

Sometimes, though, even when I knew the right decision, I still couldn't make it because I was so tightly bound to my personal plans.

Yet with faith, forgiveness, and love, my mess has become my ministry. I learned to take what I'd learned from my trials and shape them into triumphs. I hope my story will help you realize that everything has its purpose. In the end, you'll see how the adversity I faced throughout my life readied me for the destiny and purpose God had designed for me.

I pray this book inspires you never to allow someone else to define, diminish, or limit you, but instead empowers you to push through your perceived limitations—bad decisions you've made, words spoken to you to wound your spirit—and open your heart to your own unique and wonderful purpose. As I've learned all too well, the only way forward is to PUSH . . . persevere until something happens!

prologue

SECRETS IN A BOX

It was a beautiful late spring day in Dixon, Illinois, but my sisters and I were not going to enjoy it. We all dreaded the task at hand: cleaning out my mother's house after her death.

Here we were, already struggling with the tension, assumptions, hurt feelings, and resentment so common among grieving families. But now we had to sort through the mountains of belongings she had accumulated during her four decades living in the house.

I was working alone in the basement when I moved into the furnace room, a small space with its own door. This room housed the incinerator, water softener, and furnace, and one wall was lined with shelves. When I walked into the room, I found it surprisingly tidy, especially compared to the rest of the basement. The shelves were stacked with old books, magazines, and boxes. I went through the boxes one by one, discovering little worth keeping.

Exhausted, I was about to give up when I pulled out one more cardboard box, the kind that holds reams of paper. As soon as I lifted the lid and started thumbing through the papers inside, I knew this box was different.

It contained a collection of secrets—some answering questions I'd asked my whole life and others raising questions I had never known to ask. I knew what an intensely private person my mother had been, and I couldn't believe what I was uncovering. It was as if she had left this box, albeit well tucked away, for me to discover.

I unfolded a lawn chair, sank into it, and pulled the box onto my lap. I sifted through the contents of the box, feeling like an archaeologist discovering a gateway to the past. There were her old paycheck stubs, college report cards, diplomas, transcripts, letters, and other documents.

Then my breath caught. I opened a yellowing envelope and discovered three birth certificates, all announcing the birth of the same baby.

Me.

I was born on Wednesday, November 14, 1951, in Kansas City, Missouri. All three birth certificates agreed on this. But then they started to disagree.

The first birth certificate, registered on December 7, 1951, showed my name as Carolyn Gracie Johnson, born to a twenty-three-year-old mother named Lydia Johnson, from 6134 St. Lawrence Avenue in Chicago, Illinois. The time of birth was noted as 4:30 p.m.

A second certificate, registered on January 12, 1952, showed my name as Carolyn Gracie Williams, born to a twenty-nine-year old mother named Zelodious Pinkye Williams—the woman I would know as my mother for most of my life—from 606 Monroe Avenue in Dixon, Illinois. My time of birth was noted as 4:45 p.m. As with the first birth certificate, there was no father listed. On this birth certificate, though, I was marked "illegitimate."

I sat and stared at that word. I'd heard it a thousand times, but seeing it used to describe my birth made me feel debased. It's difficult to explain how terrible and ugly it felt so see my triumphant entrance into the world labeled that way, as an event unauthorized by the law, not in accordance with accepted standards. No birth should ever be labeled "illegitimate."

A third birth certificate appeared to be a copy of the second one, but the name Carolyn Gracie was crossed out. In its place was a new name: Alversia Harolyn Williams. This copy, too, listed no father and said I was illegitimate.

I was shocked. Even as I felt slapped by that cruel word, I also had the feeling that I now held the key to mysteries that had confused me my whole life—mysteries created by the lies my mother told.

Mother-daughter relationships can be complicated. Often these relationships grow softer and easier over time, but even as we both grew older, that wasn't the case for me and my mother. There were unspoken lies that lingered between us, always seeming to prevent us from making a true connection. I have a lifetime of memories of trying in vain to connect with my mother.

While clearing out her things, I found a letter I'd written to her two months after surgery revealed she had cancer. She had hidden the letter in her lingerie drawer. In it, I wrote, "Being your daughter has been one of the most difficult challenges of my life . . . but as difficult as I've found it to be your daughter, I know that was God's plan." I asked her for a chance to spend time with her. I wanted to ask questions to understand her better. I told her, "I want to see beyond the image and see what caused the pain, disappointment, and sense of loss I hear in your conversations. When I know that, I'll know the woman who is my mother."

I remembered asking my mother if she'd received the letter, hoping to start a conversation. I remembered her saying it had never been delivered.

Little did I know, while writing that letter to my mother, that a trove of her secrets sat on a shelf in the basement, waiting to be discovered. In the box, I found more letters—letters condemning the choices my mother had made and letters that made it clear how much I did not know. My mother was a keeper of secrets, and now I realize that those secrets formed a veil between us, keeping us from truly seeing one another. Her generation, her brothers and sisters, contributed to this culture of secrecy. There were things we children simply didn't need to know or understand, they thought.

I didn't feel the same way. I thought I had a right to know my history, to find out where I came from.

Archaeologists use their discoveries to teach the world about the past. Using my discovery, this box of history and kept secrets, I was determined to understand my past, finally fitting together the pieces of the puzzle.

In my search for answers, I pushed through a cloud of memories. Words I thought had been forgotten, things people had said to me long ago, returned to me.

You're nothing but a bastard.
Hold your head erect, and command all men's respect.
You're the worst thing that ever happened to your mother.

Some of these words shaped who I would become—either because they inspired me or because I resolved not to let them become my truth. I felt certain there was more for me to discover. I was determined to uncover the truth, which I thought would finally set me free.

I needed to know.

chapter 1

A MYSTERIOUS MOTHER

To understand where I came from, I first had to understand who my mother was and where she came from—which was no easy feat. My knowledge of her family history is a puzzle I put together gradually. Some pieces of the puzzle I found in the box in her basement, and others I found in conversations I overheard, answers to questions I asked, and research I did based on what I knew about her past. The puzzle is large and complex, and there are still some pieces missing, buried in questions that have never been answered.

Growing up, I realized that people were drawn to my mother. She was a natural beauty who seldom wore makeup, with a rich ebony complexion, high cheekbones, almond-shaped deep-set eyes, and chiseled features. She carried her long-limbed figure elegantly. She had strong, broad shoulders and black hair that covered her long neck. She had a hearty, robust laugh, but she also had a tongue that could cut like a knife. With a slightly raised eyebrow or a drawn-tight mouth, she conveyed her disapproval, her condemnation. She showed no sympathy for human weakness or for excuses. She had strong opinions and political views, which she expressed through her community involvement and activity in volunteer programs. She was generous, but she never forgot a loan. She was a study in contradictions.

I learned there were many elements at play early on in my mother's life that could impact the way she viewed the world and the decisions she would make later in life. She and her family endured life before the Civil Rights Movement, and I'm sure the conditions of our country shaped her character and the decisions she would make.

Zelodious Pinkye Williams—everyone called her "Zee"—was born in 1922 in Mound Bayou, Mississippi, a small, all-black city in the Delta's bottomlands. My mother's parents had twelve children, but only eight survived to adulthood. Mom was the fifth of those eight. Her father was a veteran of the Spanish-American War; history and his Army papers suggest that his colored regiment likely fought alongside Roosevelt's Rough Riders in Cuba. A farmer by trade, he was also a visionary inventor and entrepreneur. I found an expired patent he'd filed for a device designed to register the number of people entering and exiting streetcars. He died when he was fifty-five years old, and my mother was just eight. My mom's mother died two years later at just forty-three years old.

By age ten, my mother had lost both her parents.

Aside from the deep personal losses she suffered, the historical conditions of the Deep South in the 1920s tell me that my mother's life, as a dirt-poor colored child growing up in Mississippi, was not easy. It was a tremendously difficult time to be black. The year my mother was born, the Dyer Anti-Lynching Bill—which would have imposed punishment on those found guilty of lynching and other mob violence—was filibustered and defeated. Over the next seven years, the Ku Klux Klan lynched more than three hundred African Americans in the South. Mom grew up during the era of Jim Crow laws, which subjected black people to constant humiliation as they lived in a state of unrelenting fear. The Supreme Court had sanctioned explicit racism, saying that white and black children could not even attend the same schools. Black Americans faced not just the threat of physical violence, but also severely prohibitive voting restrictions and dramatically limited educational, workplace, and financial opportunities.

This was the world my mother had to exist in—and attempt to overcome.

Mom would tell me of her childhood hardships while she hot combed and braided my hair. Sitting between her knees, I gazed down at her dark, scarred feet. She told me that she had worn shoes only for school and church. I remember running my finger over one particularly nasty scar on her leg, a gash from a line of barbed wire she jumped while white boys chased her.

When the Great Depression hit the country in 1929, the family's life was further weighed down by poverty and loss. Once my mother's parents died, her oldest sister, Willie Corotha, lovingly called Tutta—who was nineteen years old when the children were left orphans—assumed responsibility for raising the family. Tutta demanded that everyone get a job in order to financially contribute to the household. Eventually, the family moved to Clarksdale, Mississippi.

Whenever my mother reminisced with her siblings about growing up, I listened closely, my curiosity insatiable. I imagined them supporting each other, arguing, forming alliances. Florida-Carolina ("FC"), the next oldest after Tutta, and Otha ("Papa T"), the oldest boy, left home soon after their parents' deaths to fend for themselves, floating in and out of the family circle from then on. Jesse, the baby of the family, was taken to live with an uncle. Canthon, a free spirit known also as "Kent" or "Buddy," would catch a train and be gone for months. Occasionally he'd come back rundown or ill—once from a bad case of syphilis that temporarily blinded him—and needing to be nursed back to health, only to leave again once he was better.

With FC and Papa T gone, Buddy off riding the rails, and Jesse taken away, no-nonsense, practical Tutta was left taking care of two girls, my mother and her younger sister Cleretha, and the youngest boy still at home, Narvell—even as Tutta was often sickly herself, nursing a chronic stomach condition.

Uncle Narvell, who would grow up to be tall, slim, and sharply intelligent, would play devil's advocate in arguments just to show he could win. "If someone would just pay me to think," he liked to say, "I could make the family rich." I loved hearing stories about the close relationship between Mom, Aunt Cleretha, and Uncle Narvell.

But it was the closeness between Mom and Aunt Cleretha I heard about the most. Just seventeen months apart and similar in appearance, Zee and Cle, as they were known, liked to pretend they were twins. They spent many nights lying awake planning for their futures while Uncle Narvell snored.

Aunt Tutta told me that Aunt Cleretha was the happy-go-lucky one, the partier who loved to laugh and have fun. She always had a boyfriend, whereas Aunt Tutta couldn't remember my mother dating. Aunt Tutta always said Mom was the serious one—focused, strong-willed, and industrious—and she could squeeze money tighter than anybody. When she earned money working in the cotton fields or cleaning wealthy white folks' kitchens, she would always squirrel some away for emergencies. When someone in the family needed help, my mother was the one to pull up a plank in the shotgun house or dig up a can from a hole in the backyard to dole out some of her stashed funds—a part of her character that never changed.

Aunt Tutta was the relative who was most willing to tell me about my family and my early years. Sitting at her kitchen table or in her living room, we would chat while she petted her dog and ate the peculiar food she favored: brick-hard toast dipped in creamy, overcooked oatmeal. She preferred to eat without her teeth in. Aunt Tutta was a slender woman who cared nothing for fashion, pulling back her fine hair with combs and often wearing her clothes in a disarranged way or without a bra. She always seemed more like my grandmother than my aunt, having very little formal education but the wisdom of Solomon. She was someone I always trusted—I don't believe she ever lied to me. It was she who gave me strength when I needed it.

Growing up together in such hard times, my mother and Aunt Cleretha made a pact that they would always be together and would always support one another. I imagine being orphaned at such a young age made them think seriously about family and responsibility. They agreed that if either of them died before their children were grown, the other would care for those children—an agreement that would one day serve as justification for changing the course of a family.

Many of their conversations revolved around forming plans that would take them far away from the harsh life of poverty and the stifling chokehold of racial violence. They understood that education was the key to a better life, and so my mother and Aunt Cleretha vowed to be the leaders of the Williams family, bringing them out of hardship and into opportunity.

Even high school diplomas would have made them the most educated members of the family, but they set their sights on college degrees. For two dirt-poor colored girls in the '20s and '30s, this was a lofty ambition, but they were determined. They had very big dreams, and they never saw failure as an option.

When my mother described her childhood to me, she spoke most often of the rays of light that came into her life and guided her, like beacons, toward her dreams: her teachers. She was influenced by the numerous black business owners and community leaders she saw working in Mound Bayou and Clarksdale, watching as they fought back against the Great Depression and the forces of racism to manage successful businesses.

In the midst of hardship and turmoil, as the family struggled to work and survive, the promise of education rang louder in my mother's ear than anything else. Seeds of greatness existed in my mother, and the powerful voices in her life tended those seeds, nurturing her ambition and confidence. My mother's passion for education was the instrument that would draw out the potential God had placed in her.

At the age of twenty, Mom was able to begin her college education. She worked hard not only to finance her own education, but to help Aunt Cleretha attend college as well. Both sisters received degrees from Alcorn A&M State College, now known as Alcorn State University. My mother graduated in 1945 with her degree in Home Economics, but she wasn't finished. At that time, opportunities for young black women were still severely limited. She knew that to compete in the white-dominated workforce, she would need a master's degree in order to achieve her dream, which was to become a teacher.

But the tides of life shifted, and her dream was deferred.

• • •

Mom had just been accepted to the University of Iowa to pursue her Master of Education degree when she met my biological father, Harold, on a Mississippi-bound train where he worked as a porter. I never knew much about him, and I would meet him only once before he died—after I was already grown up and starting my own family. Always intensely curious, I gathered snippets of information where I could. Uncle Narvell and his wife Aunt Kathleen once recalled the one time when Mom brought Harold to meet them, and he refused to get out of the car because he didn't want to get mud on his shoes. He was stylish and fastidious about his clothes—a trait I would inherit.

When my mother learned she was pregnant, she assumed that her condition would result in Harold proposing marriage in order to make things right. Instead, when she revealed her predicament, he revealed his own: he had a wife and son safely tucked away in another town.

Now what? The timing was bad, but the situation was even worse. In the '50s, racism was deeply institutionalized. The country was still living under the "separate but equal" Supreme Court ruling of 1896. Schools, restaurants, restrooms, and even drinking fountains were set up for "Whites" and "Colored" only. For my mother—a black woman striving to be a teacher—the odds were already daunting. Having a child outside of wedlock, she believed, would dash her dream completely. People held far stricter values and morals then. Being an unwed mother was a disgrace, and abortion was illegal. My mother wanted a piece of the American Dream for herself, and she knew what it would take to get it.

So there my mother was: proud, determined, furious, and ashamed. The plans she had established for her life were slipping away, and her dreams would need to be delayed. I was a threat not just to her dreams, but also to her image of herself. Had I been conceived after the Supreme Court's *Roe v. Wade* decision legalized abortion nationwide, I would almost certainly never have been born. In my late twenties, while I was dealing with some medical concerns, my doctor asked me whether my mother had ever taken a drug called DES to prevent miscarriage. When I asked my mother about this, her response was dry and sarcastic, containing no hint of apology. "No ma'am," she retorted. "I never went to a doctor, and I certainly wasn't taking drugs to keep you. I did everything I could to lose you." She tried inserting hangers into her uterus, she told me, and she drank a concoction that promised to cause miscarriage. She went so far as to fling herself down a flight of stairs—but I hung on.

I endured.

Mom came up with a plan. She told everyone she would be attending school full time in Ames, Iowa, but instead she would go into hiding. She planned to have me in Missouri, where it was easier to put a baby up for adoption without leaving a paper trail.

My mother traveled to a small resort town called Excelsior Springs, about thirty miles from Kansas City, Missouri. She got a job as a maid at the historic Elms Hotel, a palatial building constructed of native limestone with grand ballrooms and inviting verandas. Guests at the hotel relaxed in mineral spring baths and soaked up sunlight on the balconies while my proud mother swept and scrubbed.

She used the alias Lydia Johnson, the name I would see on the first of my three birth certificates, and said that she was from Chicago. She claimed she was twenty-three, when in fact she was twenty-nine. Carefully and methodically, she created a lie that would allow her to place her unwanted infant up for adoption undetected and get back to the life she had planned for herself. All these lies were designed to prevent me from ever finding her, thereby enabling her to deny my existence.

This was Mom's life for four months. She would one day describe to me how she kept her swelling stomach bound by tight clothing during the day, allowing me to move freely in her belly only at night. There would be no baby showers, no affectionate pats on the stomach, no assurances of a warm and accepting home awaiting me. I was hated and cherished at the same time.

I believe I felt the anguish of her emotional rejection while I was still in her womb. I know this about her: she could have never embraced something she was planning to give away. I was persona non grata before I ever drew my first breath, and I would continue to feel that rejection and abandonment from her in some form or fashion for the rest of our lives together.

When my mother could no longer deny her condition, she confided in another woman working at the hotel. This woman introduced Mom to a priest, hopeful that he could provide some guidance and assistance. My mother explained her plan to the priest, who told her about a place called Florence Home for Colored Girls. At the Florence Home—a counterpart to the city's many similar organizations for white women—black unwed mothers received shelter, medical care, guidance, and education from volunteer physicians, nurses, counselors, teachers, and religious leaders.

Florence Home was in Kansas City, Missouri, a major hub on the railroad line. The city was known as a place where women went to dump babies.

As quietly as my mother had arrived at the Elms Hotel four months earlier, she left. She had never had a medical examination, so she was unsure of her due date. Instinctively she felt it was time to make a visit to the place the priest had told her about. She took a bus trip to Florence Home, arriving at the four-story colonial-style facility the evening of November 13, 1951. She was taken in and examined, and the next morning, while she was eating breakfast, her water broke.

I was born on November 14, 1951, after eight and a half hours of labor. My mother had attached only one hope to my birth.

"Is it a boy?" she asked the nurse.

"No," said the nurse, "it's a pretty little girl with a full head of hair."

My mother wanted to be released immediately after giving birth, eager to get back to the life she'd put on hold. The spring semester of her graduate program would start in January, and she planned to be there. She saw other young mothers at Florence Home receiving their newborns, but she didn't want to see me.

I believe she had willed herself not to care about me, not to get attached. She just wanted to get out and get away from everything that reminded her of this diversion from her path and the decision she had made.

But the staff at Florence Home counseled her to remain there for a few more days to recuperate. Forty-eight hours after my birth, the head nurse—who had met my mother only once, when she was admitted—acted on some feeling, something she had seen in my mother beyond the words they had exchanged. There were policies in place designed to separate mothers from the babies they had decided to put up for adoption, but something compelled this nurse to break the rules.

Every year on my birthday, I used to play a game with my mother. I would say, "Just think, this time eight (or nine, or ten) years ago, you were giving birth to me." I wanted her to talk about my birth. During one of these conversations, my mother told me the story of when she and I first set eyes on each other.

She remembered: "The nurse never even asked me. She just walked into the room with you in her arms and said, 'You'll never be able to forgive yourself if you don't at least look into her face and tell her goodbye. You have to know who she is, or you'll never know what's missing.'"

Looking down at me in her arms, my mother named me Carolyn Gracie—Carolyn from her grandmother, I believe, and Gracie from her mother. She requested that this name remain with me after I was adopted.

The nurse, whose name was Alversia Eaton, changed the course of all our lives. She spoke honestly with my mother, telling her she wasn't like the other girls who came to Florence Home with no hope and no options. "You're an educated, mature woman," she said. "You have so much more than most of the girls who come in here. You are well able to raise your baby."

These words she spoke to my mother were powerful. These words created in my mother a new image of herself and her situation. My mother was so affected by the nurse's influence that she would decide, with my third birth certificate, to rename me Alversia—and she even asked my new namesake to be my godmother.

By the time I was two weeks old, Mrs. Eaton's counseling had resulted in my mother changing her mind. I was not put up for adoption. She decided to keep me—but for her whole life, I felt I lived in the shadow of her disgrace.

chapter 2

A CONFUSING START

During my first four years of life, I was cast into three different families. This is a period my aunts and uncles were always reluctant to talk about, even after my mother died. Rather than discussing the details of how or why I was shuffled around among various relatives like a foster child, they would simply reassure me, saying, "Zee loved you." I managed to get some answers from the letters my mother kept. But gaps remain, and even where I *know* what happened, I don't necessarily understand it.

This is a period in my history I have never been able to come to terms with. It has never made sense to me. My mother had such a strong sense of family, yet her choices and decisions during this time conflict with everything I thought I knew about her.

It was not unusual in the African American community for a child to be raised by other family members. In fact, it was and still is commonplace. But it was out of character for my mother. When my Aunt FC died in childbirth several years before I was born, and her husband struggled to accept the child he felt had caused his wife's death, my mother came in and took her newborn nephew to live with her until his father was ready to reclaim him. The way she allowed her own daughter's life to play out seemed completely against what she'd stood for in the past and what she would stand for in the future.

She may have felt that having a child outside of marriage was disgraceful, but in my mind, the disgrace was her standing on the sidelines as other people raised me, allowing me to think they were my mother and father. I still struggle to come to terms with what she did to me, her baby. She would give me away over and over again.

My mother had lied to her family and virtually disappeared without contact for nearly five months, hiding her pregnancy and my birth from them, and she was slow to dismantle her lies, preferring to keep my existence a secret as long as possible. Uncle Narvell and his wife, Aunt Kathleen, were the first to know. My mother visited them before assuming her false identity and going into hiding, and Aunt Kathleen noticed some extra weight on my mother's normally trim figure. No one could confirm her suspicions, however—Aunt Cleretha found it implausible that my mother wouldn't have confided in her, and Aunt Tutta, shocked by the suggestion, refused to entertain rumors.

Four months later, when my mother summoned Aunt Kathleen and Uncle Narvell to come to Florence Home, Aunt Kathleen saw that she'd been right. There I was, two weeks old, resting in my mother's arms. Aunt Kathleen told me, "Zee was so proud of you. When we got there, she brought you out all dressed up, with a ribbon barely attached to the wisp of hair you had."

I don't know how the arrangement came about—whether she asked, whether they offered, whether it was settled before they arrived at Florence Home or proposed once they arrived. This was one of the answers I could never draw out of my relatives. However it happened, when I was six weeks old, I was taken to live with Aunt Kathleen and Uncle Narvell in Edwardsville, Kansas—some eight hours from where my mother and most of the Williams family now lived in Dixon, Illinois. Aunt Cleretha had moved to Dixon to marry Gene, a handsome army sergeant, and some of her siblings had followed. The plan was for Aunt Kathleen and Uncle Narvell to raise me as their own. I was, for the time being, *their* baby.

They already had three children of their own to care for, all under the age of five. Aunt Kathleen was patient and steady, soft-spoken, a reassuring force to whom I would grow extremely attached. She was biracial, with a light complexion from her white father and shoulder-length wavy black hair. She and Uncle Narvell were married when they were teenagers, but even after many years of marriage, Uncle Narvell liked to say she looked no different than she had when they first met. As I grew up, I would come to admire their marriage, which I viewed as a true love affair. Uncle Narvell would dream, and Aunt Kathleen would keep him grounded. Uncle Narvell seemed like the disciplinarian, but Aunt Kathleen had a quiet, feisty strength. She was a practical, no-frills woman, but she loved her family wholeheartedly and was protective of them. When I was near them, I felt love and acceptance.

At the time when I was brought to live with them, they operated a dry cleaning business and would take us along in the car on their driving route as they dropped off garments. Uncle Narvell told me that when Aunt Kathleen would get out of the car, I would scream and reach after her, wailing for the person I thought was my mother.

Aunt Kathleen and Uncle Narvell called me "Versie," the name my mother provided. They never knew what my original name had been. They didn't even know the full name that nickname came from—Alversia Harolyn Williams—until I was five months old, being christened on Easter Sunday in Kansas City, Kansas. My mother was at the baptism. At some point she moved from Dixon to Kansas City to be a dietician at Wheatley-Provident Hospital—I assume she did this to be near me.

My mother's appearance at my baptism was typical of how she floated around the edge of my life, popping in and out, never becoming completely committed to the role of mother, while Aunt Kathleen and Uncle Narvell cared for me and loved me as if I was their own child. I even called my Aunt Kathleen "Mommy."

Especially now, having my own children and grandchildren, I wonder, *How could my mother have allowed me to call someone else Mommy?*

She wouldn't be there to hold me, feed me, calm my fears, rock me to sleep, see me turn over for the first time, see my first smile, or hear my first words. When I began to recognize faces, hers was not the one I would seek. When I took my first steps, I didn't stumble into the safety of my mother's arms, trusting her to catch me. I'm certain I could feel the severed connection between me and my mother, and I believe this feeling resulted in my persistent fears of rejection and abandonment.

I am told I cried all the time, one of the few things my elders told me about myself as a baby. They said I loved oatmeal and had a deep voice, but I was given no details that connected me to anyone. Perhaps my constant crying was how I expressed my anxiety and confusion. I know I was always determined to have my voice heard.

Until I was more than a year old, it seems, my mother managed to keep me a secret from her sister Cle, despite their close relationship and long-held pact that they would always support each other. In one letter I found, Aunt Cleretha wrote to my mother saying she wanted to send me a dress. My mother wrote back asking how her sister managed to find out about me. She confessed, "I have been trying to bring myself to tell you all about her but was too ashamed, and you were the last person I felt free to tell when it seems that you should have been among the first."

As it turned out, this would be one of their last exchanges. My mother didn't talk about me with her closest sister, another letter revealed, until after Aunt Cleretha had given birth to a stillborn daughter in January 1953. Aunt Cleretha, who already had two children, had been fighting tuberculosis throughout that pregnancy, and her illness progressed rapidly after the loss of her child.

In May 1953, when I was one and a half years old, Aunt Cleretha, my mother's beloved sister, died at the age of twenty-nine. This was a seismic upheaval, causing a sudden and radical shift in two families and altering many people's lives forever. Just as an earthquake triggers other catastrophic events, Aunt Cleretha's death caused aftershocks in the family, changing the lives of everybody and setting many other events into motion.

Aunt Cleretha's family was left adrift: her husband, Gene, was left to raise their five-year-old son, Melvin, and their four-year-old daughter, Brenda, alone.

My mother and her siblings were devastated. Aunt Cleretha, the lighthearted girl from their youth who loved to laugh, had been the change agent of the family, the one who inspired the others. Their destinies had been intertwined, and now a link was missing. No one could make sense of this tragedy.

My mother brought her niece and nephew back to stay with her in Kansas City for that summer. When they returned to Dixon at the summer's end, they were surprised to learn that Gene had remarried. He'd wanted someone to help him raise his children, but his new wife wasn't well suited for this task. The way I heard it, she was a heavy drinker, loved to entertain, and mostly ignored the children. My mother would send money and clothes, but she got reports from Aunt Tutta that the children were always unkempt and often neglected. My mother began to fight a fierce battle to get custody of her sister's children.

During that summer in 1953 when Melvin and Brenda stayed with my mother in Kansas City, other family dynamics unfolded. Aunt Kathleen and Uncle Narvell learned that Aunt Kathleen was pregnant with her fourth child.

As Aunt Kathleen would later explain to me, "Versie, you were so attached to me. If I got out of your sight, you wailed. When I began to have morning sickness so badly that I could hardly get out of bed, Zee decided that it would best if she took you to live with her."

When I was almost two years old, my mother brought me to her apartment in Kansas City, taking me from the only home and parents I had known.

Once I came to live with her, she had to find a babysitter for me. The woman she found lived outside of walking distance of the apartment, and Mom didn't own a car. So she took me on the bus and left me with the babysitter throughout the week, picking me up on her days off.

Amazingly, I have several vivid memories of that time in Kansas City. Once, later in my childhood when I was riding in the car with my mother and Aunt Kathleen, I began peppering them with questions, asking about some of my memories. Both of them were astonished that I had retained any impressions from when I was so young.

I remembered eating candy and cashews from a dining room cabinet, and my mother confirmed that the couple living in the apartment below hers was very fond of me and often allowed me to stay with them instead of going to my babysitter, because I never adjusted to being with the babysitter. My mother told me that this babysitter kept several children and was very strict; she didn't allow me to suck my finger, so I would just walk around with my right index finger lying on the side of my face, near my mouth, never daring to suck it.

"I remember sleeping next to the wall in a room," I described, "and I often climbed over someone to go to the bathroom and then someone would come in and get me and make me come back to bed." To this day I cannot stand sleeping on the inside of the bed.

Mom would laugh, "You remember that?" It was her I'd climbed over. She said, "I'd wake up and find you, just a toddler, scrubbing the bathroom floor with cleanser." She told me how she often dressed me and returned to find me undoing my clothes—apparently to re-dress myself, ensuring everything was tucked in and smoothed down to my liking.

These sparse memories are like breadcrumbs leading back to my time spent with my mother, back when it was just the two of us. I wish I had more of them.

For some reason, and at some point, the trial period of me living with my mother ended. I have conflicting accounts of why and how the next transfer occurred. My mother's version: "You stayed sick. You picked up whatever illness went through the babysitter's house. I was always taking off work to take care of you. Then you ended up in the hospital with pneumonia. It was just too hard trying to work and care for you." Whether my constant sickness was the real reason or whether it was something else, my mother began making plans to cast me off again, this time into a situation that would scandalize friends and family.

My mother was so determined in her attempts to rescue Melvin and Brenda, but so dismissive of her own child's well-being.

Mom's older vagabond brother, tall, slim, dapper Uncle Kent, had married a heavyset, outspoken woman, Etta Mae. Their family was the next one I would join. Before finding the box of documents and letters in my mother's basement after her death, I hadn't even known when I went to live with Uncle Kent and Aunt Etta, but a letter in the box from Aunt Tutta to my mother says I arrived in March 1954, when I was almost two and a half years old.

My mother told it like this: "Tutta wanted you to come stay with her. Buddy and Etta Mae were moving to Dixon, and they were supposed to take you to Dixon to deliver you to Tutta, but instead they just kept you."

This never made sense. How does someone simply *keep* your child? Also, I'm certain that if Aunt Tutta had demanded me, I would have been brought to her. Aunt Tutta's word was law, and no one crossed her, although I was always told my mother was strong-willed. Aside from that, Aunt Tutta already had five children. My mother had already taken me from Aunt Kathleen and Uncle Narvell, not wanting them to be burdened by too many children; it doesn't follow that she would add me to Aunt Tutta's already large family, her youngest just nine months younger than me.

My cousin Sheila, Aunt Tutta's oldest daughter who was nine years older than me, remembers things this way: "Aunt Etta and Uncle Kent didn't bring you to Dixon. Aunt Kathleen and Uncle Narvell brought you to Dixon and left you with Uncle Kent and Aunt Etta."

She remembered being shocked that Aunt Kathleen and Uncle Narvell would give away the child she thought was their baby.

"No one told us who you really were," she told me later.

However it really happened, I went to live with yet another family, separated again from the mother who had given birth to me. Buddy and Etta were childless and sending me to their home may have seemed like the perfect solution for them, Uncle Narvell, Aunt Kathleen, my mother—everybody but me. Was anyone emotionally impacted by my absence? Did anyone care what all this was doing to me? Was anyone questioning or challenging my mother's decisions? What was going on in my mother's life and in her head? What was so important and unsolvable that she could abandon me and allow me to call someone else Mommy?

Aunt Etta and Uncle Kent could never have a child of their own. They fostered other little girls, but they could never keep them. As much as my aunt and uncle wanted a child, their home wasn't the best place for one. Uncle Kent, who never settled down much after his days of hopping trains, had become a heavy drinker, a gambler, and a womanizer.

I had to have been confused and anxious to be thrust into a new home—to be taught to call another set of caretakers "Mommy" and "Daddy"—but I remember liking it there. My aunt and uncle were crazy about me and spoiled me. Plus, there was always something exciting going on. Another young girl around my age was staying there around the same time, and my aunt and uncle rented out a room to a man who rode a motorcycle. He taught me to empty the mousetraps, opening them and lifting the dead captives by their tails. People came and went all the time, and my aunt and uncle often had friends over who drank, smoked, cussed, and played cards into the wee hours of the night.

At these parties, I was the little darling, the helper who ran errands for the grownups. When it was time for me to go to bed, I could never sleep. I think it was during this time that I learned to be independent and fearless, mostly out of necessity. If Uncle Kent couldn't take me with him where he was going or find a babysitter, he would leave me, his three-year-old niece, at home by myself.

Aunt Etta and Uncle Kent didn't have a daycare solution for me, but they worked out a plan so someone would always be home with me . . . sort of. They both worked at Dixon State School, a mental institution on the outskirts of town. My uncle worked seven a.m. to three p.m., and my aunt worked three p.m. to eleven p.m. I would ride to Dixon State School on the bus with Mommy, she would be dropped off at the cottage where she worked, and I would stay on board and wait for Daddy to get on at his stop.

Then he and I rode home together, and that's when the action really got started.

Uncle Kent had no intentions of being tied down to a toddler. He had a posse of friends he ran with, and I was his sidekick. I went with him to gambling games, taverns, bootleg spots, and anywhere else his nightly plans took him. I remember going with him to a shoeshine spot where the men huddled on the floor throwing dice, and my uncle taught me how to blow on the dice to give him good luck. I always got some candy. My uncle had a friend who drove a taxi, and many nights that was how we got around. I'd stand on the front seat between my uncle and his friend, my small arms wrapped tightly around their seat backs, holding on for dear life as they drove through the streets, both men often drunk.

For most of my life, I believed my mother must not have known what was going on with me—she must have thought I was safe and sound living with her brother. But the letters I found in the box in the basement after she died, the box full of secrets, showed me this wasn't true.

People wrote to my mother telling her of several incidents that would have caused any responsible parent to come running for her child. I learned my Uncle Kent was in and out of jail all the time for one infraction or another, usually related to his drinking and associated activities.

Regina Jones, one of my mother's close friends who lived in Dixon, had found out the truth of who I was when Uncle Jesse's wife slipped and told her. Regina wrote to my mother, "Zee, if she is your baby, you should really be ashamed to toss her from hand to hand the way you are doing. There's no way in this world I would disown my own baby. You are ruining her life. She is going through life calling this one and that one 'Mama,' not even knowing who her Mama is. I wouldn't let people make my baby call me Aunt. I often wondered what kind of parents Narvell and Kathleen are to give a sweet baby like this away. I'll tell you one thing, if you don't take her away from Etta and Buddy you are going to regret it. The lives they live aren't fit for a child."

In another letter, Aunt Tutta was more emphatic that Mom needed to either come get me immediately or allow me to live with her. She told my mother a story: The Dixon police came to the house one evening because they'd received a complaint from a neighbor about hearing a child crying in the dark house next door. The police couldn't get into the house, so Aunt Tutta's husband, Mr. John, followed the police there, let them in, and brought me back to Aunt Tutta. Aunt Tutta had Mr. John take her around town, searching for Daddy. She must have given him a mighty tongue-lashing, but he only told her, "Having that girl was Etta Mae's idea. If you want her, take her." Aunt Tutta wrote to my mother, "Buddy has no business with a child!"

Still my mother did not intervene. I continued living with Mommy and Daddy while my mother continued to wage her own personal war to ensure Melvin and Brenda were well cared for, even as her own daughter cried out in the darkness.

I have flashes of memory of my mother visiting me at Aunt Etta and Uncle Kent's house. I loved Westerns and pretending I was a cowgirl, and once my mother brought me a complete cowgirl outfit: a tasseled skirt and vest, a cowgirl hat, a stick horse, and a Hop-Along Cassidy watch. On a different visit, she brought me a puppy I named Skippy, after my favorite peanut butter. I cried when the nice lady left, and Aunt Etta pulled me from her and said, "Shut up all that screaming, you don't even know who you're crying for!"

During this time, my mother was weighing her options. She was still fighting for her sister Cle's children, honoring their childhood pact. On some level, I believe she must have been thinking about me, too, though her actions didn't show it. She was trying to figure out a solution.

Eventually, a strange solution presented itself.

Gene's brief second marriage had ended, and he was still struggling to care for his and Aunt Cleretha's children. They were spending a lot of time next door at Gene's parents' home. My mother tried to persuade him to send them to her, but Gene wouldn't allow it. In one letter, he tried to encourage my mother to return to Dixon to help with the children. He admitted that Tutta was against this, but he said my mother should do what was best for her.

Then, in a later letter, Gene made a proposal of marriage. "Your daughter needs a father," he wrote, "and my children need a mother."

On January 15, 1956, when I had just turned four years old, I was in bed at Aunt Tutta's house. I was sick with the mumps, and I always stayed with Aunt Tutta when I was sick. She had a home remedy for everything, she knew how to pinch and wrap a wound, and she always knew from our symptoms, even before calling the doctor, what medicine we needed.

On this particular day, my cousin Evelyn, Aunt Tutta's youngest daughter, was running around, excited about a wedding that would take place later that afternoon. "Don't worry," she said, "I promise I'll bring you a piece of wedding cake."

An image is emblazoned in my memory of a woman walking into my sick room. My cousin Sheila, standing beside my bed, could see I was confused. It was the nice lady who visited me sometimes. She was wearing a soft peach-colored, full-length taffeta dress, and she appeared to be floating. She was bringing me a piece of *her* wedding cake. I stared at her, uncertain.

When the beautiful woman left, my cousin Sheila whispered, "That's your momma."

chapter 3

IT TAKES A VILLAGE

I've often wondered what other plans, if any, my mother considered. Why was this the only way? She was ashamed to be an unwed mother, but she had lied before—couldn't she simply claim my father had died and move to Dixon as a widow? She could have raised me that way, and she could have helped raise her niece and nephew. Or, if she needed a husband to complete her picture of a family, couldn't she have met someone else? She was a beautiful, educated woman.

Life is complicated, and there were many factors to consider. Did her childhood promise carry an obligation so strong that she would move into her beloved sister's home, marry her husband, and raise her children? Did she think this was the best answer for all of us?

After my mother married Gene, I was cast into my third family. My mother and I moved into the two-bedroom house that Gene and Aunt Cleretha had built in Dixon. Now it was me, my mother, Gene, and my cousins, Melvin and Brenda, who were now my stepsiblings. There were no celebrations, no explanations. It was just another quick acclimation to a new life with a new family.

One day we were simply brought together and labeled a family. By the pure definition of "family," I guess that's what we were—relatives living together—but this was the family in which I never felt I belonged. I felt like an outsider. I would always call us the "patchwork" family, because in my mind, we had been pieced together like a quilt.

We were given a rigorous education about who we were to one another. We were no longer cousins, we were told, and we were to call each other brother and sister. Not long after we began to live together, Brenda, Melvin, and I were photographed together posing innocently, the image of the family we were expected to become. Brenda and I were often dressed alike. It was a complete indoctrination.

If my life had been confusing before, it became even more confusing as I tried to figure out my place in this new family. We were all coming together from situations that had left us a bit bruised, and we all needed extra love, emotional support, and a great deal of patience. But this wasn't what we got. Instead, as was the norm in those days, it was expected that children would just adjust, with no questions asked.

From the beginning I felt I was at a distinct disadvantage. Melvin and Brenda had been given the opportunity to establish an ongoing, loving relationship with my mother that I didn't have. It wasn't only that they had spent that summer with her after their mother died; she had been in their lives since they were born and lived in Dixon, just around the corner from their house, until moving to Kansas City. Melvin and Brenda had lost their own mother, so sympathy was heaped on them. In my mother's mind, she had always been there for me, even if I only saw her occasionally. At the time I became part of this new family, my memories of my mother were like fleeting shades of gray in my mind.

Melvin and Brenda had their father, their grandparents—who lived next door—and, most of all, each other. I knew no one. I had no common bond that connected me to anyone, and the adults in our life took no special measures to ease the transition for me or my cousins.

I'm not sure how my new siblings felt about me. They may have felt somewhat threatened by me because they had not long before had another stepfamily come through—which hadn't gone very well for them. Yet I just saw them as a united front, siblings who would gang up against me for the fun of it. I suppose my mother assumed that instinct would fill in the gaps left by the missing years, that we would eventually form the bonds of family. But I could never figure out where I fit in. I just wanted to belong.

I was taught to call her "Mommy" instead of "Aunt Zee," although Melvin and Brenda were still allowed to call her their aunt. I was taught to call Gene "Daddy." If I slipped and called them the wrong name, either at home or in public, I was chastised. To make matters more confusing, I still called Aunt Etta and Uncle Kent "Mommy" and "Daddy"—as I would until they died—and I saw them frequently. I didn't know any other children who had two sets of parents.

My mother was dealing with her own struggle to be accepted, facing her own adjustment period. She had married her deceased sister's husband and finally claimed a child no one had known was hers. In the eyes of the small, judgmental community we lived in, she had entered into an unholy alliance. The gossip was cruel. At church, I would hear adults whispering about me. "Poor thing doesn't even know what to call her own mother." Some members of my mother's family spurned her. She had to deal with all this judgment while taking on a mothering role she would prove emotionally ill-equipped to handle.

I remember my mother's forced efforts to make us quickly appear like a respectable family. My friends would later tell me that we seemed like the perfect family, but within the walls at 515 West Sixth Street, the constant tension and misery hung over our lives like a fog. Family gossip was that Mom laid down the law and told Daddy he could drink his beer, but he had to do it at home—no more running with his buddies. She was determined to create the family image she desired. I don't recall a lot of laughter in our house, unless someone came to visit. My mother may have kept her word to her sister, given me a father, and—in the end—gained the legitimacy she needed to function in society with her illegitimate child. But I believe she felt trapped in the life she had chosen, and she punished herself and all of us for her unhappiness.

I would later discover that Mom had still been enrolled at the University of Iowa when she got married and had returned to Iowa to finish out the semester after the wedding, while I returned to Aunt Etta's and Uncle Kent's until she finished. Then, four months after the wedding, she was awarded a teaching certificate in Kansas City, Missouri, but she never accepted the position. I can only assume she was hoping to escape from the knowing eyes and judging spirits she faced in Dixon. But in the end, for whatever reason, they stayed there, and she was forced to live out her charade.

As a result, I believe, she was frequently on edge, snappy, and irritated. I'm not sure what her work schedule was, but I know she was at home with me in the afternoons when I returned from morning kindergarten and Brenda and Melvin were in school.

Mom and I would eat lunch together while she watched *As the World Turns*. After lunch, when she laid me down for my nap, she held my hands together and asked me, "How much do I love you?" She'd pull my hands apart little by little until they were spread out all the way. She'd say, "I love you this much," and then she'd hug me tight, and I would give my usual response: "And I love you more than all the money in the world." I treasure these memories—one of the few times when I truly felt her love and a real connection. Most of the time, though, I would fear her judgment, exasperation, and condemnation.

I had to grow accustomed not only to my third Mommy, but also to my third Daddy. Gene was slim, with wavy hair. I was fascinated by a permanent dimple he had in his cheek, the result of bad dental work he'd had while in the army. Of the three children, I always felt I was the most affectionate with him. Brenda and Melvin found him very strict, but I would throw my arms around him enthusiastically. Sometimes I would sit with him on the couch, his feet on my lap, while we watched Westerns together. Before he married my mother, he'd come visit me at Aunt Etta and Uncle Kent's, sometimes taking me to buy popcorn so we could go to the river and feed the ducks, but he never singled me out once we were a family.

At the same time that I was becoming attached to Daddy, on some level I was also conflicted, believing he was keeping me from my real father. Everyone marveled that Brenda looked just like Aunt Cleretha and that Melvin looked like Daddy. I was searching for the person I looked like. I was always on the lookout for someone who could be my real father.

I took creative license to design my father in whatever image I chose. Any time I saw a strange black man in town, I would say, "That's probably my father coming to check on me." If I saw a black man with a feature I shared, like my gapped front teeth or my unibrow, I suspected he was my father.

For a time, I was convinced that a deacon from our church was my father. He had a gap in his front teeth, and every time he called me "darlin'," it sounded like it was addressing me as a daughter. I imagined we were purposely living across the street from him so he could watch me grow up.

One day I asked his aunt, "Are you my aunt?"

"I'm everyone's aunt," she responded.

"No," I said. "You're my aunt, because Uncle Wink is my real father."

"Oh, baby," she said softly. "What makes you say that?" I told her, and she responded, "I know Wink probably wishes you were his little girl, but it's not so." Then I heard her say under her breath, "I wish folks could see that all these lies do is cause trouble."

The community was nearly as curious as I was about my real father—I was a great mystery to everybody. My mother held things to herself, so people created their own truths. As my mother fought and eventually succeeded in her career, many in the community admired her; yet she was also a target, a proud and determined woman whom people felt called to tear down. And because my mother never revealed her secrets, people's gossip and speculation would persist for many years.

At the same time I was learning what to call my new parents, I had to learn to call myself another new name. When Mom was enrolling me in kindergarten, she gave my name as Carolyn Grace Alversia Ashford. I had never heard that name before—I had only been called "Versie." I wasn't the only one who was confused. I remember my cousin Sheila asking, "When did she become Carolyn? I thought her name was Versie."

But it was settled: I was Carolyn now, and I was fascinated by my sudden possession of two middle names. I loved to rattle off my name in a quick lilt: "My name is Carolyn Grace Alversia Ashford."

People seemed to like the way I said it—they asked me to repeat it over and over again. "That's a big name for such a little girl," they would say.

Meanwhile, I became very protective of my nickname, Versie. I didn't like being teased about my name or trying to explain why I had two names. This was my family name, and it was very personal. Only those closest to me could call me that. Carolyn was my school name and how I introduced myself to new people; anyone else calling me Versie felt like an invasion of my privacy. I hated when my family would call me Versie at school. My classmates would tease me about having two names—or worse yet, they'd start calling me Versie in attempts to ridicule me. My name was my identity, and I wanted control over it.

For their part, my mother and Daddy were still getting used to each other and their new arrangement. Quickly, my mother asserted her authority over the household finances, Daddy's friends, and most other matters. I recall only one blowup they had, about money. Mom and Daddy were yelling at each other and slamming doors. I remember Mom sleeping with me that night. From then on, whenever any of us needed money, Daddy told us, "Ask Zee." She was the one who held the control in our house, with a sharp tongue and an iron fist.

In the beginning, the three of us kids shared a bedroom with bunk beds, Melvin on top and me and Brenda on the bottom. Ours was a restrictive life, with lots of rules. We weren't allowed to spend the night at anyone's house except relatives. If friends came over, I was always nervous because they could never be caught sitting on our nicely made beds. They either sat on the floor or weren't invited into our room. The only activities we could participate in were school- or church-related. In the summer, we were expected to spend mornings weeding Daddy's garden and picking vegetables.

We knew that on Friday evenings we had to clean the whole house, and we risked being spanked if it wasn't done well. When we were assigned to do the dishes, one of us washed them, one dried them, and one put them away. If Mom found a single dirty dish or dirty piece of silverware, she would empty all the cabinets of all the dishes and make us wash every single one, including her special occasion china. Her opinion was that with three sets of eyes on the dishes, *somebody* should catch a dirty one. You can believe we learned to keep a watchful eye as we did the dishes.

Growing up, I was the typical pain-in-the-butt little sister. I was four years old when I learned to read, and when it was my turn to read the comics section of the Sunday newspaper, I always read them out loud. It drove Melvin and Brenda crazy.

Because I was the youngest, I was teased a lot. Melvin was mean to me and Brenda both. He got himself into trouble often—one time he shot Brenda in the foot with a BB gun—and he often talked me into taking the blame for his mischief by promising me his allowance, which he never delivered. He once set the couch on fire after proposing that we have dinner by candlelight, and he tried unsuccessfully to blame me. Brenda, on the other hand, was the most afraid of Mom's wrath. While our parents were at home, she always lived by the strict rules of our house. When adults weren't around, though, she wasn't afraid to gang up on me with Melvin.

Unlike Brenda, I was a tomboy who wasn't afraid of consequences—Mom's constant response was "No," so the only way I could do anything was to sneak. Brenda would ask, "Why do you do things knowing you're going to get into trouble?" I would tell her, "She can whip my butt, but she can't take away the fun I had."

I may have felt strange in my own family, but I loved growing up in Dixon, a quaint town with a population of just fifteen thousand or so. A large Veterans Memorial arch spelled out "Dixon" in wide letters above Galena Avenue, the city's main thoroughfare, heading up the three-block historic downtown. Rock River ran right through the city, partitioning its north and south sides, the water gray and choppy. Cars drove under old limestone railroad bridges.

Dixon had a very small black population, less than five percent. The vast majority of black families lived in de facto segregation on the south side, largely west of the railroad tracks, where the projects were. We grew up east of the railroad tracks, where most people owned their own homes. I often heard us called "the uppity Negroes on the hill." We weren't allowed to go to the West End unless we were visiting Aunt Tutta and her kids, a six-block walk from our house.

We spent a lot of our time with these cousins. I loved being with them. This was the family I looked like and felt at home with.

I was a sensitive child who cried at the slightest insult. One day when I was eight years old or so, a neighborhood kid punched me in the stomach and I ran to Aunt Tutta crying, waking her while she was sleeping after her night shift. She marched me out to her children. "Somebody teach this girl how to fight," she commanded my cousins. One of her sons showed me how to ball up my little hands and throw a punch. It didn't help me much, but I always liked feeling I wasn't defenseless—feeling reassured I had people on my side.

We lived in a very tight-knit neighborhood that felt more like a private compound. More than a dozen children, mostly girls close to my age, lived near us. All the backyards opened into one huge playground with no fences and no locked doors. We ran freely from one house to the next, playing games together and running through the ditch that cut through the neighborhood and filled with water when it rained. When the ditch was full we waded in it, and when it was dry we followed Melvin throughout the city's underground pipes, pretending we were explorers.

When the summer heat became unbearable, we made our pallets in the backyard and slept outside, with no fear of intruders or wayward animals. We rode our bicycles everywhere, and on Sundays we often played softball in the park. We watched television after dark, if at all. When the streetlights came on we had to be close to home, but we stayed outside and played hide and seek or sat on the neighbors' patio eating homemade ice cream and watching home movies.

The adults grew much of the food we ate. Daddy had a vegetable garden he tended carefully. There was also a large family garden full of rows of corn, grape vines, and fruit trees, managed by my step-grandfather. In the fall, after harvesting the corn, we children would bind together the cornstalks with ropes to make a hut we could play in, pretending to be Indians.

Many afternoons we kids would load up a wagon of fresh vegetables and go into the white neighborhoods to sell our produce. In the fall, the women worked canning food, freezing the vegetables to carry us through many winter meals. The grapes went to make jelly, and Daddy also used them to make his wine. During the summer the backyards filled with the smell of barbecue. Daddy and his siblings loved a cold beer, and their barbecue often suffered as evenings wore on and they focused on drinking rather than minding the meat.

It was a community of laughter, love, caring, and sharing. We were growing up in a segregated environment, but in many ways this enriched our upbringing. Our mentors and role models were among us. They looked like us. It really felt as though the entire black community raised us, not just our own families. We knew if we did something wrong, we'd be disciplined by any adult who had seen us, and then again by our parents once we got home. We referred to the adults as Mr. and Mrs. or Aunt and Uncle, even when they weren't related to us. The only adults we called by their first names were Leon and Regina Jones, because they insisted on it—being called "Mr. and Mrs. Jones" made them feel old, and they were a stylish, cool couple.

Some of my most loving memories are of Uncle Oscar and Aunt Gladys, an older couple, who were close friends of our family. They never had any children, although they certainly babied their dog, Mitzy. Brenda and I often spent part of our summer with them when Mom was away working on her master's degree. I liked to pretend they were my grandparents. They were very proper, teaching us to keep our napkins in our laps and our elbows off the table. They always ended our meals with something sweet, a scoop of sherbet or a bowl of peaches.

We spent a lot of time with Daddy's siblings and their children, as well as with his parents, Nana and Pop Major, who lived next door. This was the family I wanted to fit in with, but I learned I had two things working against me—things that stigmatized me as being different and therefore inferior: I was born out of wedlock, and I had dark skin. Pop Major taught me the social disgrace of both of these conditions. In the '50s, whether you were light-skinned or dark-skinned mattered in terms of class and status, and I stood out among the lighter complexioned Ashfords with my dark skin—I looked like a Williams.

Nana was mild-mannered and kind, always slipping us sandwiches she made with homemade jam. She looked white, but she said she was part Native American and African American. She had waist-length salt-and-pepper hair she would braid and wrap around her head. Pop Major's complexion was as dark as mine. He was baldheaded and always had a wad of chewing tobacco in his mouth. He was mean-spirited and kept a rather stern expression on his face. He was a lay minister, although I was never certain about whether he'd really been ordained, and he was also—as I would come to discover—what we would today call a pedophile.

It was from Pop Major's lips I first heard the word "bastard."

Each year for Christmas, Mom bought the gifts we would give Nana and Pop Major. One year when I was around eight or nine, I decided to give them my own gift. Nana had baby pictures of all her grandchildren and great-grandchildren in frames around her living and dining rooms, but she didn't have a picture of me. I wanted to be in her "Hall of Frames." I rummaged through Mom's boxes, found the only baby picture I had ever seen of me, framed it, and gave it to Nana. From her reaction, you would have thought I'd given her a gold nugget. She immediately placed my picture on top of the TV for all to see, and I brimmed with pride and a sense of acceptance.

I wanted to get Pop Major something special, too, so I had carefully wrapped in toilet paper the little gold cross necklace I'd worn for my christening. I held my breath, hoping he would be as glad as Nana with my gift, but when he pulled out the necklace, he threw it back at me and snapped, "What do I want with this? I don't need another cross, and I sure don't need one from a little bastard!"

I stood there and felt tears welling up to the rims of my eyelids, waiting for one blink to send them spilling down my cheeks. I lunged and tore my little cross from his hand and ran from the house. I heard Nana say, "Major, why'd you say that?"

I burst into our kitchen, surprising my mother.

"Girl, what is wrong with you?" she asked sharply.

I didn't tell my mother about the necklace—I was afraid I'd be punished for giving it away. Instead I just said, "Pop Major called me a bastard. What's a bastard?"

"He's ignorant," my mother replied. "There's no such thing as a bastard."

Months later I spotted Pop Major sitting in his old wooden swing, cutting a piece of snuff with his pocketknife. I sat on the swing next to him. I was wearing the cross necklace, and he noticed it. "That's supposed to be my necklace," he said. "Why you got it on?"

"You said you didn't want it," I reminded him. "And you don't have to worry," I shot. "I'll never give you anything else!" I jumped off the swing, preparing to have my say and run. "My momma says you're ignorant!"

He laughed and spat his tobacco. "Get on out of here," he said. "I told you, you ain't nothing but a little darky bastard."

I put my hand on my hip. "You don't know what you're talking about," I yelled. "My momma says there's no such thing as a bastard!"

Pop Major grabbed me by the shoulder and pulled me into the house. I was a bastard, he told me, because I had no father. Then he pulled his Bible from under the sofa and showed me Deuteronomy 23:2: "A bastard shall not enter into the congregation of the Lord." Just in case I still didn't understand who I was, he said, "And just so you know, my son is *not* your daddy, and you can tell your mammy it's her fault you ain't got a daddy and can't ever go to heaven!"

I knew what *that* meant. We went to Sunday school and church every week. I was frightened not only by Pop Major's declaration that I'd be barred from heaven, but also by the venomous way he said it. I ran out of the house crying to tell my mother what Pop Major had said.

She didn't blink. She didn't betray any emotion at all. Instead, she looked at me and said firmly, "Stop crying! You're going to have to learn to hold your head erect and command all men's respect."

She was reminding me of an important lesson that she had been teaching me and Brenda. My mother had been showing the two of us how to walk around the house with books on our heads, standing very straight with our shoulders squared back. She wanted us to walk with dignity so that it became instinctive for us. When we would walk past her during these exercises, she would say, "Hold your head erect, you'll command all men's respect." It was a lesson my mother modeled for us well. In 1962, she became the first black schoolteacher in Dixon. She put the Ashford name on the map. Leon and Regina held a tea at their house in her honor, and the entire community proudly celebrated her accomplishment. It had been a long road for my mother, but she had achieved her goal of becoming a teacher—largely because she never stopped pursuing her dream and holding her head high, commanding respect.

I didn't get the consolation from my mother I was looking for that day, and I had no idea what walking with my head up had to do with the cruel words I'd just heard, but I never forgot my mother's reminder, and eventually it took on a new meaning. To this day I remember my mother's phrase of empowerment. It resonates with me when I face pivotal moments with defiance and confidence. Today, I share these words with my granddaughters and others who find themselves in difficult circumstances: "Hold your head erect, you'll command all men's respect." My mother didn't give me what I wanted—demonstrative love or comfort—she gave me what I needed.

And I would use those words again and again.

Pop Major, as I said, was a disgusting pedophile, although that word wasn't really used when I was growing up—nobody ever talked about it at all. He would hide on his dark back porch, and if I was sent over to Nana's to borrow milk or sugar, I would find him standing in the shadows, his erect penis poking out of his pants. He would shake it and try to get me to stroke it. If I screamed, he'd zip up his pants and laugh as if he'd just been trying to scare me.

Sometimes he'd offer a quarter to touch him. He did this to Brenda, too, and she was the one who showed me how to get the money and run. The first time I tried this, he caught my wrist and pulled me so hard he tore the skin, but I screamed and he let me go.

One summer when I was about nine years old, he called me into the toolshed on the back of his property. The shed was dark and smelly—and when I went in, Pop Major grabbed me and kissed me, trying to put his tongue in my mouth, his breath reeking of tobacco and peppermint. I thought I would vomit. In the dark, I didn't see that he had dropped his pants to his ankles. He never penetrated me, but he pushed me up against the door, pulled down my panties, and moved his penis back and forth between my bare legs until he let out a grunt, and then he was done.

He spat his chewing tobacco. "You better not say anything to anyone, you hear me?"

I didn't.

It sounds unbelievable now, but back then, this was just one more thing that children weren't supposed to talk about. Brenda didn't talk about it. I didn't talk about it. I'm sure there were other girls who didn't talk about it. I don't know how much Nana knew—but the adults must have known some of what was happening.

After Pop Major molested me in the woodshed, he would come over to our house every day once I was home from school, before Brenda and Melvin got home. He wanted more. He wanted me to touch it. I was afraid, so he took my hand and showed me how to rub it so it felt good to him. I don't remember how long that went on.

One day he pulled me into the bedroom. He lay on the bed and told me to get on top of him. We were both fully clothed, but he started bucking me as if he was a horse and I was riding him, rocking up and down on his stomach. I thought we were just having fun together.

A scream pierced the air, and I turned to see my mother, who'd come home from work early.

The rage on her face would have stopped the devil himself, and I was filled with terror—but her anger was directed at Pop Major, not me. Pop Major jumped up, and I fell to the side of the bed.

"What are you doing?" she yelled. "Get out, get out of this house!" She pointed at the door with a trembling hand and yelled even louder. "Don't you ever come back when I'm not at home!"

Once he was gone, she inspected me. "What in the world did you call yourself doing?" she asked harshly.

Now I was frightened. What *had* we been doing? I told my mother we'd been playing.

"Grown men don't play with little girls like that," she told me.

When Daddy came home, she was still at the top of her anger. She told him what she'd walked in on, and she said that Pop Major was never again to step foot in our home. There was never another mention of the event. I don't know if Nana was ever privy to what had happened or if Daddy ever said anything to his father, but I know Pop Major never darkened our door again.

Words do have power. During this time of my life, Pop Major's angry words and name-calling pierced my heart, but his words also sparked defiance in me. I hated the loneliness of always being under attack. As I grew up and developed spiritually, I would come to understand the battle much differently—I would come to connect with and fully understand the words of Ephesians 6:12 (NIV): "For our struggle is not against flesh and blood, but against the rulers, against the authorities, against the powers of this dark world and against the spiritual forces of evil in the heavenly realms." As a child, I didn't have the clarity that I do now about who the war was against.

I just knew it had to be fought.

I remembered my mother's words to hold my head erect, and I designed my own words of self-affirmation. When anyone tried to diminish me, I would think to myself or say under my breath, "That's okay—one of these days, you're gonna know my name!" I laugh now, because I'm not sure where I got this from or what I was thinking with this sentiment, but these words empowered me, making me certain that anybody who messed with me would be sorry. With these words protecting me, other people's cruel words lost their power.

I was fighting back the only way I knew how. When I told myself to hold my head erect, and when I told people they would know my name, those words meant something.

They made me feel big.

chapter 4

WHAT THAT CHILD NEEDS

Every year on Children's Day, we heard a sermon preached at Second Baptist Church based on Ephesians 6:1–3 (NIV): "Children, obey your parents in the Lord, for this is right. 'Honor your father and mother'—which is the first commandment with a promise—'so that it may go well with you and that you may enjoy long life on the earth.'"

But the verses that followed, directed at parents, were never the basis for a sermon that I can remember: "Do not exasperate your children; instead, bring them up in the training and instruction of the Lord."

Growing up in my home with my mother, Daddy, Melvin, and Brenda, we had no choice but to honor our parents. My mother could have chosen to accept the assignment given to her and bring us children up in a nurturing, loving way, but instead she wielded control over us through strict rules and whippings. We lived in a cloud of anxiety, never knowing what she would criticize or what would upset her. It seemed like she had a demon inside of her that would come out on her tongue. Her words were designed to cut to the core, and she used them like a weapon to discipline, humiliate, and condemn. I was her constant target.

It is so difficult to explain in words how powerless I felt during the years of my childhood. Still I desperately wanted to understand where I came from, and I wanted to feel like I belonged somewhere.

I was twelve years old when I decided I wanted some real answers about who I was. At that point, no one in our family ever talked about me as a baby except Uncle Narvell and Aunt Kathleen. I had waited long enough to ask the questions I'd been harboring for years.

I knew Daddy wasn't my real father; I wanted to know who and where my real father was. I was used to my mother resisting questions about her life before marrying Daddy, but I was determined to get answers from her.

One Saturday morning I marched into my parents' bedroom while Mom was folding clothes and dropped a very direct question: "Who do I look like?"

Calmly, without turning around, she said, "Me, I guess."

I knew I had pushed open a door to a secret room, so now I figured I might as well walk through it. "Who's my real Daddy? Do I look anything like him?"

Mom put down the sheet she was folding and sat on the edge of the bed. She told me my father's name—Harold—and where he lived and worked and came from. I couldn't believe she was finally telling me something.

"What about me looks like him?" I asked. I wanted to feel connected to him in some way.

At that moment her face shifted, and I could feel the door to the secret room closing. "Nothing," she said. "Besides, I don't remember what he looked like."

"Do you have a picture of him?" I asked.

When she answered, her voice was like ice. "I destroyed all evidence of his existence in my life."

I thought, *Except for me.*

I said, "Did you love him?"

She said, "I thought I did."

Then, when I was certain our conversation had ended, she rose and walked over to her jewelry box. She lifted up an inlaid shelf and withdrew a folded piece of paper. She handed it to me and said, "Here's the last address I have for him. That's all I've got."

I took the piece of paper to my bedroom and gazed down at it, the only connection I had to a man I'd fantasized about my whole life. The moment my father had a name, he became real. I began to imagine his face and dream of how he'd come to find me one day. I put the slip of paper in my shoebox of special rocks and other collectibles.

I was sure my father would want to know I was alive and well. Of course he'd want to come and find me someday, I believed. I sent him many letters about myself, pouring out my soul to him, sure that he was thinking about me. I never received a response.

Now that my mother had given me this valuable information, I went looking for more. She had a close bond with her five siblings, so I decided that talking to them would be a more expedient way to get additional information. When I talked with Uncle Jesse, he told me that he and Uncle Narvell had gone looking for my father with a shotgun to get him to marry my mother, which I found very noble—although I would later learn that Uncle Jesse had made it all up.

Then Uncle Jesse thought for a moment and said, "To be honest, you were the worst thing that could have happened to Zee. She's never been the same."

I stared back at him without responding. I pushed back my tears, not wanting him to see the effect of what he'd said. But as I walked back home from his house, I wondered, "Am I the reason she's never happy? Why did she have me?" I believed what my uncle had said. I could tell my mother wasn't happy, and now, I thought, I knew the reason why. Those are words a child never forgets.

In most ways, I was a model child. I didn't have disciplinary problems in school, I was polite, I had friends, I followed the rules for the most part, and I was an average student. Yet during this time, I was starting to find my voice. I began to challenge practices that didn't make sense to me.

When I was in third grade, we learned cursive writing. I turned my paper on a different slant than everybody else, because I was left-handed. In those days, however, they tried to make everyone right-handed. Mrs. Swan, my teacher, would always take my pencil from my left hand and place it in my right hand, tilting my sheet of paper in the same direction as everyone else's paper. I've always hated being made to conform to someone else's expectations without explanation. I also hated the way Mrs. Swan made me feel like the odd one out.

I took it for as long as I could. One day, when the bell rang, I stayed behind as all the other students filed out. When Mrs. Swan returned, I was still sitting at my desk. "Carolyn," she said, "is everything all right?"

I walked up to her at the front of the room as she erased the day's lessons from the blackboard.

"If I can write as good as everyone else," I said, "will you stop turning my paper when you go past my desk?"

She was surprised—maybe by my question, my boldness, or both. After thinking for a moment, she agreed.

I practiced my cursive letters over and over again, using my left hand, doing it my way. By the end of the school year, I was receiving A's in penmanship, and Mrs. Swan was using my penmanship as an example for the other students. My stand to write with my left hand was my way of taking control of who I was and standing up for who God had made me. Society's rules wanted me to fit into a certain norm, and I stood against it.

I may have felt strong in some situations, but I often felt full of emotions that overwhelmed and confused me, full of questions I could not give voice to.

Sometimes I had inner stirrings that would be so strong and unsettling that they scared me. I had a sensation that someone was speaking inside of me. I was consumed by restlessness and a sense that I was supposed to be doing something I wasn't—a feeling that I wasn't living out my destiny. Sometimes I thought I had been here before or knew something no one else knew.

One night, I was overcome by the stirrings in my spirit. I needed to tell someone, and I wanted to express it all to my mother. She wasn't home; she was visiting some of her students' parents, as she often did.

I stayed in my bedroom, crying uncontrollably, seemingly for no reason, and I didn't let Melvin or Brenda come near me. Uncle Jesse came over for a visit and tried to calm me down, but I wouldn't let him touch me. "I need to talk to Momma!" I screamed. "I need her now!" I went under the bed and refused to come out until my mother came home.

When she finally returned, she came storming into my bedroom. "What is *wrong* with you, girl?" she asked. "I can hear you all the way to the street!" She pulled me out from under the bed and said, "You are so jealous and selfish!" She thought my crying was because she wasn't home. Her angry reaction to me stifled my need to share with her the urgings in my spirit.

In a state of frenzy, I just screamed back at her, "You don't know anything about me!"

She made no effort to find out what was really happening with me that night. She said I was having "crazy fits" and brushed me off as hysterical and dramatic. That would not be the last time I felt an overwhelming pull on my spirit—like something unexplainable and important was happening to me—but it would be years before I tried again to share my feelings with anybody.

I needed someone to listen to me and explain what I was feeling, but instead my mother mocked me and made sarcastic comments about me. She had no patience for behavior she felt was intended to get attention.

My mother claimed, for instance, that after I came to live with her, I became a bed-wetter for attention because Brenda was a bed-wetter, too. I hadn't wet the bed until I went to live with my mother, that was true—but she never considered that rather than being a bid for attention, this may have spoken to my psychological distress.

I asked her once, "Why would you think I like waking up in a wet bed? I don't do it on purpose!"

She shot back, "If it bothered you, you'd stop. You've got the whole house smelling like pee!" She didn't tolerate weaknesses in anyone, and that included my inability to control my bladder.

She spanked me every time I wet the bed, reasoning that I needed punishment for being too lazy to get up to use the bathroom. When that didn't work, she made me drag my mattress outside, scrub it with a brush and hot water, and prop it up to dry on the deck along with my sheets. "Now all your friends can know that you pee in the bed," my mother said. She thought humiliation would break me of my "nasty habit."

When that didn't work she took me to the doctor, who suggested that I stop taking in any liquids after six p.m. When Mom and I were out together and someone offered me a drink or even watermelon, my mother held up a hand and said, "No liquids for her because she'll just end up sleeping in it later." This got a snicker out of everyone but me.

I was filled with shame, but this didn't keep my bed dry. In the box of letters I found in my mother's basement after she died, I found one that I'd written to God when I was ten years old. "Dear God in Heaven," I wrote, "I know people like me but it's just that I don't do what they want me to do. Oh God please help me not to wet the bed. God please help me. In Jesus' name, Amen." Could my mother really not see I needed motherly compassion, rather than scorn?

She wasn't much easier on Brenda, although I don't remember her humiliating Brenda so publicly. Eventually we began hiding our wet sheets, sneaking them down to the ditch, and burning them along with the rest of the day's garbage. "The cleaner's is always losing our sheets," my mother would snap, and Brenda and I shot each other secretive glances.

After Brenda stopped wetting the bed, but I didn't, Mom purchased an apparatus guaranteed to stop bedwetting. I remember the salesman coming to the house and doing a demonstration with a cup of water.

Every night I turned on the device, which was placed beneath my sheet. It was a metal plate studded with electrodes. Whenever moisture hit the sensors, the device gave me an electric shock and set off an alarm. The shock, the salesman had explained, would stop the impulse to urinate, and the alarm would make sure I was awake—along with everyone else in the house, it turned out. I would hear Daddy cursing from across the hall when the alarm woke him and my mother. I was supposed to go to the bathroom, empty my bladder, splash water on my face to wake up completely, change into dry pajamas, dry off the metal plate, and put a fresh sheet over it. Several times, exhausted and wanting to avoid changing the sheets, I tried tricking the machine by putting a dry towel on top of the plate, but the alarm went off again each time. Other times I slept on the floor to avoid being awakened in terror by the alarm. After two weeks, the machine had mostly done its job, and the rest came with maturity. Eventually, the bedwetting stopped.

The shame, however, lingered. I often stared at my reflection in the mirror, wondering what it was about me that everyone, especially my mother, seemed to hate. It seemed there was something about me that was different, something in me that people felt had to be destroyed. I felt like I had been born in the middle of a war, a battle was being waged from the inside out, and I had to fight back in some form every single day to keep my spirit alive.

My closest confidant during my worst moments was our family's mutt, Toy. I would go into the basement to pour all my secrets into Toy's ear, telling myself he'd been sent by God to carry my burdens. I always felt better after talking to him; the beauty of his confidence was that he never judged me or told anyone my secrets.

Sometimes I felt I'd struggled so hard and long, and my moods became so dark, that the logical solution seemed to be death. My spirit sometimes sank so low that I concluded everyone would be happier if I was dead.

One Saturday afternoon, I was coming upstairs from the basement, and at the top of the steps, I turned and gazed down at the cement wall at the bottom. An idea presented itself, and I seized upon it.

I threw myself down the stairs and knocked myself unconscious. My parents heard my body thumping down the steps and rushed to get me to the hospital. The staff there thought I may have a concussion, along with some bumps and abrasions, but they sent me home.

Mom asked, "What happened to you?"

"I got dizzy and fell," I told her. This was a plausible explanation—I often suffered from debilitating dizzy spells and had even been to doctors, who weren't able to pinpoint the problem.

Did she know this wasn't true? I think she did, but she never put words to it. Instead she told relatives, "Versie wants some attention. She's just crazy."

I knew I wasn't crazy. I'm sure I craved her attention, but there was so much more than that going on inside me that I couldn't explain—and that no one tried to understand. I was sick of the life adults were inflicting on me. I hated being a kid with no power. I hated that life was happening to me and that I had no control over it.

But I was not left alone in a wilderness of hatred and animosity; I was surrounded by many people who showed me love. The community we lived in, my extended family, was very generous with expressing warmth and acceptance. Throughout my childhood, my saving grace was the religious foundation that was established in our lives at an early age. This foundation was the rock I would build my life upon, providing me inner strength to make it through so many difficult times.

• • •

In Dixon, the church was the heart of the Negro community and the epicenter for social activity. In the '50s and '60s, the black church was the governing body of the black community, providing a moral compass for all to follow. At church, you received communion and also got fellowship, counseling, mentoring, and social support.

The church not only worked to ensure your salvation and your seat in heaven—it also acted as judge and jury when it came to social wrongdoings. If a woman had a child out of wedlock, she would be excommunicated until she came before the church members, confessed her sin, and asked to be reinstated. Just as members were voted into the church, they were also voted out. This may sound harsh, but it was effective; when I was growing up in Dixon, it was virtually unheard of for black kids in Dixon to drop out of school or go to jail.

Of Dixon's relatively small black population, almost everybody attended Second Baptist Church. The Ashford family was among the tiny percentage that attended Lee's African Methodist Episcopal (Lee's AME). From some pictures I've seen, I believe there was a time when Lee's AME was the religious mecca of Dixon's black community. I have no idea what happened to shift the congregants away from Lee's AME and into the pews of Second Baptist Church, but by the time I arrived on the scene, Lee's AME members totaled about twelve, and ten of them were from the Ashford family. Lee's AME didn't have a Sunday school program, so we would attend Sunday school at Second Baptist before going to Lee's AME for church services. Both churches were very close to our house—we could walk out of our front door and through the neighbors' yards and be there in minutes.

My mother allowed us to play in the neighborhood, but she was strict about where else we could go. When I couldn't get permission to go anywhere else, I could always get permission to go to church. I had friends I wasn't allowed to associate with during the week, but I could see them at Sunday school, in the choir, or at Baptist Youth Fellowship. My social life consisted of church activities organized and run by adults who gave tirelessly of themselves to create events and outings for us. There was always something to do or get ready for: picnics, roller skating parties, softball games, Easter egg hunts, and holiday speeches that required new outfits—whether handmade or store bought—and new shoes. Our church community was an extension of our family, and we were never disrespectful of the adults.

I disliked going to Lee's AME for church. The pastor was none other than Pop Major, my step-grandfather who molested me. He may or may not have actually been ordained. Nana, my step-grandmother, played dual roles. As the pastor's wife, she was the mother of the church, and she also prepared the communion for First Sunday services. She made the unleavened bread the evening before, and I liked to watch her carefully pour Jesus' blood—Welch's grape juice—into the communion glasses. I found the services stiff and somber, just as the Ashfords were in their daily lives, and I longed to experience the exuberance and soulful emotion that I saw at Second Baptist.

The Lee's AME church building was also run-down and rickety, lending it a haunted appearance. Brenda and I were embarrassed to be seen walking into the dilapidated building, so we would hide behind trees until we were sure there were no cars coming before making a mad dash for the door.

Inside, you had to be careful where you walked, because the wood floors were decayed and threatened to collapse, sending you into the cold, moldy-smelling basement. In the sanctuary hung a single picture of Richard Allen, the former slave who founded African Methodist Episcopalism. The church's old wooden folding chairs were cracked and would pinch the skin on your legs if you weren't careful, and they surely put runs in every woman's stockings. The piano, which was as old as Richard Allen, was missing a few ivories and needed to be tuned and restrung. Before we got a piano at home, we had to go to Lee's AME to practice, which we dreaded.

Eventually, when Melvin was around fourteen years old, he wanted more social engagement and asked to attend First Methodist, an all-white church where many of his classmates went. Brenda followed him. My mother gave me a choice: I could attend First Methodist, or I could attend Second Baptist, staying for the service after Sunday school. It was an easy decision to stay at Second Baptist. My friends all went to Second Baptist, and I loved the emotion and rich gospel music of that church. My mother split her time between the two churches. She said she wouldn't join Second Baptist, because she knew if she did, she would have to be fully immersed in the baptism pool. The Methodist church initiated followers into the body of Christ by sprinkling them with water. She had been sprinkled, and as far as she was concerned, that should be enough. I really didn't know where my mother stood when it came to her actual faith and beliefs—when I had questions about those things, I would talk to Aunt Tutta. My mother faithfully attended church every week and didn't talk much about the rest.

Church was the first place I remember feeling acceptance. Church was my personal realm—especially because I didn't have to share it with Melvin and Brenda. It was my own place to shine, and I needed that.

The pastor of Second Baptist church, Rudolph Shoultz, was the man who married my parents. He was a large-framed man with an egg-shaped head, a warm inviting laugh, and a heavy Jamaican accent—we all teased him when he mispronounced an English word. He loved the children of the church and poured a lot of time and effort into our Christian development. He started the Baptist Youth Fellowship, which sponsored most of our social activities. Reverend Shoultz played a major role in molding my perception of my own capabilities.

He was also the one who positioned my heart to receive the call of Christ. His sermons began to ignite the spark in my spirit. I remember a few of his sermons had a profound effect on me. In one sermon I remember well, Reverend Shoultz talked about how God calls us. He said, in his heavy Jamaican accent, "When God calls you, He isn't calling you, He is calling out what He put in you." That message was incredibly powerful for me, and my imagination seized upon it. This language, I thought, explained the pull I felt inside. I became fixated on drawing out the potential that had been placed within me, and I prayed for God to bring out what He had put in me. An intense belief grew in my mind and spirit: I was predestined for something, meant to do something, although I wasn't sure what.

My experiences in the church provided me with a clear connection to a greater destiny. I developed a deep curiosity about God and a hunger for greater spiritual understanding. Church was important to me, because I realized at a very young age that God had chosen me for a personal relationship with Him. I knew there was something different about the way I embraced my life—I was always seeking answers. When most of my friends were content going to Sunday school and church, I was attending the adult Bible study class, trying to understand how the Bible applied to my life. But it was all so confusing. I wasn't able to make the "thees" and "thous" come together in a meaningful way, and I grew impatient. I wanted to read something that would explain the feelings I was struggling to understand. Everything I was being taught seemed focused on how to get to heaven, but I was trying to understand how to live the life God had called me to live while I was on earth.

Reverend Shoultz was the only person I trusted enough to share these feelings with. He never laughed at me or discouraged me when I described my restlessness and sense of predestination. He took me to the Bible and showed me Romans 8:29–31 (NIV) to show me I was right: "For those God foreknew he also predestined to be conformed to the image of his Son, that he might be the firstborn among many brothers and sisters. And those he predestined, he also called; those he called, he also justified; those he justified, he also glorified."

Reverend Shoultz told me, "I've never met anyone your age who felt this spiritual awakening so strongly."

I just kept believing I was supposed to do something to change the world—my frustration lay in not knowing what that was.

I wasn't particularly enjoying my childhood. I found my mother's strict rules oppressive and her opinion of me hurtful. We only had fifteen years to live under the same roof, but I spent most of those fifteen years planning and daydreaming about my life as an adult, far away from her control, living life on my terms. After experiencing so many personal assaults, I understood that I needed to protect my spirit so who I really was didn't get lost or weakened. I began to plot out a survival plan to get through my remaining years under my mother's control. Rather than looking at everything in terms of years, I focused on milestones I would achieve.

Celebrating my birth was always extremely important to me, and becoming a teenager held great significance in my plans for independence. I looked forward to my thirteenth birthday with great anticipation, feeling its importance.

I planned a symbolic gesture that would signify and celebrate my sense of empowerment and personal independence. When the big day came—Saturday, November 14, 1964—I quietly dressed, put on a jacket, and tucked my rock collection box under my arm. Without saying a word to Daddy, who was already at the kitchen table sipping his cup of coffee and reading the morning paper, I slipped out the side door.

I ran down to the ditch behind our house. I selected the thirteen shiniest stones from my rock collection and balanced them in my right hand. I cast them into the water one by one. I felt like David, who had picked up five smooth stones with which to slay Goliath. After throwing all the stones, I proclaimed aloud, "From this day on, I declare I will never need *anyone* anymore!"

I was done expecting people to take care of me. I simply didn't *want* to need anyone, because by now I knew that needing people only led to disappointment.

This same year, Reverend Shoultz's sermons and all I'd learned in church brought me to the altar to accept Jesus Christ as my personal savior. I'd always felt like an outsider, and the story of Christ was easy for me to embrace; it brought me peace and confirmation. Even as I was becoming independent and resolute, I was nurturing an understanding that I needed a spiritual connection to a power greater than me to sustain me.

The day of my baptism was the only time I remember Daddy coming to Second Baptist. I remember being submerged in the baptism pool and coming up, surprised that there were no doves flying to commemorate this momentous occasion. I remember knowing that this was a very important moment in my life.

I stepped into my thirteenth year with a determination to make it on my own, based on the rules, plans, and dreams I established for my life. I was ready to take charge.

chapter 5

FINDING MY VOICE

Every night, as a child, I prayed to make my mother happy. I wanted to be the one to soften her eyes and bring a smile to her face. Although discipline and order were the cornerstones of our life, I longed for my mother's warmth, love, and affection.

I often cried myself to sleep while kneeling beside my bed, talking to God. I always said the same thing: "God, it's okay if no one loves me today, because when I grow up I'll have someone who loves me all the way." It brought me some relief to think this way, reassuring myself that childhood was only a short part of my life—that I could endure anything if someday I was with someone who would love and accept me just as I was.

So I lay in bed imagining my life as an adult. I may have wanted to please my mother, but I was certain I could make better decisions for my life than she and Daddy were making. I was convinced that armed with the right tools, I could be completely independent. "If I could get a job and drive a car," I wrote in my diary, "I could take care of myself."

I was still too young to drive, but getting a job would bring me closer to the independence I so desperately craved. On the Monday following my thirteenth birthday, I went to the post office and got the form to apply for my Social Security number and a work permit.

During the school year, I made money babysitting the children of my mother's teacher friends. During the summers, though, I could put my work permit to use.

My first official job was working as a carhop at the A&W drive-in, where I wore an apron and a little coin-changer cylinder on my belt. Customers drove into stalls underneath the A&W awnings and placed their orders through the speakers. Once their orders were ready, I'd bring them out, and the car's driver would roll down the window so I could latch the tray onto the outside of the window frame. The trays were heaped with hamburgers, hotdogs, and A&W's specialty—root beer floats in frosted mugs. My career as a carhop came to an end when I accidentally tipped a root beer float into a customer's lap.

I also worked at the Dixon Theatre, a pale brick building with a stately façade located on Galena Avenue, Dixon's main thoroughfare. I worked at the concession stand selling candy and popcorn. When I first started, I didn't know how to count back change; one customer saw me behind the counter, doing the math on a piece of paper, and gave me a lesson on how to count back change. The best part of the job was getting free popcorn and getting to see free movies.

But church was the place I demonstrated my leadership and developed my talents and independence. My mother had always wanted to learn to play a musical instrument, but she'd never had the privilege, so she wanted all three of us kids to be musical. We took tap dancing lessons for a short period. Then she insisted that we each play an instrument for school—drums for Melvin, clarinet for Brenda and me—and also the piano. None of my friends were involved in these activities, but my mother was determined to give us exposure to cultural opportunities she hadn't had herself. For the times we grew up in, we were the whitest acting black family in Dixon.

From the time I was six or seven years old, on Saturdays we went to the north side of town to the home of our piano teacher, Mrs. Chasteen. When one of us had our lesson, the other had to play in the back of the house with our teacher's granddaughter, watching cartoons or playing whatever games she thought up. Mrs. Chasteen held lessons in her parlor at the front of the house. If we did well during a lesson, we were allowed to lift the top of the antique coat seat and select a candy bar. She taught us songs that we would perform at her annual grand piano recital, an event she and her students took seriously. Posture and the way we held our hands was as important as how we performed. I still value the discipline that those lessons instilled in me.

Even when I was a young child, people teased and mimicked my rich, deep voice. Aunt Tutta sometimes came by our house and asked me to play the piano and sing for her—usually her favorite hymns—and I enjoyed singing, but I hadn't really thought of my voice as a particular gift.

One Saturday when I was thirteen years old, during Junior Choir rehearsal, our director, Mrs. Hughes, was trying to find a soloist. She had each of us try out to see who could sing the selected song best. When my turn came I opened my mouth and let the song explode. Reverend Shoultz came out of his study and asked, "Who was that? Let me hear that child again."

So I sang for him again. The solo—"I Believe"—was given to me, and on the Sunday I was set to sing it, my mother left First Methodist early to come hear me. For weeks afterward I would replay in my mind the expression of pride on her face. Whenever I sang after that, I would search for my mother in the audience and sing directly to her, because it seemed her face softened while I was singing.

One day after choir rehearsal, Reverend Shoultz called me into his study. "How are you coming along with your piano lessons?" he asked.

"I'm doing good," I told him.

"Well, I have an idea, for something you can do," he said. "I want to start a young children's choir, and I want you to play for them."

By age thirteen, my personality had taken shape: I was a person who took ideas and built plans upon them quickly. Once Reverend Shoultz sparked the idea, my imagination created the possibilities and the plans. He saw something in me and nurtured it, not even asking if I thought I could take on this responsibility. He said I would do it, and I believed him.

As I walked home that afternoon, I began putting together my ideas for the choir. When I returned to church on Sunday, I approached Reverend Shoultz.

"I'll do it," I told him, "but I want to lead it on my own." I didn't want the adults coming in, trying to tell me how to run things.

Reverend Shoultz laughed. "Girl, you're something else, you know that?"

I made a list of the children ages five to twelve, the range I'd set for the choir. Some of the kids were just a few years younger than I was, but already I considered myself their leader. I went to visit those children's parents to share my plans with them. I told them when to drop their kids off for practice and when to pick them up, and each of them agreed. I took my plans to Reverend Shoultz, and he just smiled and patted me on the shoulder.

I selected hymns and other pieces largely based on what I could play on the piano, especially because at thirteen, my hands couldn't span very wide ranges of keys. I used my babysitting money to buy sheet music. After a month of practice, I made flyers to give out at church, advertising the youth choir. My first rehearsal drew more than a dozen children.

We rehearsed on Saturday afternoons in the sanctuary. The children were respectful, never challenging my authority, and I never considered failure—only what I could accomplish. The kids' parents would drop them off, and I'd teach them the words to a song until they had them memorized before adding in the music. I liked to teach them interesting techniques; I taught them vocal percussion to go with "Little Drummer Boy," and when they sang "Up From the Grave He Arose," they all stood up in unison.

Reverend Shoultz dubbed us the "Angelic Choir," and we sang on the second Sunday of each month. On the Sundays we sang, all the children wore dark pants or skirts paired with white shirts. Reverend Shoultz bought red ties for the boys and red ribbons for the girls. During rehearsals he stayed in his study, never interfering. The choir's size fluctuated, growing as large as eighteen children at some point. I drew out the most reluctant children to sing solos and the shyest children to direct the choir as I accompanied them on piano. One boy was so small he had to stand on a chair to be seen. Following the director's hand gestures, the children stood, turned, and filed in rows up to the sanctuary steps.

In summers, we sometimes sang at the white churches, whose choirs took summers off. At Christmas I planned caroling parties and prepared chili and Christmas cookies for everyone all by myself. All we needed parents for was to drive us around town to houses not in walking distance.

I sometimes invited the kids to my house for black history lessons, wanting to share what I was reading and learning. I grew to love those children, and I wanted them to be proud of who they were—to hold their heads erect and command all men's respect. I would lead the Angelic Choir until I left for college. Having the trust and confidence of Reverend Shoultz and the parents to guide these little people, especially when I was so young myself, gave me a sense of purpose and maturity and bolstered my self-confidence.

During this time between childhood and adulthood, when I was maturing and growing independent, our family changed again.

My mother had a college classmate living in Indiana whose niece had gotten pregnant. My mother's friend and her husband reached out to my mother to see if she and Daddy would adopt the baby. When I was eleven years old, Mom, Daddy, Brenda, Melvin, and I went to Indiana to visit their family. I remember being sad for the baby, who was in a room by herself, crying but getting no comfort from anyone. We visited once more, and I would discover later that my mother wanted to adopt the baby, but Daddy said no.

Aunt Etta and Uncle Kent, though, still desperately wanted a child, so arrangements were made for them to adopt this baby girl. I was so excited for them—I knew they had wanted a child for so long.

One afternoon I was helping Aunt Etta prepare for the baby's arrival, hanging up some little dresses she had bought. I remarked, "Boy, this is one lucky little girl." I paused. "I wish *I* was your baby."

Aunt Etta came over and snatched the dresses from me. She said, "You were *supposed* to be our baby. This ain't nothing but Zee's guilt. She's trying to make up for taking you away from us. She told us we could adopt you, but then she got Gene to marry her. When she had what she wanted she got all high and mighty and took you back."

I stood and stared at her, shocked by her outburst. This was a story I had never heard.

As if to convince me, she added, "I've got the papers to prove it!"

Once I was home, I asked my mother about what my aunt had said. "I don't know why Etta Mae told you that," she said, taken aback. "I have never told anyone they could adopt you!"

So I went to Aunt Tutta, hoping she could either confirm or deny this new information. "That Etta Mae is just a bitter woman always trying to stir up trouble. I wish she would just keep her mouth shut!"

It was this kind of secrecy and contradiction that kept me confused and full of questions. How many more secrets and lies were there? To this day I do not know.

Mom and Daddy drove my aunt and uncle to Indiana and came back with their new daughter. I still called Aunt Etta and Uncle Kent "Mommy" and "Daddy," and the instant they returned with the six-month-old baby, I claimed her as my sister. Right away, I was crazy about her.

Her name was DeShon, but after she grabbed for a piece of candy from Uncle Kent's hand, we began calling her Candy. We all doted on her. Aunt Etta and Uncle Kent were beside themselves, giving her everything she ever wanted. I often kept Candy, and sometimes when we couldn't get her to sleep, Brenda and I rode around town with her in the car—Brenda had her license by then—until she dozed off.

At this time, Aunt Etta and Uncle Kent lived just one block over from us, so that they could stand in their backyard and see through the neighbor's yard and into ours. By now Uncle Kent had lost his right leg to poor circulation, likely from his heavy drinking. By the time his leg was amputated, it was black from him putting it in the oven, trying to keep it warm. Neither he nor Aunt Etta had a car, and Uncle Kent got around by getting rides, or swinging on crutches, refusing to wear the prosthesis he'd been fitted for.

Aunt Etta was still working, and Uncle Kent was carrying on as he always had—even with one leg, he hadn't stopped hitting the streets in search of a good time. There were rumors he was seeing several women behind Aunt Etta's back. He'd come to our house two or three times a week, usually looking for a babysitter and a ride, with Candy toddling in front of him. He guided her with a crutch, and if she fell, he extended one crutch so she could hoist herself back up. Unlike when I lived with him, his baby girl didn't hold him down—I was always willing to watch over the adorable child I considered my sister.

I remember once, when we were doing yard work, Uncle Kent came over asking Melvin to drive him somewhere. Daddy said no, and as Uncle Kent walked away on his crutches, I ran after him.

"Don't worry," I told him, "when I get my license, I'll take you anywhere you want to go."

Uncle Kent laughed. "Okay," he said. "Get on back."

He had his faults, but he was an easygoing man, a kind man whom all the kids loved. Unlike my mother, he was living life on his own terms, though imperfectly. He added more colorful dimensions of life to the family. He was still the same Uncle Kent who'd left home as a teenager to ride the rails. He liked to listen to jazz and the blues—Etta James, Sarah Vaughan, Sam Cooke—which I didn't hear in our buttoned-up, holier-than-thou household.

It was important to him that I acted like a lady. When he saw me playing crazy eights with my friends, he slapped the cards out of my hands.

"Ladies don't play cards," he chastised. But how often had I seen him playing cards with Aunt Etta? He was fond of saying, "A whistling woman and a crowing hen always come to a no-good end," yet he was the one who taught me how to whistle. He taught me many of life's lessons, but the most profound one was the ugliness of being drunk. When Uncle Kent was drunk, he would slobber, slur his words, and talk meanly, and his handsome face would take on a different look, his eyes red and his eyelids sagging. His clothes would become disheveled. He became someone different, someone I didn't like. I vowed I would not drink so I wouldn't lose control of myself like that.

A week before my fourteenth birthday, Uncle Kent's drinking, smoking, and fast living caught up with him, and he had a heart attack. He went to the hospital, where he stayed for most of a week. Mom and I had planned a trip to Rockford to get our hair done, and Mom promised me we could visit Uncle Kent in the hospital once we'd returned—but before we left, Aunt Tutta called.

"Versie," she said, "Versie, Buddy just died."

No, it couldn't be true. I never got to see him. I kept thinking that if I'd only been able to visit him, things would be different. Here I was, a freshman in high school, just days away from my fourteenth birthday, and my beloved "Daddy" was gone.

Their little girl, Candy, was three years old, too young to attend the funeral. I marched in with Aunt Etta, and I was the most emotional mourner, completely devastated. I couldn't bear watching them close that casket lid on his face. The funeral director, knowing Uncle Kent had a daughter, addressed me as Candy. When a church deacon corrected him, Aunt Etta said, "She should be listed as his daughter—he's the only father she's ever had." By this time I felt that Gene Ashford was my father, but I had always felt torn in my allegiances, and hearing Aunt Etta say this made me feel the loss of Uncle Kent even more strongly.

For the first time, I felt the deep, irrevocable loss and pain of death, a pain that would eventually be replaced with happy memories. Several months after the funeral, I dreamed I saw my uncle headed up to heaven, and as he neared the clouds, I saw his leg grow back. I didn't know if he was heaven material or not, but he had left an indelible impression on earth during his fifty years of living.

I continued caring for Candy to help Aunt Etta after she lost Uncle Kent.

Every Sunday morning, I walked around the block and picked her up to go to Sunday school. One Sunday I walked into the house and realized something was wrong.

Four-year-old Candy was crawling on the kitchen counter, trying to make herself a piece of toast. I found Aunt Etta still in bed.

She tried to speak, but her words were unintelligible, and her eyes were open but filled with fear.

I called my mother, who came over right away. When she took in the eerie scene, she called for an ambulance and told me to take Candy to church.

We learned that Aunt Etta had suffered a stroke. Over the next few weeks she had several more strokes, leaving her partially paralyzed and unable to speak beyond the word "No." She was eventually placed in a nursing home. The light went out of her eyes, and she died long before she took her final breath ten years later.

After this, my patchwork quilt family took on another patch. We brought Candy home, and she simply stayed with us.

About six months after Aunt Etta's stroke, we were returning home from a Dixon High School musical, and we found a police car parked in front of the house. A police officer and a woman—I assume a social worker—approached us.

The police officer spoke only to Candy. "Are you DeShon?" he asked. Candy didn't know that name.

My mother pulled Candy behind her, putting herself between Candy and the officer. "What do you want?" she asked.

The officer said he was there to serve papers to DeShon and take her into custody by order of the Department of Children and Family Services.

My mother grabbed the papers out of his hand. "You wait until ten o'clock at night to show up here and give papers to a five-year-old?" she shouted. "Are you crazy? We've had her all this time, and no one is taking her anywhere."

She began ushering us into the house. "I'll get an attorney and see you in court," she called back. "Until then, you know where she is—she isn't going anywhere. Don't you come here again waving papers at a child!"

They never came back. No other attempts were made to remove Candy from our family. I was impressed with my mother and how fiercely she'd protected my little sister. God had placed another solitary one in her care.

I had spoken aloud that Candy was my little sister, and it had become reality. Candy was my sister, and I believed there was a reason she'd been brought into my life. From then on, I protected her as if she was my own child.

I was a daughter, but I felt like a mother. I was a student, but I felt like a teacher. I was a child, but I felt like a grownup. I was still finding my voice. Soon, though, I would learn to use my voice even more powerfully as I tried to make a difference.

chapter 6

ANSWERING THE CALL

Once my talent had set me apart, I became serious about singing. I idolized Mahalia Jackson, "The Queen of Gospel," whose soulful, bluesy singing style I often tried to mimic. I once wrote her a letter asking for the privilege of training under her. She wrote me back saying that she was looking for a building to record and train in, and she told me to keep in touch. Nothing came of it, but that single correspondence served as fuel for the fire of my passion.

I sang anywhere I was asked to perform. I continued to sing in the church choir and the choir at school. I tried out for talent shows and won a few awards singing in the Dixon Petunia Festival talent shows. Each time I placed, I got $25 and my picture in the paper. I was often invited to be a guest soloist at area churches, and I sang at weddings and funerals.

A large part of what drove me to continue with my music was the smile that brightened my mother's face while she watched me sing. She told me I had gotten my gift from my grandfather. When I sang, I felt she saw me as special. Ironically, she would play a role in limiting my dream of developing my singing talent.

Reverend Shoultz, wanting me to add some gospel rhythm to my by-the-book piano playing, offered me the opportunity to study music with a very talented and accomplished musician and singer in St. Louis,

Missouri. I would be able to stay with her for the summer.

Reverend Shoultz came to our house to discuss it with my mother, and I felt sure he would be able to convince her. "The church would cover all the costs," he explained. Yet in the end, she wouldn't be persuaded to let me spend the summer with someone she didn't know.

Once Reverend Shoultz had left and I saw my mother wasn't going to relent, I was full of indignation. Brenda and Melvin went on a two-week church trek each summer, seeing places like Mount Rushmore and the Grand Canyon. "How come Melvin and Brenda are allowed to go on their treks with people you don't know, but I can't do this?" I argued.

But I knew my mother. She wasn't going to budge. I was used to her telling me no.

Mrs. Hughes, our church organist, went instead, and she ended up becoming this singer's accompanist. They toured Europe and eventually came to Dixon to perform, and I believe that then my mother understood the opportunity she'd denied me.

As time went on, I came to see that my voice was an instrument for the moment, rather than a lifelong dream to pursue. Still, I believe every gift has a perfect purpose. Nothing is lost—everything is in preparation for what God has planned.

If my singing career did nothing more than prepare me to stand before an audience and be unafraid, then it was a lesson that would serve me well. As I grew up, I was learning to use my voice for other things—namely, to speak out against injustice and work for real change.

I was coming of age in the 1960s, at the height of the Civil Rights Movement. We watched the race riots going on in the South on TV. It was frightening to see black men, women, and children being knocked off their feet by the force of water hoses and then, while they were down, being attacked by dogs. I remember when civil rights activist Medgar Evers was gunned down in his driveway in Mississippi. I remember the gathering at our church and my mother's shock and profound sadness.

When our family made trips to Mississippi to visit relatives, I saw black chain gangs along the highway. I saw water fountains marked "For Colored Only." I remember my mother sneaking us to the fountain marked "For Whites Only," shielding us from the white attendant's view so we could drink from a cold, clean fountain instead of using the warm, filthy one reserved for us. Mom believed that white patrons had used our fountain as a urinal.

Once, on a summer trip to Houston, Texas, we had to spend the night in Arkansas. The only hotel that gave rooms to black people was a filthy spot over a black juke joint. I don't think Momma or Daddy ever closed their eyes.

I used to wonder where I got my burning desire to make a difference. I've learned it's part of my DNA—I would one day discover that not only my mother, but also my biological father fought on the frontline for civil rights and racial equality. They fought to overcome every obstacle that might have prevented them from pursuing their inalienable rights to strive in their careers and provide for their families. Their efforts opened doors for future generations.

I would one day learn that my father was a porter with the railroad. It was a service job, but he held it with honor and dignity. He was chairman of his union, a position he used to challenge the long-held Jim Crow laws giving his white coworkers preferential treatment in benefits, pay, and job responsibilities. He spearheaded the efforts that helped the Porters' Union and the national branch of the NAACP win a landmark discrimination suit against the Frisco Railroad.

My mother, for her part, never stopped fighting against the pervasive strongholds of racism. She didn't allow anything to stop her from achieving her dream of teaching in the public school system. This fight may have played a role in her bitterness, because it certainly required tremendous sacrifice—she was even willing to sacrifice her own child—but big dreams cannot be lived without some sacrifice.

When my mother was blocked from teaching in Dixon Public Schools, I watched her work two other jobs instead, biding her time. During the day, she taught patients with intellectual and developmental disabilities at the Dixon State School, a mental hospital. At nights and on weekends, she often catered parties for Dixon's wealthy white society. She prepared fancy dishes for their parties, served the food, and cleaned up afterwards.

Sometimes my mother's rich employers would send home their children's unwanted hand-me-down clothing. I loved one of those outfits—a white pleated skirt and a blue blazer with an emblem on the breast pocket—until I bounced into class and one of my classmates shouted out, "That used to belong to me, but I didn't want it anymore!" I couldn't wait to get home and get out of those clothes.

Knowing how proud my mother was, I often wondered how she must have felt going into those people's homes and working for them, even while she was qualified for so much more. Never once did she complain. She told me, "Don't you ever tell me you didn't get something because of the color of your skin. Whatever barriers are in front of you, you just work to overcome them." She was determined to defeat the system that was trying so hard to hold her back. The system kept telling her no, but she just kept on pushing.

She had a bachelor's degree, but she was told she had to have a master's degree, even though this wasn't required of white teachers. She didn't falter. She had not finished getting her master's degree at Iowa State after marrying Daddy, so she enrolled at Illinois State University and often drove to Normal, Illinois, after work to take her classes, a two-and-a-half-hour trip each way by herself. During the summer she packed up us kids, rented an apartment, and enrolled us in summer school while she focused on her studies. It was a strain on the family and the finances, but she accomplished what she set out to do.

I was in sixth grade when Mom became the first black teacher in Dixon. There was true jubilation in the black community when she broke through that color barrier. I was proud to be her daughter. Her picture was in the paper, and our close family friends Leon and Regina Jones hosted a neighborhood tea in her honor.

Over the years, Leon and Regina became woven into the fabric of our family. Eventually they moved around the corner from our house, and I often walked to school with their oldest daughter, who was a few years younger than me. Regina and Leon made a beautiful couple, both of them tall, thin, and stylish. Regina played the piano by ear, and I marveled that she could do that—or anything else—with her long painted fingernails. She was someone I could always talk to, and she encouraged me to think for myself.

Living in Dixon, segregated though it was, I felt cushioned from the racial war and rage I saw on TV, safe in my corner of the world. But if I believed that the suffering and hatred I saw on TV only happened to the colored folks in the South, I would soon begin to adjust my naive thinking and receive an in-depth education on what it meant to be black.

Leon, who was my Sunday school teacher, was a committed activist whom some labeled a militant. He was determined that the young students he had been assigned to teach Bible lessons would learn the lessons of what it meant to be black in America. Every Sunday he came in with a book on black history, and he taught us solidarity and pride in our heritage instead of the assigned Bible lessons. He taught us what the history books were leaving out. I was completely engrossed in what we were learning. I began to feel even more confident as I held my head erect.

I admired Leon and Regina because of what they stood for. They weren't sitting around talking about the injustices—they were actively involved in fighting them. Every Saturday, they went into Chicago to attend Reverend Jesse Jackson's Operation Breadbasket, growing more and more militant. They stood out in our conservative community with their Afros, stylish dashikis, and Afro-centric artwork. Leon and Regina were passionate about the operation's mission to organize boycotts that would pressure white businesses into hiring black people and purchasing from black contractors. I could always count on a rousing conversation when I visited their home.

During my freshman year of high school, Malcolm X was assassinated. His death struck a chord with the black people in Dixon, and I began to see a shift in attitude. We began to transition from being "Negro," and from being "colored," to being "Black and Proud!" I got permission to go with the Joneses to Operation Breadbasket meetings. My mother, a lifetime member of the NAACP, would bring me to local meetings with her. There I heard the rhetoric of backlash and conversations about how to bring about change, such as by boycotting businesses that didn't hire black workers. Mom and I would sit together among those gathered at the Loveland Community Building—where my piano recitals were held—or in the basement of Second Baptist Church.

In the summer of 1967, between my sophomore and junior years, Mom chaperoned a trip for a few of us young members of Dixon's NAACP branch; we traveled to the 58th Annual NAACP National Convention in Boston, Massachusetts. A month earlier, there had been a race riot in the ghetto district of Roxbury, and witnessing the riot's aftermath—the sheer destruction in these people's neighborhoods—truly opened my eyes to a world I'd never been exposed to. I had thought of my own neighborhood as a ghetto because it was segregated, but nothing compared to the poverty I saw in Roxbury. Windows were boarded up, and fires had destroyed many buildings. People were sitting on broken front stoops and leaning out of windows with no panes. Children played in the spray of fire hydrants.

Until then, I'd seen the civil rights war through other people's experiences, but seeing it firsthand convinced me I had to take a stand wherever I could. I had a stronger sense than ever of the change I wanted to be a part of, and I knew I had to do something with my life to make a difference in other people's lives—especially my own people. I began reading every book about black people I could find. Making a difference became my obsession.

Every time I saw an opportunity to take the path less traveled, I took it. It seemed that a rite of passage for youth in the black community in Dixon was working at the Dixon State School. The pay was probably decent, but doing what everyone else did felt common to me, so I promised myself I would never work there. I wanted to take a different path and open an alternative possibility for other black kids. I decided I'd work as a Park District counselor. Before I even got an interview, I approached one of the teachers at my school who I knew was on the Park District Board. I declared, "I plan to work at the Park District this summer." He just saluted me.

I had made up my mind.

"Go ahead," Daddy said with a smirk. "You're going to get your feelings hurt." He was convinced I wouldn't get the job.

But I did get the job, and I was assigned to a park just a block from our house. A photo ran in the newspaper of me with all the other Park District counselors. When Daddy's sister Lillie Mae saw it, she exclaimed, "Look at you, the only fly in the buttermilk." I knew this wasn't a major strike against the status quo, but it was my small way of opening a door that no one else had considered passing through.

In my quest to be authentic, I urged everyone to call me by my "real" name—Carolyn, no more Versie. But there happened to be another girl at Second Baptist named Carolyn, spelled the same way. Then, to make matters worse, our church got a new minister, Reverend Savage, whose wife's name was *also* Carolyn—again spelled the same way! I decided it was time to set myself apart. I decided to add an extra "n" to my name. I even insisted it was pronounced with an emphasis on the final syllable, trying to create my own identity and differentiate myself from the other Carolyns. From that point on, I would be Caro*lynn*.

In school, I had a bit of a reputation for challenging what we were being taught. I didn't understand why biology and chemistry were a requirement for everybody planning to go to college. I had no intentions of being a doctor or a scientist. Algebra made no sense, and I just wanted to learn conversational Spanish, not memorize and fill in charts of verb tenses in Spanish.

Most importantly, I didn't understand why there was no mention in our history books of African Americans' contributions to our nation's development.

I'd spent my entire school career learning about every culture but my own. We'd learned about slavery, but beyond that all anyone heard about was Booker T. Washington and George Washington Carver. Once I began learning from Leon during Sunday school, and doing my own reading, I felt empowered and angry.

Then, for my junior year of high school, I got Mr. Jordan for American history. He knew I loved to debate, and he wasted no time in challenging me. When we began studying the Civil War, he asked me to research racial conditions of the country during that era and the war's impact on slaves.

Back then you couldn't just use Google to find your information. I did my research at school and in the public library, meticulously writing down card catalog numbers and hunting down books that might be helpful in my mission. There weren't many books about the topics I was researching, but I gathered everything I could. I interviewed Leon and other black leaders in the community. My mother, knowing that Mr. Jordan was working on his master's degree, suspected he was using me—using my research to help him write his papers.

Even if he was, I didn't care. Because once a week, Mr. Jordan turned the class over to me so I could teach my fellow students the half of history our books left out. I rose to the challenge. I felt such a sense of pride standing in front of my white classmates, sharing with them the role African Americans had played in the building of America and in fighting the Civil War. I showed them the role slavery played in the Civil War and the atrocities inflicted on freed slaves and their families after the war had ended. I told them about the active participation of African Americans in the South's politics and economy during the Reconstruction years. A few of them seemed interested, but they were largely apathetic. I don't remember anyone raising their hands to ask questions.

At that time, black history was a new field of study at the college level. Mr. Jordan invited me to go with him and my Civics teacher, Miss Woods, to a black history conference at Southern Illinois University during spring break. I was surprised when Mom agreed to let me go, and I felt grateful to be exposed to such a wealth of information.

I was using my voice—doing my part to raise awareness, provide perspective, and open a dialogue with some of my more empathetic white classmates. My assignment didn't just fuel my insatiable appetite for information; it also made me realize that my voice was powerful and credible.

During this time, Dr. Martin Luther King Jr. was preaching nonviolent civil disobedience. He was working with the Southern Christian Leadership Conference to organize the "Poor People's Campaign" to address economic injustice. Back when I was twelve years old, I had seen his famous "I Have a Dream" speech on television. It was August 28, 1963, and I was at Aunt Gladys's house. I would often visit her to keep her company, do work in the garden, and play with her dog, Mitzy.

On this particular day, Aunt Gladys made me come in to rest, have a glass of iced tea, and watch the march on Washington. I didn't want to spend all day watching these people speak, but she wouldn't let me get up—she made me stay on the sofa, her knitted Afghan draped over my legs.

I had no idea I was seeing history in the making. I was excited to see my singing idol, Mahalia Jackson, on stage with Dr. King, who requested that she perform. "My soul looks back and wonders how we made it over," she began, her rich voice filling Aunt Gladys's living room.

Then, once Dr. King was delivering his speech, I started really sitting up and paying attention. He spoke with so much power and conviction. Midway through his remarks, Mahalia shouted out, "Tell them about the dream, Martin!"

His passion grew even larger as he spoke, his words like thunder rumbling on the steps of the Lincoln Memorial, describing the future he imagined. "I have a *dream* today!" he repeated, over and over, stirring the crowd into frenzy. Tears gathered in my eyes. Dr. King painted a picture with his words, his voice trembling with emotion, describing a day when everyone in the world would join hands and sing the words of the old Negro spiritual: "Free at last!" he roared. "Free at last! Thank God Almighty, we are free at last!"

Aunt Gladys and I stood up and applauded. Wiping her eyes, Aunt Gladys explained how much courage this speech had taken. I felt a deep sense of black pride and a deep sense of hope.

It was during my junior year, the same time I was teaching my white classmates in Mr. Jordan's American History class, that Dr. King was assassinated.

The rage and pain I felt were difficult to contain. It felt like a scary time to be black. The day following the assassination, we black students came to school with an attitude of new defiance, growing bitter when we saw no sadness in our white classmates' faces.

At the beginning of choir class, a classmate and I requested to lead everyone in singing the black American anthem "Lift Every Voice and Sing." Our teacher refused our request, so the two of us waited until class began, stood up, and walked out. A few others followed, and more black students walked out of other classrooms. We all met under the big clock in the main lobby, and together we marched off campus. It was a quiet act of defiance, but we felt like we were showing our unity after the death of the leader of our people.

I was full of fire and the determination to make my life matter.

Soon after Dr. King's death, Mr. Jordan approached me with a new idea. "Carolynn, you should run for a Student Council position. I believe you can do it, and I think you'd be the first Negro to win it. Think about it!"

This was the spark that ignited a fire. Walking home that day, I decided I would run for vice president. After that moment, I never considered losing.

Ideas began popping in my head like popcorn. I began to design the strategy I needed to run a successful campaign. I charted everything out: I wrote out my action plan and the resources I needed. I would make campaign posters and put them up around school. I would need campaign buttons, and I'd need to write and deliver a speech. I was excited, and I was determined. I knew I would be victorious, because I believed what I said, and I believed what I said would happen.

My campaign platform was based on creating change in restrictive school policies, whether that meant loosening the dress code or creating open study time for seniors. My greatest supporters turned out to be my mother and my cousin Evelyn. I wasn't surprised by my mother's support—she fully backed all of our educational endeavors—but it felt good to be on the same side, fighting for a common cause. It felt good to know that something I was taking a stand for made her proud.

Mom recruited her student teacher, a talented artist, to create my campaign posters. Mom handmade the campaign buttons while Evelyn helped me practice my speech, making me repeat it until I thought I'd lose my voice, ensuring I expressed the right inflection. I decided I was going to make being black a cool thing—my campaign slogan was, "Put soul in your stroll and pride in your stride and vote for Ashford!"

My whole community was rooting for me, awaiting the results of the election. The winners would be announced at a school dance, and when that weekend arrived, Brenda even came home from college to cheer me on. As I was getting ready for the dance, Reverend Shoultz called to say, "Whether you win or lose, we're all so proud of you." My neighbors shouted out encouragement as I got in the car to go: "We're praying that you win, Versie!"

When the results were finally announced for student council vice president, it was my name they read out to the crowd.

I felt like I'd won the Nobel Peace Prize or an Academy Award. A photographer from the Dixon Evening Telegraph was taking pictures, the flashbulbs blinding me, and I was swarmed by people hugging and congratulating me. The next day, my picture was on the front page of the paper. Finally, people were beginning to know my name.

During my senior year, as student council VP, I worked to make practical differences in students' lives. I was named ambassador for our foreign exchange student. I worked with our assistant principal to get us a senior lounge area with a jukebox, and the dress code was adjusted to fit the styles of the day. I was also allowed to choose new African American artwork for the halls.

As graduation approached, I considered my life after high school. I had two distinct goals: to be a wife and mother, and to change the world. The first one I dreamed about, and the other I planned to do.

• • •

During my sophomore year, I'd begun dating a boy named Ron. At least, we called it dating, although I wasn't allowed to go anywhere. My mother's rules were clear: I couldn't date officially until I was sixteen, once I was a junior. So I would cheer for Ron at basketball games and go with him to school events. Ron was tall, good-looking, and smart, with a dry sense of humor. I liked him a lot, but after a while I realized there was just no spark between us, no excitement.

During that same time, my girlfriends and I met some boys from Freeport at a football game between the Dixon Dukes and the Freeport

Pretzels. Freeport was about a forty-five-minute drive north of Dixon. After that game, virtually every weekend a carload of the "Freeport boys" came to town and camped out at spots in Dixon where they were allowed to congregate. They would come in on Saturday evening, or sometimes Friday, and stay until late on Sunday. Many visits they could be seen at my neighbor Barbara's house just three doors down the block. Often on Sundays when I was walking to church for the evening service, I had to walk past Barbara's house, where they were often hanging out. They would catcall or attempt to introduce themselves, but I had been taught that to respond to such tactics was not ladylike, so I just kept walking, even though I was secretly delighted by the attention and intrigued by their presence. Every Monday after the Freeport boys visited, I was eager to hear the weekend's details from my girlfriends.

For nearly a year, I lived vicariously through my friends, but I remained loyal to Ron—until one particular Saturday night.

A friend of mine named Debbie was in town from Rockford to spend the weekend with me. I'd met Debbie through Aunt Gladys and we became good friends; her parents were the kind of respectable people Aunt Gladys liked to introduce us to. We'd planned a double date to the movies, but she got stood up, and Ron was grounded, so all our plans were shot. I was desperately seeking something exciting for us to do.

As usual, the Freeport boys were in town, hanging out at Barbara's house on the corner. Debbie and I decided to venture over to see what was going on.

We walked past a couple necking on the porch, not acknowledging anybody. We went into the house, where the lights were dimmed very low and R&B music was playing. It was a small party, probably fewer than ten people.

My friends had told me about a shy Freeport boy they thought was perfect for me. Curious, I agreed to be introduced to him. We said hello awkwardly, and that was it.

I stood around while Debbie talked to other people—she seemed to be doing better than I was when it came to attracting male attention. Eventually, though, we decided we weren't interested in anybody there, and we decided to leave the party.

I approached Barbara to say goodbye. "We're going home," I told her. "He's not talking, and I don't have time."

From the shadows came a voice: "Don't go, I'll talk. What do you want me to say?"

I shrugged and turned on my heel, not caring to waste any more of my time. Debbie and I left and walked back to my house.

We sat in my bedroom discussing conversations we'd had at the party. Suddenly, my telephone rang. Figuring it was Barbara asking us to come back, I answered with a short, "Yeah, what?"

The voice wasn't Barbara's—it was the voice I had heard from the shadows.

"Oh," said the voice, "you just knew I was going to call, didn't you?"

This guy wouldn't believe I'd been expecting Barbara. He tried to convince me to come back and talk to him. His name, I learned, was Greg. I was intrigued by his brashness, so different from Ron's polite, reserved manner. Still, I felt guilty when I thought of Ron, so I told Greg I wasn't interested. He refused to end the conversation until I agreed to write to him.

It certainly gave me and Debbie something new to talk about that night.

Greg and I began writing each other letters. In his first one to me, he wrote, "I'm my own CO (Commanding Officer)." Right away I recognized that Greg was different from the other guys I'd met. I was immediately drawn to his independence and cocky self-assurance. He was direct and honest and had a bit of a bad boy demeanor, which I liked at the time.

I learned he was one of ten siblings. He told me that several years before I met him, he and all his siblings but his oldest sister had been taken to St. Vincent's, a Catholic orphanage. When I met Greg, he was planning to leave the orphanage at the end of the school year. By the time we started talking, when I was a junior in high school, he'd gotten out and was living with his grandmother.

I learned he had competed in Golden Gloves boxing and had some martial arts training. He was also an artist and had won a few art contests. He was well-built, and I thought he had very nice hands. He was about 5'10" with a very light brown complexion and a bad case of acne. I never considered him particularly good-looking, but I was continually attracted to his decisiveness, the boldness with which he approached his life.

Greg and I started seeing each other during my junior and senior years of high school. We wrote each other frequent letters and learned how to call each other from payphones and run away after a few minutes to avoid depositing coins. My mother hated him—this out-of-town "thug," as she called him. I found it ironic that she approved of "straight-laced" Ron, but loathed Greg. I wonder how she would have felt if she'd known Ron was the one who tried relentlessly to get me to have sex with him, usually in his family station wagon. Greg, though, never pushed me to sleep with him after I declared I wanted to remain a virgin.

The difference was, my mother approved of Ron's family and trusted his upbringing, whereas she considered Greg's background and upbringing objectionable. She tried hard to keep me from dating Greg, but by this time I was a bit of a rebellious and resourceful teenager. I saw my mother's rules as being about controlling me, rather than building trust, so I broke them—which earned me my share of beatings and punishment.

What my mother failed to realize about me was that I had set my own rules for living my life. My rules were based on my religious beliefs and a fierce desire to do the exact opposite of whatever my mother had done.

My mother had gotten pregnant with me before marriage, so I decided I would save myself for my future husband. I certainly had no intentions of becoming pregnant before marriage, and if I ever had premarital sex, it was going to be with the man I would one day marry.

So once I finally felt ready to consummate my relationship with Greg, after my senior year and before I left for college, it was because I felt sure that this was the person I would spend my life with. Even Greg didn't fully understand the meaning that this moment held for me.

After it happened, I believed in my heart our fate was sealed. I was his forever.

• • •

So when it came to my first goal—being a wife and mother—I felt a sense of clarity. I could dream vividly, picturing my future with Greg.

I wasn't as sure about how exactly I would change the world. I simply knew I would; it was my plan, so I would make it happen somehow. I knew that college would play a large role in helping me to shape my plan.

Back when I was a freshman in high school, our guidance counselors had administered aptitude tests to determine whether we would be placed in school-work programs or college-prep courses. My guidance counselor summoned me and my mother to his office to show us my test results.

Out of the full list of occupations included on that piece of paper, my counselor had circled three: mechanic, hairdresser, and telephone operator.

He looked at my mother and said, "There really isn't any reason for Carolynn to go to college—you can save your money. Her aptitude tests indicate careers that don't require a college degree."

If only he had known who he was speaking to. If he had any appreciation for my mother's difficult and demanding journey—to get her own degree, to get her present job, and to raise a daughter who could follow in her hard-won footsteps—he would have never said such things.

My mother stood and snatched the piece of paper from his hand. She snapped, "Don't you ever speak to me or my child again about what she can and cannot do!"

Shortly after that, I was placed in college-prep courses and assigned a new guidance counselor.

Once I was a senior, I thought constantly about how to make a difference in the world while also earning a living. After running my campaign for student council, I seriously considered politics, but I couldn't see myself playing the games, and Daddy dissuaded me, saying, "You can't make a living being a black politician!"

After studying other service careers and learning the statistics on blacks in the penal system, I considered being a probation officer so I could help my people get back into society after prison. Daddy told me judges assigned these jobs and the system was too racist and too political. I thought about being a social worker, but I soon learned the pay was too little for the very hard work and commitment required. I considered teaching, but I believed it would bore me to tears. All my potential career aspirations would allow me to fight for the disenfranchised and change the world, even if it was one person at a time. Ultimately, like most other seventeen-year-olds, I didn't have a clue what I would major in or what I would do after college. I just knew that it had to be something that would make a difference.

My mother had fought hard for her education, and she believed that college was our destiny—that we wouldn't be complete without college degrees. I was proud that this was expected of me.

Despite being dedicated to her own alma mater, Alcorn State University, my mother had told me once—during a family vacation to Washington, D.C., and touring Howard University campus—that she had always hoped one of her kids would attend Howard University. Howard, a historically black university in D.C., was to most African Americans the equivalent of Yale or Harvard. I was ambitious, and feeling radical, I wanted to be surrounded by black culture. I wanted to know how it felt to be the majority instead of a minority. My passion for developing my black identity and my desire to right the wrongs in the world made Howard University the perfect choice. For once my mother's dreams and my plans aligned.

Leon's black history lessons, current events, my desire to be a bigger part of the Civil Rights Movement, and even my small role in student government had opened my eyes, and now I felt like I was standing up, shaking my fist, and raising my voice. I felt as if a storm was gathering, and I intended to be at its center.

We don't see events as history until time passes. We don't understand that while we live our lives, we're having experiences and making decisions that will change our paths forever.

At age seventeen, I headed east to Howard University. It was there that my path, which I felt certain held such purpose, was going to change forever.

chapter 7

AN EDUCATION

In late august of 1969, my parents and I drove the thirteen hours to Washington, D.C. When we got to the Howard University campus, we checked in and brought my trunk up to my room. Students milled about everywhere, the dorms buzzing, but my roommate hadn't yet arrived. Room 414 in Truth Hall was strangely silent, and it seemed like an army barrack with its metal beds and bare walls.

Coming from Dixon, this school and this city seemed enormous and daunting. Six-year-old Candy looked around my room, bewildered, and asked, "Are we going to leave her here all by herself?"

Once my family had left, I ventured out of my room, wearing a tank top in the summer heat. I passed some men sitting on a low wall, and when one whistled at me, I gave no reaction. "Hey, Stuck-Up," another man yelled. "One of your boobs is bigger than the other."

I was in a whole new world.

My roommate, it turned out, had been raised like me, in a strict home. Her father was a minister. Together, we began exploring the world outside the limited confines of our parents' standards. One of the first things I did to support my black image was cut my straightened hair and fashion it into a full, thick Afro.

My roommate and I tried cigarettes together, and I decided I didn't like them—this, I thought, was not a ladylike smell. I drank my first beer, one Schlitz Malt Liquor at a welcome party, and spent all night vomiting. I never drank beer again. My mother sent me money for meal tickets, but my roommate and I decided we would use our food money to buy new clothes, because we felt like our clothes weren't stylish enough, setting us apart from the other, more fashionable students. Our plan was to live on peanut butter and jelly sandwiches and sardines and crackers, and we would use a hotplate to prepare food—we kept it on the windowsill outside our room, because hotplates weren't allowed in the dorms. But our peanut butter meals got old fast, and when we couldn't get enough to eat by commissioning our friends to bring us extra food from the cafeteria, we took out student loans just so we could eat.

During orientation week, the freshmen took a boat trip and then went to see the monuments. At the Lincoln Memorial, I was reading the engraved Gettysburg Address when I turned around to find myself alone. I panicked when I realized the bus had left me—I didn't have a clue how to get back to campus.

A nice-looking young man approached me. "Are you a Howard student?" he asked. I said I was. He was tall and soft-spoken, and he seemed kind. "Looks like the bus left both of us," he said. "Want to get a cab?"

I didn't know how to get a cab—in Dixon, you called a cab for pickup. The young man showed me how people in the big city got a cab, stepping out into the street with his hand up until a cab pulled up.

After that we forged a friendship and spent a lot of time together. His name was Frank, and he was a music major who played piano and composed his own music. I was still loyal to Greg, but I didn't see why that should prevent me from spending time with other guys.

I would eventually tell Frank all about Greg and my commitment to him. Frank was willing to have a relationship without any sexual ties, so we became inseparable friends with an air of romance. He held my hand when we were together, he'd always kiss me good-bye, and I sat with him for hours while he composed beautiful music and played it for me.

It took a while for me to learn the rules of life outside of Dixon. I remember doing my laundry in the common laundry room on my dorm's basement. Someone came to tell me Greg was on the phone for me, so I asked another girl to watch my things—my clothes, my wallet. When I came back, she shook her head and said, "Don't you ever do that again. You don't know me. Someone else would've taken all your stuff."

For a couple of months, to earn some extra money, I taught piano and singing to kids in an inner-city daycare. My only way of getting to and from the daycare was by city bus. One day while I was on the bus headed to the school, a man on the bus stood up and threw a knife at another man. The knife lodged firmly in a seatback one row behind me. Nobody else on the bus seemed to think this deserved a reaction, but I was terrified. I sat as still as possible until the next stop, where I got off the bus as fast as I could and took a bus going the other way straight back to Howard. I immediately quit that job and never went back to the daycare.

I loved college life and the newfound freedom and friends I had. I attended the campus church chapel on Sundays and became a member of the choir. I became close friends with a diverse group of women, all of them from different cultures with different life experiences. They were from different large cities, had different accents, and wore different clothes. We laughed, had fun, studied, and became like family. The girls on the fourth floor of Truth Hall laughed at me and mimicked me for the way I dressed, talked, and danced. They said I acted "too white." The only area they could try to improve was my dancing. Before a party, they would pull me out into the hall and try to teach me the new dances.

Of course, dancing wasn't the only thing I was learning. I was a dedicated student, intent on doing well in my classes. I carried a full load, taking biology, English, Spanish, theater, and math. I was hopeless at Spanish and eventually dropped it, but I always got the highest score on English papers, thanks to the diligence of my high school teacher. I was considering majoring in psychology, political science, or black history.

Three months after arriving at Howard, I celebrated my eighteenth birthday. My mother sent a chocolate cake, my favorite, packed in a box and surrounded by bags of popcorn for both cushioning and eating. My friends at Truth Hall joined me to wash down the cake and popcorn with Jr. Hot Shoppe screwdrivers—orange slush with vodka added.

In my mind, now I was grown. I was independent.

I spent Thanksgiving with a dorm friend in New Jersey, but when I went home for Christmas, I discovered that being eighteen meant nothing once I was back in my mother's house. The moment I crossed the threshold, all the rules and limitations I'd left behind were reinstated. Things were different with my hometown friends, too, our bonds strained by different life experiences.

The only thing that hadn't changed was my relationship with Greg. I spent as much time with him as my 11:30 curfew would allow, our romance blossoming into true love. We didn't really go anywhere, except maybe to A&W for a bite to eat or the movies. Greg was always supportive of my mother's rules, and whenever he brought me my favorite Fannie May peanut brittle, he always brought her some, too. Yet she persisted in disliking him.

When the Christmas vacation ended, as sad as I was to leave Greg, I was ready to go back to school. I'd had a taste of freedom outside my mother's house, and I was eager to regain that freedom.

In January, my friends and I began thinking about joining sororities. I felt that familiar pull to make a difference. My militancy was in full bloom, and I was not interested in belonging to some bougie social sorority that didn't seem to serve a meaningful purpose on campus beyond partying and snobbery. I decided I would join a service sorority so I could give back to the community.

Delta Sigma Theta was serious about public service, and that was where I saw my life's mission. During my pledge days, I spent several weekends going to an orphanage called Junior Village. I did activities with the young children, most of them black, who lived there. They just needed to know someone cared about them and get some attention, and I was glad to give it to them.

I went through the Delta Sigma Theta initiation rituals—memorizing chants, handshakes, and songs—with the other pledges, and I made it in. I was proud to be a Delta Sigma Theta. Every step I was taking was intentional. I believed the Deltas would serve as a channel for me to work through to change the world.

Although Howard University wasn't the safest place—men who weren't students sometimes came into the dorms, and I'd heard of several girls who'd been attacked—I wasn't afraid, especially when I was with my friends at Truth Hall. I considered myself a cautious person who stayed away from trouble.

I didn't understand then that dangerous people aren't always so easy to recognize.

In late February, when all the new pledges were announced, there was a party in our honor. The other new pledges and I showed up in the required black dresses. I recognized an upperclassman from my theatre class. He had dreads and usually wore army fatigues, but tonight he was wearing a suit. He was staring at me, and he finally came over to talk. His name was Charles.

"I'm really impressed with how confidently you carry yourself," Charles said. As always, I was holding my head erect and commanding all men's respect. He wasn't bad looking. He was an upperclassman, so my ego got a little boost that he had even noticed me.

By the end of the party, Charles had asked me out. The company he worked for was hosting a party, and he wanted me to be his date. It sounded like a very adult affair, and being eager to appear sophisticated and mature, I accepted his invitation.

I fretted over what to wear. He'd seen me in my black sorority dress, I didn't have the cash to buy a new outfit, and I hated borrowing clothes. I finally decided to wear the dress I'd worn for New Year's Eve in Dixon. It was a purple silk cinched-waist dress, with a V-neck and a scarf that hung around the collar.

I was nervous. Because of my mother's strict house rules, I had very limited dating experience.

When Charles picked me up, he admired my dress. "You really look nice," he said.

"Thank you," I said with a smile.

As the evening wore on, I started to feel more comfortable. We went to a reception, followed by dinner and dancing. I had set certain rules for myself that I would not bend, and Charles seemed impressed when I declined his repeated offers to buy me a drink.

When the evening ended, he asked if I wanted to go back to his place for a while—he had an apartment off campus. Another of my rules was never to go back to a man's apartment alone, so I respectfully declined.

"Wow," he said, "aren't you a good little girl."

It seemed like he was being very understanding.

Charles pulled up in front of the Quad, and I reached to open my car door. He said, "Can't you stay and talk for a while?" Before I could answer, he quickly put the car in reverse and made a sharp turn into the small alley between the Quad and the new dorms. At first I thought he just wanted to find a private place to talk.

Instead he started ranting. "Who the hell do you think you are?" he yelled. "You think you're better than me? You can't drink with me? You can't spend time alone with me?" He banged his hands on the steering wheel and balled his hands into fists.

I was scared out of my mind.

I thought, *I have no idea who this person is.*

"I've seen you walking around here with your nose up in the air," he screamed, "thinking you're so special. I just wanted to see who you really were. You ain't shit!"

I tried then to get out of the car, but he grabbed the collar of my pretty purple dress and yanked me backwards. I heard the fabric of the dress tearing. He began choking me with the scarf of the dress.

I gasped for air as he picked me up by my neck, pushed my torso over the seatback, and tore my pantyhose and underwear. Things were moving so fast. He assaulted me with his mouth. He moved violently, pushing me back against the seat, holding me there.

And then he threw me down on the front seat like a rag doll, bashing my head into the steering wheel.

He started unzipping his pants. I knew what was going to happen next, but there was nothing I could do to stop him. He had me pinned in a small space, and he was overpowering me. I begged him, "Please, I'm sorry—please don't do this!"

Suddenly, without warning, he began to cry, his body falling limply onto mine. He pulled himself off of me and got out of the car, sobbing like a baby.

I got out of the car and ran. I could hear his voice behind me, asking for forgiveness. My glasses had been knocked off in his car, and my vision blurred before me. Hysterical, I started yelling out for help.

Someone took me to my room. Someone called the dorm mother, someone called the police, and someone called my parents.

When I talked to Daddy, his voice was kind and consoling. He whispered, "Did he actually rape you?"

I assured him I had not been raped, but I was too embarrassed to explain what had happened. Daddy didn't want to hear the details. He told me I should tell the police I'd been assaulted and leave out the sexual part. I agreed—my bruised body and torn clothing were the evidence of my attack. My dress and panties were taken for evidence. A few weeks later, Daddy wrote me a letter expressing sadness for what had happened to me and offering his loving support. He told me this incident didn't have to define me, and he assured me that he loved me. His was the only voice of support I heard from home, and it wasn't enough—it was like a bright flare that burned away, leaving me in the dark again. My mother offered no kind words.

When I called Greg, he wasn't nearly as supportive. After I told him what had happened, I was surprised and then crestfallen by his response. It was obvious from the tone he took and the questions he asked that he didn't believe I'd been attacked. He seemed repulsed, believing I'd had sex with someone else and thought this was the only way to tell him.

"If I had sex with someone I wanted to have sex with," I said, "why would I call to tell you? You would have never known." I hung up on him.

When a court date was set, Mom came without Daddy. She didn't comfort me or provide any consoling words. She stared at me coolly, her expression impassive, as if I were a stranger. I saw what looked like disappointment in her eyes.

When my attacker was brought in and she laid eyes on him and his dreads, she was appalled that I had even gone out with him—in those days, dreads were a sure sign of drugs and hippies. She hissed at me in a whisper, "You went out with *that*? Well, what did you expect? You got just what you deserved!" She treated me with complete disdain following the hearing.

No one from the University offered me any support before or after the hearing. Charles was found guilty, but if he was punished, no one ever shared his punishment with me. I believe he was president of the Howard University student body. As far as I know, he didn't suffer any consequences.

Everything had been thrown off balance by the attack and by the sheer rage Charles had demonstrated toward me. I badly needed help, but I didn't get it from the university, Greg, or my mother.

Mom decided my dorm friends were a bad influence. Before she returned to Dixon, she pulled some strings and had me moved into the Quad Annex, a new dorm facility with suites that held four private rooms and a common living room. I was right across the alley from the place where I had been attacked. Mom set me up in my private room, new dorm mates, and a portable TV and felt she had gotten me out of harm's way.

I had my own room, but the isolation felt like I was in a prison. My new room had a bed on one side and a study area on the opposite side; it felt narrow and confining, like a jail cell. I missed the camaraderie of my friends from Truth Hall. They visited sometimes, but it wasn't the same as being part of a community. I kept to myself. Charles was in my theatre class, so I skipped it, along with some others. A fog of depression settled around me.

Before my mom had left, I'd begged her not to tell anyone in Dixon what had happened to me. I just wanted some time to get through the shame of the attack and not have everyone in my hometown discussing what had happened.

But soon after her visit, I got a call from the pastor of Second Baptist Church, Reverend Savage. He seemed uncomfortable talking about what had happened. He offered to pray with me.

I hardly heard a word he said. I was seething, livid. My mother, who hated us discussing anything that went on in our home, had revealed my private business. I wasn't as close to this minister as I had been to Reverend Schoultz, and I didn't appreciate my mother telling him my private business after I had asked her not to. I was devastated by her hypocrisy. A few days later, my best friend Irma called from Dixon to console me. She said my cousin Roger had told her what had happened.

It felt as if everyone I knew had betrayed me—especially my mother. There was no one I could express my fears to or talk with about how I was feeling. I had been completely abandoned.

Growing up, I'd experienced severe episodes of vertigo, ringing in my ears, accompanied by extreme vomiting. My doctor had never determined what was causing my symptoms, but he'd given me a bottle of Valium to take with me to college in case I should have another attack. It didn't really cure it, just allowed me to fall asleep until my vertigo subsided.

That night, after finding out that everyone was talking about what had happened to me, I was mortified. I emptied the bottle of Valium into my system and waited for it to take effect. I didn't know what to expect from the drug or when it would kick in, but my purpose for taking the pills was certain. I wanted to end all the accumulated pain.

Soon after I had taken the pills, Frank called to see if I wanted to get a sandwich from Pork Chop Alley. I walked with him across campus, not mentioning what I'd done. On our way back to the dorms, the Valium kicked in and I started throwing up. I collapsed and lost consciousness.

I awoke in the hospital, surrounded by my friends from Truth Hall. I tried to get up to leave, but I had been restrained. I finally stopped fighting and simply slipped into a darkness that had no light, no dreams, and seemingly no end.

When I next woke up, I was in a mental ward at the Howard University hospital, still in restraints. They brought me food in a wooden bowl, my only utensil a plastic spoon. Once I was allowed to have visitors, I had just one: Frank. When I asked to leave, a nurse informed me I'd been scheduled to see a psychiatrist. Apparently when they'd contacted my family to say it appeared I had attempted suicide, my mother had responded, "Keep her, maybe you can help her."

The psychiatrist told me this and then asked, "What kind of help does your mother think you need?"

"I guess you should ask her!" I said.

I never spoke with her. She never came to see about me. What kind of mother leaves her child alone in a mental hospital?

She abandoned me again.

They made me go to group sessions, but I refused to talk. They told me that unless I opened up, I could not be released.

Each day rolled into the next without my knowing when one day ended and another began. I lost track of time. My only contact with the outside world was Frank. He brought me a white teddy bear with a ribbon around its neck that said, "I Love You." The bear would keep me company, Frank said.

I grew angrier every day. I was angry that my efforts to end my pain had failed. I was angry that my mother had allowed me to be institutionalized like I was crazy. I wasn't crazy, and I resented being treated and housed like I was. I was just in so much pain.

After a week had passed, I was allowed a phone call. I waited until I knew my mother would be at work. I called the house, and Daddy picked up. "Daddy," I said, "if you don't get me out of here *today*, when I do get out, you'll never see me again." Before another day had passed, I was released.

I left the hospital and returned to my dorm room—but I didn't know how to move beyond what had happened. I tried returning to classes, but I felt lost and detached from my body. I couldn't feel like my old self again.

About a week after returning to my dorm, I was walking across campus with my head down. I'd always walked with my head held high, but now I avoided meeting people's gaze. Someone, I realized, was standing right in front of me, blocking my path. I looked up.

It was my attacker! He spoke calmly, trying to apologize, but I was paralyzed. I stood frozen. I didn't speak. I only stared at him, my heart hammering in my chest, until he walked away. The terror I felt just knowing he was able to get close to me again sent me into a place I hated to be—fear and panic!

I didn't feel safe. I'd lost my sense of purpose. Worst of all, I felt powerless. I'm not a fragile person, and I'm not a victim, but I just didn't know how to put it all back together again. This act of violence had knocked me off my planned course. I didn't have the strength to fight back on my own, and the people and system whose support I most needed weren't fighting for me.

Finally, I gave up. I withdrew.

I packed up my things and bought a train ticket home to Dixon. I said goodbye to all my friends. As the train pulled out of Union Station, I stared out the window and cried. I hated the weakness I felt—I hated failing.

When I returned to Dixon, the house was full of eerie silence. People in town, I would find, were eager to ask me what had happened, quick to pry. Yet Mom and Daddy never spoke of what had happened, so I wondered about their feelings. Were they embarrassed? Were they angry?

I struggled with not only the shame of my ordeal, but also this sense of failure. I still felt like there was a cloud of sadness engulfing me, but I couldn't talk to anybody about it. I couldn't hold my head up.

I had once had dreams of changing the world, but now I had only nightmares. I had a recurring vivid nightmare of a cat viciously eating my vagina, tearing at my skin with its needle-sharp teeth. Again and again I woke up screaming, until Mom decided I needed counseling.

She took me to a clinic where I spoke with a counselor about the attack; during our sessions, other painful experiences in my life came up. After three sessions, the counselor asked Mom to come into the office at the end of my session. "We're making great progress," he said, "but I think that one of her problems is her relationship with you. Would you consider group sessions?"

"I'm just fine," my mother said in a clipped tone, shooting the counselor a withering look. She marched me out of the office and into the parking lot. As soon as the car door was closed, she scowled and asked, "What have you been telling them in there?"

I never went back to the clinic. My nightmares gradually subsided, although to this day the sight of cats unnerves me.

About a month after I returned home, Howard shut down due to campus riots, and everyone got credit for the remainder of the school year. I was dismayed—if only I could have made it another month. I was so disappointed in myself: I had allowed my fear to prevent me from moving forward. It wasn't just the attack that had crippled me, but also my reaction to the attack.

My attack and my inability to overcome the fear it caused served as the catalyst for me to follow a new dream. I never wanted fear to control me again. As I look back over the span of my life, I see that in the greatest battles I fought and lost, my defeat could be attributed to my response to fear. In order to succeed, I had to learn to push through the fear.

I went into an introspective circle of one, retreating into myself to think and rebuild. It was obvious that everyone who knew me had heard about my situation by now. I hated the stares and the empty, prying questions, so I tried to avoid human contact.

Too much was happening, too many things were standing in my way, preventing me from pursuing my purpose. Where was God in all this? Was anyone listening, and did anyone care?

It was during this time that I saw I really had no religious foundation for this situation or for my life. All church had taught me were the rules to get to heaven. I had no spiritual footing to get me through this life until I got to heaven. This was the beginning of my disillusionment with the church, starting me on my intentional journey for a deeper understanding of how to get from birth to death without killing myself along the way.

College had been my plan, but it was gone now. It was time for me to figure out what I wanted next from life, and then figure out how to get it. I'd had such big plans—plans for the world. I hadn't known exactly what they were, but college was supposed to help me sort it all out. Now my life felt like a joke, a slap in the face. I had to do something.

Life wasn't over—I just needed a new plan.

chapter 8

CHANGING COURSE

I've always been an intentional person: I always get a vision for how to move forward, and it's this vision that sparks the plan and drives me into action. When I returned from college, I didn't know what to do. I needed a vision and a plan, but at that time in my life I had neither. I'd never dreamed I wouldn't graduate from Howard. I'd never dreamed that I would fail, so I had no plan for failure.

I hated being at home again. The strict rules and 11:30 curfew were reinstated, making me feel like a child again, but the worst part was feeling like a disappointment. Melvin and Brenda had done exactly what was expected of them, and I had failed. My mother didn't make any effort to convince me otherwise, and the truth was that I hated disappointing her.

My relationship with Daddy was the bright spot in my life at that time. I'd been touched by the support he'd given me following the attack at Howard, and now he was the only person who showed a genuine interest in me. He wasn't much of a conversationalist, but we had frequent small talks that I still remember.

Once I asked him if he'd ever met my biological father.

"No," he said, "and Zee never discussed him. When we first got married, I asked her if I could adopt you."

This surprised me. "Why didn't you?"

"Zee was afraid the legal proceedings would go in the paper, and the school district could use her having a child out of wedlock to prevent her from becoming a teacher."

It may seem outlandish now, but teachers back then were subject to morality checks, and behaving in a way that was deemed immoral could result in them losing their jobs or never getting hired. I hadn't known this until Daddy told me; it explained some of her evasiveness, her secrecy. She couldn't risk the exposure.

A day or so later, when Daddy and I were talking again in the kitchen, he said, "Now that you're old enough, do you want to officially have my name?"

"Yes!" I quickly exclaimed. I liked knowing that I'd belong to him and that he wanted me.

He smiled. "I'll get it taken care of," he said.

In a different conversation I had with Daddy, I expressed my dream to change the world. I didn't want to return to college, I told him—"I want to join the Peace Corps." I later discovered I wasn't eligible without a college degree, but in that moment, what mattered was Daddy's support. He encouraged me to pursue a place in the Peace Corps.

And then he said: "Listen, I don't know what's wrong with Zee when it comes to you, but do the things you want in your life, and don't ever let her stop you. Don't let anyone stop you."

I kissed him on the permanent dimple in his cheek and thanked him for being my daddy.

• • •

After years of working as a janitor at Northern Illinois Gas Company, Daddy had pursued a meter reader position. He confided in me that he'd done it mostly just to please my mother. All the walking, he said, was taking its toll on him. "It's a job for a young man," he said. He started suffering persistent pain in his hip.

For as long as I could remember he'd had a loud hacking cough, a result of his smoking—first cigarettes and then a pipe. When I was younger, I'd always known he was in the audience during school events when I heard his cough.

That spring after I returned from Howard, his cough began to produce blood. In June of 1970, he went to the hospital for exploratory surgery. He was diagnosed with esophageal cancer. The prognosis was that he had six months to live—until January.

I prayed daily that Daddy would fight back and live. I wanted him to live and walk me down the aisle someday, be a grandfather to my future children. He had to overcome this enemy of his body. But I watched him lose the twinkle of laughter in his eyes, replaced by a sad acceptance of pending death. He withdrew into silence before he lost his ability to speak. I wanted to hear him sound like he was going to fight back, but instead he seemed like he was waiting for his time to run out. It hurt to see the lack of fight in him.

During this time, I didn't socialize much. Things with Greg had cooled off after the attack. For months I'd been writing back and forth with a Navy man named Chris. I'd found his name on a list of servicemen posted at the dorm at Howard; students were encouraged to write letters to our servicemen to boost morale. We sent each other pictures, and our letters grew more personal and more romantic.

Just after Daddy was released from the hospital after his surgery, Chris asked to come to Dixon for a visit. While he was there he proposed to me and asked Daddy for my hand in marriage. Daddy gave his permission, and when Chris proposed, I said yes. I wasn't madly in love with him, but I think I was desperate for a plan, a place to escape to, and something to cling to in what felt like a world of nothingness.

At eighteen years old, I was engaged to be married. I felt as though I'd been stripped of my purpose after being attacked at Howard. Now, I figured, I should focus on my other dream, which burned as brightly as ever in my spirit. I was going to be a wife and mother—this was now my path, my plan. But I would have to wait a while as Chris returned to Baltimore to finish out his stint in the Navy.

I got a summer job at the Northern Illinois Gas Company, where Daddy worked.

At the gas company, I was an office assistant. I paid bills, answered the phones, ran errands, and did anything else they needed done.

When I wasn't at work, though, I was still avoiding most people, still trying to recover from what had happened at Howard. Even as I struggled with feelings of isolation, I often retreated into my circle of one with just my thoughts for company.

During that time, when I felt so confused and lost, I was at least grateful to spend time with Daddy and appreciate him. He was a quiet, simple man with a wry sense of humor. He'd crack a joke and smirk. He seemed content just coming home to a hot meal, a cold beer, and his pipe. He liked watching baseball and Westerns on TV. He supported my mother, although he mumbled at her a lot under his breath.

One day while Daddy and I were driving back from an appointment, we went past a beautiful hill on Route 2 that I had always dreamed about building a house on. I asked, "Remember when you promised to buy me that hill for my graduation present?" I had pointed it out to him while he was teaching me how to drive on the highway to prepare me for getting my license.

"I thought you meant *college* graduation," he joked.

"No," I said with a laugh. "You owe me that hill."

"Okay," he said, "let's make it a wedding present." This was another joke. He'd always told me he wasn't paying for a big wedding. He liked to say that when it was time for me to get married, he'd just put a ladder under my window so I could elope.

Now, it seemed as if he might not even be around when I got married.

My engagement to Chris unraveled fairly quickly. In my small community, any news quickly became gossip. A friend of mine got in touch with Greg and let him know that I was engaged. Right away he came back into my life and charmed his way back into my heart. I wrote Chris a "Dear John" letter explaining that I had to break off our engagement, which I felt guilty about—he'd told me he had seen other guys get these letters and hoped he would never get one himself.

Greg teased that I'd gotten engaged just to get his attention, which wasn't true—but once we started spending time together again, I felt like at least part of my life was back to normal. Greg and I had history together, and I felt he understood me better than anybody else.

When the summer ended, my mother gave me an ultimatum: I could return to college, or I could get a full-time job and continue paying rent. She also promised if I started taking classes again, she'd return the rent I'd paid her. So in the fall of 1970, I decided to enroll at Sauk Valley Community College, a junior college halfway between Dixon and Sterling. I was a full-time student that semester, working at Brooks Drugstore part time.

I took classes, I spent time with Greg, I worked at the drugstore, and I helped take care of Daddy. As his health declined, I sometimes heard my mother crying in the furnace room, concealing the pain she was feeling. I knew better than to try to offer her any comfort.

We knew that Christmas would be Daddy's last. I was fired from my drugstore job after refusing to work on Christmas day, choosing instead to spend every moment I could with my family. Daddy was getting weaker. We all did our best to make sure he was comfortable.

Greg had always loved Christmas. On Christmas Eve, he came over to help me decorate and put up a tree. It was important to me to ensure that Candy had as normal a Christmas as possible, given the lack of festivity in our house that year. As soon as we were finished decorating the house, Greg proposed.

"I'm not sure I'm ready to get married," he said, "but I know if I don't marry you now, when I'm ready you probably won't be around."

I said yes.

We sat in the living room for a while, talking about our plans. I was excited that we were making our commitment to each other official. Then I went back to my parents' bedroom, where Daddy was sitting on the edge of the bed while Mom helped him clean his breathing tube.

I shared our news and showed them the ring Greg had given me. "We've set July 31 for the wedding," I said happily, oblivious for the moment to their suffering. Daddy, who was no longer able to speak, nodded his head. I bounced out of the bedroom before my mother could add anything.

No doubt we were very young, but I was certain we were mature enough to make it work. I had just turned nineteen years old, and I was busy creating my future—the life I wanted for myself.

On a cold evening in January, Daddy—so frail he looked like a different person—was taken in an ambulance to the hospital in Rockford. By now the cancer had reached his brain, and the doctors said it was just a matter of days. Melvin, now a second lieutenant in the Air Force, was sent home. Brenda was home, too. We all gathered in Daddy's room at the hospital.

Once he was resting peacefully, I got a ride back to Dixon, where I stayed with my little sister Candy at Aunt Tutta's house. I spent a while studying for the finals I still had to take for my fall semester classes at Sauk Valley. I fell asleep.

I woke up to someone shaking me. It was Melvin, telling me Daddy was gone.

I didn't cry—I just got up and began moving into action. I knew that we'd be getting visitors after Daddy's death, so I went back to the house and began to clean. I felt that I had to be strong.

I thought it was symbolic that—because I had returned to Dixon and Mom had slipped away briefly with Regina for a cup of coffee—Daddy had died with just his two children, Brenda and Melvin, at his side. In the end he'd never begun the adoption process, never given me his name. He was fifty-one years old, leaving my mother a widow at age forty-nine. I would deeply miss his presence in my life.

The day of Daddy's funeral, as we were lining up to go out to the processional cars that would take us to church, my mother burst into tears and ran to her bedroom.

I ran right behind her. I sat beside her and put my arms around her, but she shrugged me off, reluctant as ever to show emotion. She said, "Don't, I'll be okay." I stepped away from her, but I waited in the room until she was ready so we could leave together.

I remember thinking, *Maybe she loved Daddy after all.*

I wanted to sing one song at his funeral, but Brenda vetoed it. She, Melvin, and my mother rode in one car to the service, and Greg, Candy, and I rode in another. Their unity during this period spoke volumes about my position in the family. I was on the outside and I was deeply hurt, but I tried to stay strong for Candy. I refused to cry. At the end of the service, I watched as Melvin and Brenda bent down to kiss Daddy goodbye, but I couldn't do it.

• • •

If it had been hard living with my mother before Daddy's death, afterward it became impossible. Mom's disposition was dark and she seemed angry all the time, which I knew was how she grieved. A few weeks after Daddy's funeral, a representative from the Northern Illinois Gas Company came by the house to offer me a permanent position, one that would have been an excellent opportunity working at the company's headquarters in a northwest suburb of Chicago.

"No," my mother said firmly. "She's going back to school."

A couple of months after Daddy's death, I came home half an hour past my curfew and my mother beat me with the aluminum hose from our Electrolux vacuum cleaner.

It wasn't about discipline. She was full of rage, and this was how she showed her power. I looked at the situation: I was nineteen, engaged to be married, and paying her rent, which she'd never stopped charging even after I'd returned to school. I knew it was time to go. That was the last beating I would take from her.

By this time, I was working as a youth counselor in the young boys' unit at Nachusa Lutheran Home, a residential treatment home for wayward adolescents outside of Dixon. Each counselor's schedule included two sleepovers a week. After resolving to get out of Mom's house, I volunteered to take all the sleepover shifts so I had a place to sleep until I could find a place to live. Every day I looked for an apartment.

It didn't take long until I found a one-bedroom apartment in a large older home that had been converted into four apartments. The building was about three blocks from my mother's house. When I moved out, Candy pleaded with me to take her with me. It broke my heart to leave my little sister behind, but she was another of my mother's rescued children so I hoped she'd be okay.

My apartment was fully furnished, which was good, because I didn't have any furniture—the hardest part was knowing I was sleeping on a stranger's old mattress. The oven had only one setting, so you had to watch whatever you put in there so it didn't burn up. It was full of cockroaches, but it didn't matter. It was mine, and I could come and go without fearing my mother's abuse. I promised myself I would never live under her roof again.

After Daddy's death, I stopped attending my classes at Sauk Valley. In my view, college attendance was just another thing that someone else was telling me to do. I didn't feel like striving anymore. My original purpose was lost.

It was easy to walk away from then, but it would be the one decision I'd regret forever.

After I moved out of my childhood home, Frank made a surprise visit to see me. He went to my mother's house asking for me. She called me, but I told her it would be better if I didn't see him. He was concerned, I think, that I had simply faded from his life. I knew he would have done anything for me—he said he would have married me. But I couldn't have married Frank, because things just weren't that way between us.

Frank represented a life I'd lived a long time ago. My college education was a distant thought, seemingly from a different period in my life. Now I was pursuing the life I used to lie in bed and dream about: becoming a wife and a mother, finally having that one who was going to love me all the way. That dream seemed much more authentic and achievable to me now. I already knew what kind of wife and mother I would be. I convinced myself that what had happened on Howard's campus was meant to happen, so that I could have this realization. This was my real future.

I focused on planning my wedding so I could get on with my life as a married woman. My mother let me know in no uncertain terms that she wasn't paying for my wedding. As far as I was concerned, her control over me had ended. Her lack of financial support certainly wasn't going to stop us.

Greg and I worked out our budget and saved our money. Our wedding wouldn't be on the scale I had dreamed of, but we had everything we thought we wanted. We set about doing everything else we needed to do before getting married.

Greg worked for the electric company, and he secured a transfer from Freeport to Dixon, where we'd decided to begin our married life. Because he was younger than twenty-one, Illinois law required him to have his birth certificate and signed permission from a family member over the age of twenty-one for him to get married. The law only required women to be eighteen to marry, so I didn't actually need my birth certificate, but all these legalities triggered my curiosity. I had never seen a copy of my own birth certificate, so I asked my mother if I could see mine. She said she didn't have it, so I sent away for it. I was curious.

My name, so far as I knew, was Carolyn Grace Alversia Ashford—although I now spelled my first name "Carolynn." It took several tries before I got the document, because I didn't have the correct information to request it. I finally requested it using just my mother's name. I was completely shocked when my birth certificate arrived with my name spelled out as Alversia Harolyn Williams.

I had been seeking my identity from the moment my mother became a permanent part of my life, asking her questions and begging to hear stories, and she'd never thought about telling me my *real* name? What was so hard about just sitting down with me and laying everything on the table? My name kept playing such a bizarre role in my life.

I stormed over to my mother's to confront her. I showed her my copy of the birth certificate and exploded, "I thought you hated my father! Why would you give me that god-awful name?"

She wouldn't answer my questions. She simply looked at me with a blank expression and told me, "Because he asked me to. If you don't like it, you are free to change it." She refused to say anything more, and I just walked out the door.

Before the wedding, Greg and I needed an apartment big enough to accommodate us both. At that time, in 1971, there were few apartment buildings in Dixon. The rental property market consisted mostly of either older houses divided up into apartments—like the one I was living in by myself—or homes being rented.

I learned quickly that the kinds of apartments we were looking for wouldn't rent to black people. Every day I'd search the classified ads and find a place that sounded perfect. I'd call and make an appointment, show up, and be told it was no longer available. After this happened several times, I asked a white friend to call about seeing an apartment I'd been informed was already being rented. They gave her an appointment and an application. They were discriminating against us.

So I did what I do best—I began a letter-writing campaign. I wrote letters to the editor of the *Dixon Evening Telegraph*, the mayor, and the president of the Dixon Chamber of Commerce. I described the racism I'd experienced and called for Dixon to improve itself for the sake of the future. "I want my children to have a fair chance," I wrote, "and not walk unaware into the wall of prejudice and hidden hate." These people refusing to rent to me were certainly going to know my name.

My letter to the local paper ended up in a column called "Voice of the People." Following the letter's publication, I got a call from a man who'd been my boss when I worked at the gas company. "I'd be proud to rent to you and your husband," he said. We had the main floor of the townhouse duplex, with two bedrooms, two baths, a dining room, a nice kitchen, and a living room. We moved in a month before our wedding. We were set.

• • •

I'd always believed that once I was married, I'd be loved and accepted, finally finding that sense of belonging I had always longed for. Naively, I expected marriage to erase all the pains of the past, to fulfill all my dreams and desires.

Now I see I was so broken that any show of love felt like water to a wanderer in the desert. There were signs I should have paid attention to.

Once we were engaged, I heard rumors that Greg was messing around on me. But once he moved to Dixon and we were together all the time, I dismissed them as idle gossip. Instead I focused on all the good I saw in Greg.

I remembered how he'd patiently taught me to drive stick shift in his 1966 Chevy Impala, his pride and joy. He took me out over and over again until I could shift gears and stop on a hill and rock the car so it didn't roll backwards.

He bought me a pair of ice skates and took me skating, pulling me around the rink until I could stand on my own.

In high school, when I hadn't been allowed to go anywhere, he'd come to town and we would sit on the front porch, talking about our future; the children we would have and the life we'd build together. We pledged never to abandon our children as our parents had abandoned us.

No one in my family saw what I saw in Greg. Everyone believed I could do better, but I had no idea what "better" looked like. I was following my heart. All I saw was a caring, patient man who'd helped me through the hardest times—with the exception of how he'd reacted to the attack at Howard, which I tried to put out of my mind. No one knew him like I did or saw his potential, I thought. I saw his determination to create a good life for himself, and that impressed me. He was a man with a plan, with bold, decisive ways, and that was exactly what I wanted. He was determined to make it, just like I was.

I believed in this man. The future he painted for us and his dreams for our life were everything I wanted. I believed in his love. I believed in his plan. I believed in what I saw in him. I pushed away the doubts I should have had. I was going to prove to everyone that they were wrong. He was the right man for me—the right man to be the father of my children.

On July 31, 1971, Greg and I were married. I had loved him for five years. He made me feel whole and accepted and loved. I had no doubt I was going to spend the rest of my life loving him, building a family, and showing the rest of the world how wrong they'd been about us. My mother did everything she could to ruin our wedding. She persuaded Uncle Narvell and Aunt Kathleen not to come. They claimed they had a big print job and couldn't make it, but I never believed that. Their absence hurt me deeply. Mom tried to convince the new pastor at Second Baptist Church, Reverend Sherrod, not to perform the ceremony, her reason being that we were living together without being married. When that didn't work, she contacted all our guests and told them not to get us any wedding gifts.

When the wedding day arrived, Mom showed up in Brenda's old prom dress. It was yellow, the color I'd asked her to wear, but it was completely wrinkled, as if she'd pulled it from a pile of dirty laundry. She ruined every picture she was in, scowling with disapproval.

When Greg was late getting to the church, my mother said curtly, "I hope that Negro got cold feet and decided to leave you standing at the altar."

But Greg showed up, much to my mother's disappointment—he'd had to make a quick trip to the men's store for a new tuxedo shirt after accidentally misplacing his.

I refused to let anything or anyone cast a shadow on my joy that day. Melvin gave me away, handsome in his white Air Force uniform, and Brenda was my maid of honor. Candy was my flower girl. I did everything in my favorite color, yellow, and my favorite flower, daisies.

At our reception at the VFW Hall, during my first dance with Greg, I called out triumphantly to my new mother-in-law: "I got him now!"

She waved a hand at me. "Yeah," she yelled with a laugh. "You got that devil now!"

Greg and I took a modest honeymoon to Wisconsin Dells, Wisconsin, an old resort city located on the Wisconsin River. We had a nice several days—staying in a hotel, going on rides, and buying souvenirs like a pair of leather moccasins—we laughed and basked in the glow of being married.

I was completely unprepared for the turn that things would take.

On our way home from Wisconsin Dells, we got a little lost on our way to Freeport, where we'd planned to stay and visit Greg's grandmother. Greg blamed me. It had been my responsibility to remember the route, he said. He screamed and cursed, which was out of character for him. I was shocked and frightened by his outburst.

We arrived at his grandmother's house in late afternoon, hours after we had intended to arrive. Greg announced that he was going to the VFW without me.

My mother had never allowed me to spend time with his family, so I didn't know them very well. My conversation with Big Mama, as she was called, was awkward, and I was hurt and embarrassed that my husband of five days had dumped me on her doorstep and gone off to spend time with his buddies.

I went upstairs and read a book until I drifted off to sleep. I woke up several times throughout the night, expecting to see my husband by my side, but the bed was empty.

When the new day began to ease light into the room, I looked over to see Greg lying there, sound asleep and smelling like a brewery. I was disappointed, and knowing what I do today, I should have been afraid. I didn't know back then just how bad things could get.

It was just as my mother-in-law had said: I had that devil now.

chapter 9

TO HAVE AND TO HOLD

There was no honeymoon period in my marriage. It was obvious to me: I was married, and Greg was not. After our wedding, I learned that he'd had several girlfriends while we were dating—and he still had them. He began staying out all night, leaving me alone to wonder where he'd gone. It quickly became clear that he was nothing like the man I'd spent long nights talking with, planning a future. This was not the man I'd been defending.

Nothing I did was good enough, and Greg used my every mistake to make indictments against my mother. "Your mother acted like you were gold," he snapped, "but you ain't shit!" The most minor infraction provoked cursing, demeaning accusations, and unwarranted anger: I didn't cook his food right; I didn't fold the towels the way he wanted. "This ain't Zee's house," he said. "You're going to do things my way!"

Soon after we got married, his possessiveness lost me my job as a counselor at Nachusa Lutheran Home. He insisted on staying with me during my overnight shifts to check up on me. I received a warning, and I told Greg, "If you keep coming here, they're going to fire me." He kept coming.

I learned soon enough that what I had seen in Greg as determination was actually obsession. He was a compulsive cleaner, so nothing I did in the way of cleaning met his expectations. He attributed his cleanliness to the training he'd received at the orphanage, because the nuns there were strict about it, but he displayed such a mania about order. He wanted everything to be controlled and in its right place.

I also hadn't realized before getting married just how much Greg drank. He went out plenty on his own, but I liked for us to go out together on Saturday nights. We'd go to The Bronze Social Club, a place my mother had always forbidden, to shoot pool, socialize, dance, and listen to live music or a DJ. When the club closed for the night, we'd come back to Dixon to a house that during the weekend served as a backstreet gambling joint, run by a husband and wife. The wife would fry up catfish and pork chops and make sandwiches the patrons could buy, and everybody would smoke and drink but me. The first few times we went, I was shocked at some of the upstanding people I saw there—and they were just as shocked to see me.

Someone once saw me at the gambling house and said to Greg, "Zee would kill you if she knew you'd brought her here."

Greg replied, "It's time she sees how the rest of the world lives."

We would get home at three or four in the morning, and Greg believed in sleeping for at least twelve hours after he had come in. To be with him, I often woke up well into the afternoon on Sundays, too late to go to church.

At that time, I was trying to assess church and its meaning in my life. I still prayed and believed in God, but church attendance was no longer a priority—once I got married, church became more of a special occasion. I went once or twice a month. The Bible says you can't serve two masters, and Greg was quickly becoming my new master.

Greg's way of communicating was critical, angry, and filled with cursing. I found myself trying to go toe-to-toe with him. Before we were married, I never swore. The first time I did, Greg laughed and said, "Listen who's trying to cuss."

He had a pattern. He would find something I'd done wrong, and then we'd fight and he would leave the house. Sometimes he came back in the morning, and other times he'd be gone the whole weekend. When he'd return in the middle of the night, I often dropped the needle on the record to play "Thin Line Between Love and Hate," hoping to scare him. *The sweetest woman in the world can be the meanest woman in the world, if you make her that way*, the lyrics drifted. He'd usually just laugh and come to bed.

It didn't take long for me to see the reality of what I was dealing with, so I had to establish a plan for survival. At some point, knowing how mean my husband was, knowing he was still going around town with other women, I set two unbreakable boundaries in place for myself—limits on the bounds of my forgiveness.

If he ever gave me a sexually transmitted disease, I would leave.

If he ever got another woman pregnant, I would leave.

Just like I had always done, I tried to create order by making plans and setting rules for myself. These rules would allow me to hold on to any remaining scraps of dignity. If I had known then what I was going to live through, I would have created other boundaries, but I didn't know that then. And as things got worse, I did not add boundaries to my list. Instead I focused on the boundaries that hadn't been broken, clinging to them for hope.

The first time he hit me was so scary. It was about two months after we got married. My husband was half a foot taller than me and seventy pounds heavier. He had practiced boxing and martial arts.

I wish I could remember what set him off. He hit me across my face so hard that blood splattered everywhere. I was sure my nose was broken. Then he grabbed me by my hair and dragged me to the telephone.

"Call your mother," he screamed. "You ain't shit. Tell your mamma she can come get your ass, 'cause you can't do nothing!" He screamed and screamed. "All she raised was some shit!" He kept screaming at me to call her.

In total terror, broken into submission, I dialed a number with trembling fingers—but it wasn't my mother's. I called the church.

Reverend Sherrod, who had married us, picked up the phone and just listened to the terror on my end of the line, my voice shaking, Greg's voice thundering in the background.

"Mom," I managed to say, "this is Versie, can you come get me? I'm not shit." Tears streamed down my face. "I don't know anything about being a wife. Greg wants you to come get me *now*!"

Within minutes, Reverend Sherrod was banging on the door. "You leave," he shouted at Greg. "We'll talk tomorrow."

Reverend Sherrod cleaned up all the blood. He took me to the hospital to make sure my nose wasn't broken. He brought me home and sat down with me. My eye was swollen shut, and I kept an ice pack pressed gingerly against my badly bruised nose.

Reverend Sherrod, who had a doctorate in psychology, focused his concern on what he'd heard my husband screaming over the phone. He believed Greg's rage was directed at my mother because she had held me up as someone he didn't deserve. Greg was trying to hurt my mother, Reverend Sherrod said, by hurting me. It was his opinion that Greg would continue degrading and physically abusing me until he either permanently maimed me or left me so scarred, inside and out, that nobody would want to look at me.

"The level of rage I heard on the phone frightened me," Reverend Sherrod said.

"You need to get out before he escalates things to an even more dangerous level."

His next words echoed in my mind—I wouldn't forget them.

He said, "That kind of rage kills."

Before leaving, Reverend Sherrod said that he'd noticed my absence at church. "How are you going to be able to hold onto your faith," he asked, "if you're with someone who doesn't hold the beliefs you were raised on? You'll never be able to bring him up, but he is strong enough to bring you down."

The next day, Reverend Sherrod took my husband fishing on Rock River and talked to him. When Greg came home, he showered me with apologies. This would never happen again, he promised.

But Reverend Sherrod had been right—the abuse didn't stop, and it did escalate.

The Saturday after Thanksgiving, Greg had to work overtime. As usual, he left me with a list of chores. He needed the buttons tightened on his leather coat and a tear in the lining stitched. I cut my thumbs pushing the sewing needle through the leather, but I did what he'd asked. I didn't want anything to interfere with our plans for the evening.

We were planning to go to a holiday party that evening at the Knights of Columbus Hall—the KC Hall—a large event venue where many Dixon parties were held. It was the first official function we would attend as a married couple. I was excited to be going. I had bought a new dress and had my Afro shaped.

When Greg got home from work, I had dinner already prepared. We ate, showered, and dressed for the evening. Once we had our coats on, he put his hands into the pockets of the leather coat I'd fixed. He pulled out the lining. "You were supposed to sew this," he said.

There was a tear I hadn't known about.

He pushed past me and walked toward the door. "I'm not taking you anywhere!"

I really wanted to go to that party. I rushed after him. "You better not leave me! Not tonight!"

He made a guttural "yah!" sound, the kind a karate fighter makes as he strikes. The kick hit my chest. I hit the kitchen floor hard. I don't remember feeling the blow that knocked me out.

• • •

The next thing I remember is waking up in a hospital bed. It was Sunday afternoon. I had a concussion and was suffering from amnesia. I was having trouble putting things together in my mind.

A nurse came in. "How are you feeling, Mrs. Thompson?"

Was I married?

I looked down at my swollen hands and saw my wedding ring.

Where was my husband?

I drifted in and out of sleep.

During one of my periods of awakening, I looked up to see my mother in the chair next to me, looking at me. I didn't know how she had found out I was here. The look on her face was hard to interpret. I wasn't sure if she was concerned or angry. She didn't express any compassion for the state she found her only child in.

"What happened to you?" she asked.

"I don't remember," I said honestly.

"Well, I know this," she said flatly. "That sucker dropped you off in the emergency room and fled like a thief in the night. He showed up at that party alone and said you were at home." She fixed her cool gaze on me. "Why didn't you call me?"

I didn't answer her.

As she got up to leave, she said, "I hope now you've had enough."

My mother had never known what I needed from her—she'd never understood. If she had ever offered sympathy, warmth, or comfort, I may have run straight into her arms, but her words were as sharp and judgmental as ever. All I felt was condemnation.

On the second day of my stay in the hospital, Greg finally came to see the damage he had done. He'd been staying away, he said, because he was scared my mother had called the police. His head was down, his shoulders slumped, looking nervous and contrite.

I was still having difficulty remembering what had happened. Greg tried to help me piece it all together. He said I'd pulled a kitchen knife on him and he'd gone into survival mode.

To this day, I have no memory of picking up a knife—I only remember Greg's foot coming down on my head.

I stayed in the hospital for four days. The evening before I was released, my mother came back to my bedside.

She said tersely, "Well, I know from the doctor's report what most likely happened." Her next words were as cold as a Chicago winter. "You need to get your stuff and bring your butt back home. I'll give you the money to pay for an annulment."

I didn't answer her. What I needed was my own plan, but I didn't have time to put one together. I knew what life with my mother was like—I knew exactly what awaited me if I decided to move back in with her. I hadn't forgotten the cutting remarks, the controlling rules, the critical observations, or the beatings.

If I went home with my husband, wasn't it possible that life would get better?

Hadn't he apologized? Hadn't he said he would give me the money to buy a new coat to replace the one he had torn throwing me to the ground? That proved he was sorry, didn't it? And wasn't it possible that maybe, at least partly, this had been my fault?

Back then I knew nothing about domestic abuse. There were no Lifetime TV movies showing viewers how it looked or how it could escalate. All I had to go on was my love for Greg. I believed him when he said it would never happen again, because he was just so sorry about it. I had to give him one more chance. Didn't I?

The morning came, and I chose my husband. I made up my mind: I had gotten myself into this, and I would figure my way out. But one thing I knew for certain and would remain steadfast in: I would never return to my mother's home.

Greg brought me one of his jackets to wear home. I shivered against the cruel December wind as we walked across the frozen parking lot to the car, my whole body feeling tender and broken. I would be sore for weeks.

• • •

Writing this book, I struggled with telling this part of my story, which spans many years. Who I am now is so far from who I was then. I hate the word *victim*—I never felt like I was being passive. I fought back, but I held on to hope for too long. Writing about my marriage to Greg brought back the nightmares. I didn't want to give him the privilege of taking up so many pages of my journey. I didn't want to see in writing how long I stayed or how many chances I gave him even after I'd left. It has taken me a long time to forgive myself for the years of pain, the cycle that began then as I hobbled across the cold pavement of the hospital parking lot.

I was also hesitant to speak about domestic abuse as a larger issue, because the only life I've lived is my own. I know firsthand a woman will not leave until she's ready, which often isn't until long after she realizes she should.

But light must be shed on the darkness, even if the light is harsh and the darkness vast. According to the National Coalition Against Domestic Violence (2015), an American woman is beaten or abused every nine seconds. Women ages eighteen to twenty-four are most susceptible. Appearances can deceive, and domestic violence dwells in every zip code. I always looked like I had my act together. You never know what woman has been on the receiving end of a fist.

There are so many reasons women stay. *If I tried just a little bit harder*, they think, *I could save my marriage. It's my fault. I'll try harder not to do anything to make him mad. I have nowhere to go. Leaving will make me a failure. My vows to God say 'til death do us part. What about my children? Leaving will deprive my children of their father. It can't get worse than this; I've made it through worse than this before. I just don't want to be alone. I couldn't make it on my own. I can't support myself. He said he would kill me if I left. I still love him.*

And even in the absence of any concrete reason, there is the overwhelming sense of stress, fear, depression, guilt, anger, and shame. I was young, and I was in love. I had no one I felt I could confide in. Doctors asked no questions, and police did nothing, even when they found me alone in a blood-splattered kitchen.

I am a strong woman who surrendered my strength for too long. I am a woman who makes plans, and for many years I shackled myself to a plan that no longer served my life. Yet my ultimate victory was more precious because it was so hard-won.

You must understand how difficult and complicated it was to free myself from the ties that bound me, even if they were invisible—even if it may seem to you, reading, as if I could have stepped free from those ties many times. So many women in abusive relationships stay trying to live out some dream they thought a man or marriage would fulfill.

As you read the coming chapters, I hope you reserve judgment and reach for compassion, understanding, and love. I hope you remember there are many women in situations like the one I survived. Perhaps you are one of them. They live in paralyzed fear. They operate under the control of men they can't stop loving. Some of them will never leave.

...

It wasn't as if Greg came home every day and beat me—it wasn't like that. There were some bright spots, some better times.

Greg enjoyed showing me new experiences and teaching me things my sheltered life had not included. He loved going to the county fair, so the first summer we were married, we traveled every weekend to a nearby county fair, tasting all the different foods and buying junk trinkets, laughing and having fun.

He loved to play cards, so he taught me to play pinochle, Tonk, and poker. We'd sit at the kitchen table playing cards for hours. He showed me how to bet on my hand and win. I was a quick study and loved it when I'd beat him.

We went out to dinner almost every Friday, trying a new restaurant every time. Some were greasy spoon taco and rib joints, and others were top-rated restaurants with romantic atmospheres, where we ordered new things like prime rib, escargot, calamari, and even caviar to expand our palates beyond what our childhoods had exposed us to. Sometimes I felt like we were finishing our growing up together.

Christmas was his favorite time of the year. If he had ignored me throughout the year, he made up for at Christmas. He was his most loving during the Christmas season, becoming almost childlike.

He knew I loved dogs, and within the first couple of months after we married, he got us a Samoyed puppy I named Malcolm, after Malcolm X. Greg and I adored that dog and had fun training him.

On the rare occasions Greg spent time with my mother, he treated her well. He made sure our home had the things she liked to eat. She may have hated him, but she was cordial enough around him, reserving her spiteful comments about him for others' ears. He fully engaged himself with our family at our reunions and dinners. I believe that was the life he'd always wanted. Greg was also my rock when my mother and I had our clashes, listening and offering me sympathy for my frustrations.

He was smart and extremely handy; there wasn't anything he couldn't figure out and fix or build. He took good care of our home, the yard, and our cars. He was a good provider, but his provisions came with a price.

What scared me? His rage, his fists: I never knew when these were coming. But even aside from the beatings, there was the emotional abuse—Greg's disrespect, his silence when I failed to finish the list of chores he left me every day. He was just a mean individual who kept me walking on eggshells. Over and over I asked myself, "How was he able to hide this much rage from me so well for so long? Why did I not see this side of him before I married him?"

My marriage became an exercise in survival. Every time Greg beat me, I would pray, "Dear God, please don't let him be the one to take my life." Many nights, I would lie awake imagining my escape from this nightmare I was living. I knew my dreams and plans for love would not be fulfilled in this relationship.

Yet I had nowhere else to go. I'd promised myself I would never return to my mother's home, and I had no money, no alternatives. After losing my job at Nachusa Home, I worked for a short time as a retail salesclerk at Kline's, a department store, but I didn't make enough money there, so I applied for a position at Fosco Fabricators. I carefully handwrote my résumé, and the hiring manager admired my penmanship—but was later dismayed to discover, after giving me the position as receptionist and assistant to the purchasing manager, that I'd handwritten my résumé because I wasn't a proficient typist.

Even so, my job didn't pay enough to give me much independence. I would have to live through this hell until I could figure a way out.

In June of 1972, nearly one year after Greg and I got married, one of my cousins died in a car accident on her way home from college. I got the call about her death in the morning, and in the evening I got another call to let me know that the whole family was gathering at Aunt Tutta's house. I was shocked and grieving, but Greg wouldn't let me leave the house because I hadn't fried his fish yet.

"I won't stay long," I said.

"Just fry the fish first," he insisted.

Anger and grief swirled within me, rising. "Fry your own damn fish!" I shouted.

He slapped me hard across the face. I grabbed my purse and ran out the back door. I tore through the yard. I saw him get into the car to follow me, so I kept running, hiding behind trees and shrubs, trying to make it to Aunt Tutta's house. Uncle Jesse's wife, Sylvia, saw me. I got into her car, still crying.

Sylvia helped me get a hotel room, where I stayed for several days while the family was in mourning. Aunt Tutta confronted Greg and made him let me back into our house to get clothes to wear to the funeral. Mom learned I was staying at the hotel.

It was then that my mother told me she had been there, months before, when I was leaving the hospital. Sitting in her car, she'd watched her child leave the hospital with the man who'd put her there.

"I washed my hands of you that day," she said. "I decided all I could do was wait until you'd had enough."

Now my mother wanted to know again if I'd had enough. She offered to pay for a divorce—she'd even hired an attorney. I made an appointment.

I never went.

Greg came to my cousin's funeral and said kind things to me while I cried. I fell into his kindness. He promised that things would be different. I knew things wouldn't be different, but still I hoped they would be.

I clung to the better times, following my love and believing in happy endings.

My husband loved to fish, and although fishing bored me, he patiently taught me to bait the hook, put the worm on the hook, and pull in the fish. Because I paid more attention to reading my books than my line, the fish got fat off my worms, so Greg put bobbers on my line. He and his buddy would bring the catch back to our place, sit on the back porch, and clean the fish. Greg also enjoyed camping, and although I hated it, I tried because it made him so happy—although he took all the fun out of things by bringing his obsessive cleanliness even to the campgrounds, insisting that I clean out the tent like it was our house, rolling up the sleeping bags and sweeping out the tent with a little whisk broom.

We took a camping trip just a month or two after my cousin died. On that trip, Greg taught me to run and steer the fishing boat he'd just bought. He took us out to the middle of the lake, turned off the motor, and told me to steer us back to the dock. As he yelled at me to pick up speed, I somehow set the boat spinning in circles and got us caught up in a bunch of lily pads and moss. We went out to eat that evening and laughed our butts off, thinking about the scene we'd made out there.

When we returned from that camping trip, I discovered I was pregnant. I was finally going to be a mother.

chapter 10

NEW LIFE

From the moment I knew I was pregnant, my life changed. My body became a temple to guard the gift that God had given us. I was determined to be the best mother I could possibly be, monitoring everything from what I inhaled, to what I ate, to the amount I sleep I got. I refused to be around people who were smoking. I held my breath when I walked behind car exhaust pipes. I didn't drink much anyway, but now I abstained and ate nutritiously for my child. Everything became about giving my unborn child the best possible environment to grow in.

Following our first doctor's appointment confirming our pregnancy, I was having a reflective moment, gently touching my stomach. I spoke aloud to myself, "This baby could come out looking like its grandfather, and I wouldn't even know it." Three days later, when Greg came home from work on Friday, he said, "Pack your things. We're leaving in the morning to go find your dad."

I was shocked. This idea hadn't even seemed within the realm of possibility, but now it was going to happen—Greg knew I still had the address my mother had given me, the one where I'd sent so many letters that had gone unanswered. I was excited and nervous at the same time. I couldn't sleep for imagining what the meeting would be like.

Greg and I drove the eight hours to Springfield, Missouri, and found the house at the address. It was a simple, well-kept house, and we parked on the street.

All of a sudden I was a nervous wreck. "Nobody's home," I said, almost relieved.

"Let's just wait," Greg said.

Not much time passed before a car pulled into the breezeway, with a man driving and a woman in the passenger seat. Greg and I got out of our car and walked over. I saw the man look up to adjust the rearview mirror so he could see who was approaching. When he saw me, he seemed to freeze. Did he know who I was?

The woman got out and came over to us as we approached their car. I thought, *She resembles my mother.*

"Hello," she said. "Do we know you?"

"You don't know me," I said, "but we're here to see Harold. He knows my mother." By this time, he had gotten out of the car and was unloading groceries.

"Please, come on in," she said invitingly.

She sat us on a couch in the living room and brought us cold drinks. Once he was finished helping her, he came and sat across from us in an armchair and she disappeared into another part of the house. I guessed she might have had an idea what the visit was about.

I couldn't stop staring at him. He was a heavyset man with light brown skin who seemed to have some difficulty walking. I searched his face for my features. He and Greg made small talk for a while, but I just kept on staring.

At last Greg gave me a nudge. "Go on, say something!" he said.

"I think you knew my mother," I said carefully, "and I believe you're my father." Then I told the story. He had been a porter on the train. He had met my mother while she was traveling to Mississippi with my cousins. A relationship had developed.

He shook his head. "No," he said, "I don't remember anyone like that."

"So you're denying you're my father?" I asked, trying to keep my voice steady.

"I'm sorry," he said. "I only have one child—my son, Harold Junior." He pointed at a framed picture that showed a handsome young man. "He's twenty-six years old. Lives in San Francisco."

We kept talking for about an hour. At one point, he said, "How do I know you're not someone just showing up looking for money?"

A flash of anger ran through me. "I'm not," I said quickly. "My mother and stepfather always made sure I was well taken care of." I found it disturbing that he could assume I'd sought him out for money. "I'm married," I said, nodding to Greg, "and we're not looking for anything from you."

I had thought about telling Harold he would soon be a grandfather, but now I banished the thought from my head. He didn't deserve to know. At that moment, I completely shut down. I'd spent my childhood dreaming my father would come to town and find me. This man didn't even want to acknowledge me.

He finally admitted that he did remember a pretty woman on the train. She had some children with her, he remembered, and he'd tried to help her, but that was the whole story.

I asked, "Of all the people you met over the years, you're saying you remember this *one* woman?" I didn't challenge him further.

Greg broke the awkward silence and suggested we get ready to go. Harold asked where we were headed. We told him we were going to Kansas City to visit my Uncle Narvell and Aunt Kathleen.

"Do you know how to get to the highway?" he asked. "I'll show you how to get out of town." At that moment his kind, probably long-suffering wife came out from wherever she had been waiting, saying she would come with him to escort us to the highway.

As soon as we got into the car, Greg said, "It's obvious he was lying. He knew all about your mom. He described the scenario exactly like your mom told it to you. Besides, do you think he would have invited us into their home if he didn't believe you were his child? You shocked him showing up like that, that's all." He shook his head. "I would love to know what his wife said to him after we left."

I began to cry. It was humiliating. I had hoped we would end our meeting with an embrace and a promise to get to know one other. Instead my childhood fantasy had been shattered—it was obvious Harold hadn't spent a day worrying about me. I wished I had thought of more questions to ask that might have shed more light on the truth, but I didn't know what those questions would have been. I didn't have enough facts. I even began to doubt everything I'd been told, wondering if he might not be my father after all. Was it just another lie from my mother?

By the time we got to Kansas City, though, I decided he had lost out on a great opportunity to know his daughter. He was just another person who was supposed to love me who didn't. The only silver lining of our meeting was the news I had a brother. I liked knowing I had a biological sibling, although I doubted I would ever know him.

When we arrived at Uncle Narvell and Aunt Kathleen's house, my uncle asked what had brought us their way.

I told him, "We just left Springfield, Missouri, from meeting my father."

My uncle shared a surprised glance with Aunt Kathleen. "How'd that go?" he asked.

I told him, and the story left him shaking his head. "Versie, I'm sure glad you weren't a child of mine, just showing up on our doorstep."

We laughed, and I started feeling a little better. "At the end of the meeting he offered to show us to the highway," I said.

"I bet he *did* show you to the highway!" Uncle Narvell laughed.

Once I returned home, my mother asked me to come over. My uncle had told her about my trip, as I'd expected he would. All she asked me was, "Are you satisfied now?"

"I had to know what he looks like before the baby comes," I told her. "I'm glad I went."

• • •

Greg may have supported me when it came to finding my father, but his rage still rose to the surface often. Our frequent fighting got us evicted from our hard-won duplex. We decided it was time to leave Dixon and look for a permanent place for our growing family. We began looking for a house in Rockford, Illinois, but we were coming up short on the money we would need for a down payment. Greg was a conscientious saver, and he worked hard trying to scrape together enough.

I had no extra money of my own, and I knew if I didn't help out, he would hold it over my head and throw it in my face every chance he got.

I finally swallowed my pride and worked up the nerve to ask my mother for help. I went to her and asked if she would allow me to tap into the unused college fund she had established for me. I knew she didn't like Greg, but still I was taken aback by her response. She was standing at the kitchen sink.

She turned and looked me in my face and said, "No ma'am, I can't help you!"

It wasn't her refusal that stung so sharply—it was the tone in which she delivered it, flat and dismissive. I felt hurt and angry for humbling myself to come to her with my hands out, but I didn't say another word. I refused to beg. As I left her house empty-handed, I determined in my heart that I would never ask her for anything again.

Greg decided to ask my Uncle Jesse if we could live with him until we found a house. Uncle Jesse was the only member of my family Greg got along with, perhaps because they had some things in common—Uncle Jesse was a mean, abusive drunk. He agreed to let us live with him.

Uncle Jesse had a big house, a split-level, and he gave us the upper level for ourselves. I checked on my uncle sometimes—knowing he was smoking and drinking, afraid he'd burn up the house trying to make his dinner—but for the most part, he let us be.

On my twenty-first birthday, I was excited and wanted to celebrate, but instead all I got was a card in the mail from my mother. She had given Brenda and Melvin each a car for their twenty-first birthdays. I wasn't expecting a car, but I was insulted and hurt by her gift: twenty-one single dollar bills tucked into the generic card.

My entire life, I'd watched my mother draw lines between me and my siblings and how she treated us. Her behavior always seemed calculated to deliver the most hurtful message. Whenever I called her behavior into question, she showed no understanding of my feelings and would only joke about how emotional I was. I took the card and the money to her house and gave them back to her. We got in a terrible argument, and when I returned to Uncle Jesse's house, Greg was nowhere to be found.

I was twenty-one years old, pregnant, and alone. I decided to buy my own birthday present. I went to a department store in Rockford, opened up a credit card, and bought maternity clothes as a birthday gift to myself.

When Greg discovered what I'd done, he knocked me around. As he advanced on me to hit me again, I ran, and when I was trying to escape, I slipped on the hardwood steps and landed at the bottom of the steps on the floor. I looked up and saw my uncle looking down at me.

Uncle Jesse said, "I'm not stepping in to help you. You had no business doing that."

We continued living day to day in our hot-and-cold marriage, and Greg eventually pulled together the money we needed to make a down payment on a house. He worked as much overtime as he could and put off paying some of our bills to get us to the amount we needed.

One month before our baby was due, we moved into our new home in Rockford, Illinois, about an hour's drive from Dixon. It was a three-bedroom ranch house with a garage, a nice-sized backyard with a patio, and a weeping willow tree in the backyard. We imagined a swing set for our child to play on. The biggest attraction of the house was the very large family room with a brick fireplace. After we decorated the nursery, every day we would go into the room, stare at the empty crib, and anticipate our baby's arrival. I was so proud of Greg—finally, in some way, he was living up to the image I'd had of him when we got married.

Yet he reminded me at every turn that he had done all this without me. I had quit my job at Fosco Fabricators to move to Rockford and become a mother, so I was more dependent on my husband than ever. Nothing we had was mine. It all belonged to him.

In April 1973, on Good Friday, we went to the doctor, who said the baby hadn't dropped yet—it would probably be another couple of weeks. On Saturday, I told Greg I wanted to go out for dinner at a nice restaurant. It would be the last time I'd be able to go out for a while once the baby came.

Greg agreed, but he wanted to catch up with some friends first. I waited for him while the hours ticked away until it was far too late for dinner. Once he climbed into bed, I was fuming and suspicious. I said to him, "We need to talk," but he ignored me. His back was to me, so I tore the covers off him to get his attention.

"You'd better cover me back up," he said angrily.

I reached across the bed to throw the covers back just as he sat up, hitting him across the face. It was an accident, but that was all it took.

He got up and started beating my face and chest and head and wouldn't stop. I managed to get to the front door and run out into the night, screaming for someone to help me, my nightgown stretched over my pregnant belly. There was a laundromat half a block away, and I collapsed against the door. At that moment, I felt the pressure under my breasts lighten; I felt the baby drop into my pelvis.

I was badly bruised and bleeding from my mouth and nose. The sensation of the baby dropping took my breath away. I curled up in a ball crying. I was unable to lift myself to my feet. Greg was running after me, but when he got to me, his anger was gone. He lifted me and carried me home.

The next morning, my face looked like it had been put through a meat grinder. I thought to myself, *I have to get out of here. Look at what he's done to me.* We didn't speak to each other the next day.

On Monday morning, once Greg had left for work, I got up and packed my Volkswagen Beetle. I decided I'd stay at a hotel until the baby was born. I had some savings. I knew I couldn't tell my mother.

I pulled out of the driveway, and I broke down crying. I pulled back into the garage. I knew I didn't want to have my baby by myself.

Less than twenty-four hours later, early Tuesday morning, I was awakened by pain radiating across my lower back and ripping down my legs. I thought it might be labor, but I thought, *It's too early.* Then I felt the uncontrollable urge to pee but couldn't make it to the bathroom, so I peed in the trashcan—later I realized this was my water breaking.

I woke Greg up. "I think I might be in labor," I said.

"Well," Greg said, "Are you sure? I've got to go to work in a few hours." He got up and went into the guestroom to sleep.

I lay in bed timing what I now knew were contractions. My body clenched up and pain shot through me every seven minutes. I went to the nursery and grabbed the bag I had packed for myself and the baby. I finally went and woke Greg up. "We've got to get to the hospital," I said.

"Okay, wait a minute," he said.

He went around the house ensuring everything was in its proper place. He took out all the garbage. He got out the rake and combed it over the shag rug to make it neat. He went and got a plastic tarp to put across the backseat of his beloved car, and he instructed me to lie down on the plastic.

By the time we got to the hospital, I was pushing and soaked in blood. The doctors had to cut my clothes off. Our baby boy was born within minutes. We named him Preston. He was beautiful, with long eyelashes, and right from the start he was a perfect baby.

Greg called my mother to share the news of our son's arrival. The high school where she taught was flooded, so she was out of school. By the end of the day Mom and Aunt Tutta were at the hospital to meet Mom's first grandchild.

Once my mother arrived, her eyes lingered on my scarred and scratched face. She asked me what had happened, and I muttered something about getting rug burn. She raised her eyebrows almost imperceptibly, showing just a hint of judgment and skepticism—but then she set eyes on her grandchild. "Give me that baby," she said, cooing.

She stayed with us for three days, cooking, showing me how to bathe Preston, and making sure I knew what to do. She was a good teacher. On the fourth day, once Greg had left for work and I was alone, I walked around the house with the baby clutched to my chest. I had to give him a bath, I knew, but I was too nervous. He seemed so slippery. What if he slipped out of my hands?

At two p.m., the doorbell rang, and when I answered it I found my mother on my front step, a casserole dish balanced in her hands. "Have you bathed him yet?" I shook my head. She smirked. "I thought so," she said.

This time she made me bathe my baby by myself, on standby for reassurance. As it turned out, my mom was born to be a grandmother. Over the years she showed the kind of love as a grandmother that she had never shown as a mother. I was grateful for her help in those first days, when I was so uncertain about how to manage everything.

After that, though, I was on my own. Preston was the light of our lives, and Greg doted on him—yet nothing in our marriage changed.

I knew what kind of wife and mother I wanted to be. I'd watched my mother dominate our home so that Daddy never had a voice or really seemed happy. I was prepared to honor and respect my husband, submitting myself and working hard to bring love into our new home.

I did my best to compromise. Because going out to the clubs was still in Greg's blood, I determined that Friday would be Greg's night to go out. If I wanted to go out, Saturday night would be when we'd go out together, and Sunday would be family day. Greg obviously didn't share this vision. Things got to the point where he started his weekends on Thursday and went out every night . . . and he often went out on Blue Monday, as it was called.

Even when he was gone much of the time, he wanted control over everything. My mother called Preston "the kitchen baby" because Greg put up a gate so our son wouldn't wander into the family room and make a mess. If Preston crawled across the shag rug, Greg was behind him with the rake, combing the rug back into place. If Preston pulled himself up by the furniture, Greg was behind him, wiping away his tiny handprints. Preston was allowed to have three toys out at once—if he wanted a new one, he had to put one back. When my husband came home, he didn't want to be disturbed. Greg wanted the baby to be quiet. I was expected to have our son fed before we sat down for dinner.

Greg was determined I'd have as full a workday as he did. My list of chores was lengthy. If I didn't make the bed, Greg wouldn't go to bed at night until I'd made it. The laundry had to be done all on one day, rather than spreading it out. Once I was finished, the laundry room floor had to be mopped and the washer and dryer washed out. Greg was obsessive about conserving electricity, and if I left appliances plugged in, he made me come outside and watch the electric meter tick upwards. "See?" he'd say. When I went grocery shopping, he would give me a check he'd already made out to ensure I didn't spend too much. I had to bring a calculator to the store to avoid being embarrassed at the register.

I quickly learned that being a stay-at-home mom wasn't as fulfilling as I thought it would be. I was too focused on getting the chores done and avoiding Greg's wrath to focus my activities around our son. I started out taking Preston to the YMCA for swimming, watching him splash and bob in the water with the other babies. I soon abandoned this plan after a few stressful attempts of rushing to get back home in time to finish all the chores on my list. If a friend stopped by to visit, my eyes kept darting to the clock. Would I have time to finish all my tasks?

I realize now that I was still trying to perform to get the prize: love.

But nothing was good enough for my husband. I worked hard to keep up, scrambling to cross everything off my lists, hoping we could have a peaceful evening. I did my best to avoid provoking him. But many times it wasn't enough.

I often fought back, leaving scratches and bite marks.

Once while we were arguing, I put a pot of water on the stovetop. I was determined that if Greg came near me, I would scald him. He said to me, "I see you boiling that water. If you throw it at me, you better be ready to run, because I'll take that pot and put the bottom of it on your face." Without a word I cut the heat.

A few times, when Greg came in from an all-night party, dead drunk, I helped him undress for bed, took off his shirt, and beat him with his belt. I watched red lines appear on his back, getting some degree of grim satisfaction at my revenge. The next day, he would come over to me, wincing, and ask if I could see anything on his back. I thought it was so strange he never looked in a mirror. "No," I lied.

In all the conversations we'd had before getting married, we both imagined me being a stay-at-home mom once we started our family. To make that possible, Greg got a part-time janitorial job cleaning offices after work. When Preston was around ten months old, Greg had grown exhausted from juggling his full-time job with his part-time janitorial work. He decided I had to find a job to help out with expenses. "Just a part-time job would help," he said. He suggested that I become a grocery checkout clerk. At this point, Preston hadn't begun talking or walking yet, and my biggest concern was missing out on all my baby's firsts.

The longer I thought about having a job, though, the more it appealed to me. If I had money, I realized, I would have a little more power.

When I came home from Howard, I'd shut down all the dreams I had of changing the world. I repositioned my thinking: being a wife and a mother was a calling, and I knew it was my purpose. I was fully committed to this role.

But now that Greg was telling me I had to get a job, I was having a hard time conjuring up an image of getting *just* a job to pay the bills. If I had to go to work and leave my baby, I didn't want just a job—I wanted a *career* that took me somewhere besides out of the house every day. I felt ambition sparking in my spirit again. If I was going to leave my child with a babysitter, I wanted something that would make it financially worthwhile, cultivate my talent, and spark my passion.

I got a nursing unit clerk position at St. Anthony's Hospital. My shift was from three p.m. to eleven p.m., so Preston was left with the sitter for only two hours a day. I would drop him off, and Greg would pick him up. My job was reading patients' charts after the doctors made their rounds for notes, going to the pharmacy for the nurses, and going on other assorted errands. I liked working with the nurses, who made me feel like we were all in the healing game together. My tasks took me all over the hospital, learning the ins and outs of how things worked there. I used my time observing and asking questions. This job, I thought, could turn into a career.

Greg had to take a gravel road to work, and he didn't want his beloved '66 Chevy Impala to get dented by stray rocks, so I drove his car to work at the hospital and he used my Volkswagen Beetle. But his souped-up Impala was a magnet for vandals. After his car was vandalized in the hospital parking lot not once, but twice, he made me resign. I felt the car was just a part of the story. I suspected he disliked being tied down every evening caring for a toddler. Either way, I was back to square one.

My next career opportunity was working as an administrative assistant at a midsize State Farm Insurance agency. Unfortunately, I discovered quickly that this was not a career I wanted to pursue. Every day I was bored out of my mind. Nothing about my job sparked my imagination. This was not the kind of work I was meant to do.

One day during my lunch hour, I went to the Illinois Bell Telephone Company to pay our phone bill. I happened to know the service rep waiting on me; she'd lived in Dixon. While we were catching up, she mentioned that Illinois Bell was hiring. Everyone knew that getting a job with the phone company wasn't easy—but if you managed to get in, it was one of the best paying jobs in the area. I took an application and returned to work.

A few days later, I went during my lunch hour to drop off my filled-out application and was surprised when they offered to set up an interview that very day. They were looking to fill a telephone operator position, they said. The problem, as I saw it, was the erratic schedule. Knowing how difficult it would be to manage Preston's daycare needs, I turned them down.

My friend called me up. "If you want to work at Illinois Bell," she explained, "you have to start as an operator." She also mentioned the company's upgrade transfer plan, which would allow me to post for a new position in six months. "But you need to take the operator job to get in the door." Before beginning my job search, I had set my boundaries: I would only accept a regular eight a.m. to five p.m., Monday to Friday job with benefits and the potential for advancement.

Illinois Bell called me with another offer, again for an operator position. I turned them down again. My friend, exasperated, assured me they wouldn't call back.

A few months later, I was home nursing a summer cold. The phone rang: A woman was calling from Illinois Bell. Before she could get started, I interrupted her. "I'm not able to take an operator position," I told her.

"Actually," she said, "this opportunity is in the repair department. Are you interested?"

I thought, *But I know nothing about repair.* "Could you tell me what the job involves?" I asked.

"Your job would be to take the repair calls, fill out repair tickets, and send them down to dispatch for service calls. After the service is restored, the ticket comes back to you, and you file the ticket. How does that sound?"

Before I could answer, the caller continued. "I'll be honest, these repair clerk positions don't open up very often. They're usually filled immediately by operators, but no one applied this time, so we returned to our applicant pool. Do you think you'd be interested?"

At this point, I'm sure she was surprised that I hadn't accepted the job—but I had a plan, and I was going to stick to it.

"What are the hours?" I asked.

"You'd work eight to four-thirty and one Saturday a month, with a half-hour lunch."

I took the job.

It was late summer in 1974, and I was twenty-two years old. I had a one-year-old son, and I had a job at Illinois Bell. At a family gathering, Uncle Narvell said he was proud of me. "That's a job you can retire from," he said. My mother was less supportive, saying, "She's just trying to show me she can get by without a degree."

My mother wasn't the only one to act less than thrilled about my new job. When I started at Illinois Bell, it seemed like no one wanted much to do with me. I felt women staring at me during lunch breaks in the cafeteria, but no one spoke to me. Eventually, I befriended one woman who told me frankly, "People don't like you. You came in off the street and took a job that one of us could have used to get off this crazy operator schedule. It would have been a promotion for one of us."

"The woman who offered me the job said no operators applied," I said.

She raised her eyebrows. "Yeah, well, she lied."

Some people may have thought it wasn't fair, and I agreed—it was God's favor, and "favor ain't fair." I was full of gratitude.

The work itself wasn't particularly exciting, but I knew this new beginning was just the start. We took telephone repair calls, wrote out the repair complaints on tickets, sent them on a conveyor-like belt to the dispatch team, and filed the resolved tickets. For security reasons, the central office building where we worked had no windows. I felt like I was in a tomb all day.

All this time I kept in my mind the six-month mark, when I could write my own career ticket by applying for a more challenging position through the upgrade transfer plan. As this date grew nearer, I started spending my break time looking through the jobs manual. I wondered why nobody else seemed interested in taking advantage of this opportunity. How could they be content with the monotony of this work, when so many opportunities were within reach? I frequently asked my coworkers about their goals. I encouraged them to take charge of their futures, as I planned to do.

When I came into work one morning, Fred, my supervisor, called me into his office. He fixed me with a kind but stern expression. "Carolynn," he said, "the others are feeling like you don't fit in here. It's obvious you have more education and more ambition than they do."

I was startled—and not just by Fred's incorrect assumption that I was more educated than my coworkers. Didn't they want to move up in the company, too?

"For most of these girls, this is all they'll ever do, and they're okay with that. So please just do your job and drop the motivational talks."

The next time Fred called me into his office, it was after I submitted my paperwork for the upgrade transfer program. I had set my sights on the highest position I could post for, one that would put me in line for a management role. I wanted to use whatever power was afforded to me through the upgrade transfer plan to catapult myself as far as I could and as fast as I could.

"Carolynn," Fred said with a sigh, rubbing his graying temples, "no one goes from being a repair clerk to being a communications consultant." Fred sat me down and laid out a career path for me that would take five years and much more patience than my ambition could stand. He handed the form back to me, unsigned. "Consider the customer service rep position," he said. "I know you're ready to go, but just be patient. Your time will come."

Fred didn't understand—nobody seemed to understand. I had a sense of urgency. I had a plan, and just like any time I'd ever had a plan, I was going to work my plan. Any efforts to discourage me only sparked my determination.

I handed my paperwork back to Fred. "I'll take my chances," I told him.

Fred was right—moving into the communications consultant position wasn't an easy process. I had to go through three levels of testing: three different interviews, aptitude tests, decision-making tasks, and psychological evaluations. Every time I passed one test, I had to take another.

I made it to the final round: a full two days of interviewing in Chicago. Fred brought the team together to say I would be gone those two days. His intention was for the others to wish me well, but instead they told me stories of those who'd failed.

One girl said, "Maybe when you get this out of your system, you'll see it's not so bad working here."

I stood up and declared, "I'm going to pass this test, and if you're not careful, one of these days I'll be the boss of all of you!" They all laughed, but I was serious. I believed what I said—and I believed what I said would happen.

Nobody else knew how important this was. Nobody else knew my ambition had dual purposes. I needed a job that paid enough for me to leave my husband.

The night before the testing started, I drove the two hours to Chicago, leaving Preston in his father's care, and checked into the hotel. I went out and had a bowl of chili, savoring this time by myself, eager for tomorrow to come so I could prove myself. Once I returned to my hotel room, my bravado began to fade. I had no idea what to expect, but I knew failure wasn't an option—so instead of sleeping, I lay in bed and prayed.

The next morning, I put on the outfit I'd chosen to look professional—a black suit with a crisply pressed white blouse, a black and white silk tied scarf, a lined skirt so it wouldn't wrinkle, and a small briefcase. I knew I had to sell myself as the image of success; looking the part was as important as playing it. I tried to breathe deeply and stay calm. I walked the block and a half to the Illinois Bell headquarters, where I met my fellow candidates. There were five of us, and we went through sessions all that day and the next with different people in different situations to see how we'd react and how we made decisions and prioritized assignments.

It was a grueling two days. I spoke clearly and confidently, and every time I shook somebody's hand, I kept a firm grip and eye contact. One of the tests was an in-box simulation exercise. I went into a room by myself and sat at a desk; I'd been told I was being videotaped. I was presented with business-related scenarios and given a list of tasks that included returning telephone calls, handling correspondence, meetings to attend, and customer complaints. It was up to me to prioritize each task in order of perceived importance, giving my rationale regarding my decisions and judgment calls for how to handle difficult customers. I talked to myself out loud throughout the entire task, narrating my reasoning.

By lunchtime I was drained, craving some time by myself to regroup—but I suspected they wanted to see how we'd handle ourselves having lunch around strangers. *Okay*, I said to myself with a sigh, *I guess I'm on again.* I put on a big smile and tried my best to be engaging.

On my drive back to Rockford, I was exhausted, but satisfied. I had done the best I could. I gave God a prayer of thanks.

When I came back to the office, everybody wanted to know how I'd done. "I did my best," I said, "and when I pass, I'll take you all out for dinner."

"And if you don't," they teased, "we're stuck with you another year."

Six weeks later, Fred called the whole team into his office and announced that I had passed. "When a position in the Marketing and Sales Department opens," he said, "Carolynn will be offered the position of communications consultant."

There was a flurry of hugs and pats on the back, and once everyone else had trickled out of the office, Fred looked at me with pride.

"Well, you did it!" he said. "You should be very proud of yourself. I don't know anybody else who's done it on their first try, and I certainly don't know anyone who's passed after such a short time with the company." He went and shut the door before continuing. "I understand you're the first African American woman to have accomplished this. Some people in Chicago are interested in bringing you there to take a position."

And just as Fred had predicted, over the next few weeks, people in upper management in the company called offering me jobs in Chicago. This seemed like the perfect escape, a job that paid enough that I could take my son and leave my husband to start over somewhere new.

But I wasn't ready. I hated big cities. I couldn't envision living in Chicago alone, raising my son. I couldn't do it.

Unless you have been in an abusive relationship, you cannot truly understand this contradiction—the way it is possible to hold in your mind two different views of your world. You know the life you're living isn't the life you want, and you want to escape. Yet in some ways you grow accustomed to the way things are. Time passes, nothing really changes except your coping mechanisms, and you know that nothing will change. But still you hope, because to finish things ends your dream of being a family.

I got a phone call from a black manager, someone I'd been told had a great deal of influence within the company. I don't remember his name, but I won't ever forget his message.

"Hello, young lady," he said. "How are you doing? What's going on? Do you understand how important this is, what we're asking you to do? We finally have a black woman pass these tests, and you want to play hard to get?"

He told me there were no open positions in Rockford, and there wouldn't be any for quite some time. I explained that I had a home, a husband, and a child, and that I couldn't relocate.

He ended the call by saying, "I hope you realize you just ruined your career!"

At first I was angry that someone I didn't even know was calling me and trying to speak failure into my life. Then I began to feel demoralized and full of doubt. The euphoria of having passed the test had worn off. Yet I believed in God's plans for me, and I never lost my faith. No matter how bad my caller had made things sound, I still believed that what was mine could not be taken from me.

Five months later, Fred called me into his office again. He was smiling. "I just got a call," he said, "and it looks like you're about to become a communications consultant."

The only female communications consultant outside of Chicago had announced, seemingly out of nowhere, that she was resigning to return to college to become a veterinarian. My coworkers were literally shaking their heads at the unexpected turn of events, saying I was incredibly lucky.

I've never believed in luck. I saw God's hand holding the door open. He was urging me forward to fulfill the potential He had placed inside of me.

This was my time to push through my own perceived limitations, to dare to do things that others said I could not or should not do.

chapter 11

THOSE WHO HELP THEMSELVES

Without intending to, I became a corporate trailblazer. I was acutely aware that I wasn't just a woman in a male-dominated world; I was a black woman in that world, which brought its own set of complexities. I suddenly had people telling me how to act, what organizations would be beneficial for me to belong to, and who I should or shouldn't be seen with. As I moved into my new role, I had a strong sense of responsibility and commitment to perform well so the door I came through would remain open. I didn't want my failure to be a roadblock for the next woman or person of color. I also felt compelled to enlighten my coworkers and customers to their biases and take a stand against their prejudices. This wasn't just about me.

During my rigorous testing and interview process to become a communications consultant, I'd been asked whether I planned to have more children.

"Not at this time," I had answered.

But I'd stopped taking birth control when Preston was two, in keeping with my plan. I never intended to have just one child, and all my children had to be by the same man. Greg and I were eager to add to our family.

When I found out I was pregnant with our second child—during the six weeks when I was traveling to Chicago to be trained for my new position—I was scared. Timing couldn't have been worse. Would they fire me? Would all my hard work and waiting have been for nothing?

I went to my training instructor, who happened to be a woman, and confided in her. She congratulated me and assured me, "Don't worry, they can't touch you for being pregnant." So once the training was over and I returned to my home office in Rockford, I sat down with my new manager, Bill, and gave him the news.

Word spread to the other sales representatives, all of them men. One of them, upon hearing I was pregnant, said right in front of me, "See, this is why we shouldn't hire women—they're not reliable employees. Now she's going to want us to carry her load when she's out on maternity leave."

I had people rooting against me on all sides. There were those at work that didn't expect me to succeed, and my husband, I would learn, was jealous of my success.

When I received my first check with my promotional increase in it, I came home from training in Chicago and discovered Greg had gone to my office, picked up my check, and deposited it. Before coming home, he'd also had a few drinks—he was always his most vicious before he became completely drunk.

He threw the deposit slip in my face and told me, "I guess you think you're hot shit now." As he spoke, he advanced on me. "But I don't care what you do, you'll never make more money than me!"

I knew better than to try to go toe-to-toe with him—I was fourteen weeks pregnant, and I didn't want to exacerbate the situation.

But I was incredulous, and I couldn't stop the anger from building up inside me. I said, "Who gave you the right to forge my name and cash *my* check?"

Now it was too late. Greg's personal insecurities had mixed with the alcohol, creating a grenade I couldn't put the pin back into.

He came at me, backing me up against the kitchen cabinets. I was pinned in the corner with no escape as he began to beat me. I fell to the floor, trying to protect my body, and he kicked me again and again in my stomach, my face, and my back.

Once he had inflicted the amount of pain he felt would teach me a lesson, he stormed out of the house. I called the police, and when they showed up, they looked at my swollen face and saw the blood on the kitchen floor.

"Listen," one of them said, examining my face, "he's gone. If we find him and arrest him, he'll bail out and come back angrier than when he left. Then what will you do?" They suggested that I find a place to stay until my husband cooled down.

My mother was on her way to Rockford already, bringing Preston home from a visit to Dixon. I cleaned up the bloodied kitchen, packed a few things for myself and my son, and told my mother I was going home with her for the weekend. She saw my swollen face but asked no questions.

Exactly one week after the beating, I began having severe cramps and feeling the need to push. Thinking I was about to have a bowel movement, I rushed to the bathroom. The instant I sat down, the fetus fell into the toilet.

A scream tore from my throat. "Greg!" I yelled as loudly as I could. "Call the doctor! Call the doctor!"

Greg rushed into the bathroom to find me sitting there, our baby dangling from its umbilical cord into the toilet bowl.

He moved quickly, grabbing a bath towel and wrapping it between my legs like a diaper to hold the baby in place. He rushed me to the hospital. We both knew it was too late to save our baby—a boy. My husband didn't stay with me in the hospital as I had the remains of our child scraped from me. The hospital staff said they couldn't say for sure what had gone wrong, but I knew it had been Greg's savage beating.

He had killed our son.

In many ways, during our marriage I had to be two different people. I was one person at home, and I was a different person at work. Every evening during my drive home, I went through the mental process of dismantling the image I held of myself at work—the image of a woman who had a voice and made decisions—and I prepared to be the submissive wife whose opinion held no weight. At home, I was fighting for my life, walking through the minefield of my marriage.

At work, however, I could be confident and successful. At work, I had the freedom to create my own brand and fearlessly speak my mind. I was in control. Many people thought I was an experiment and expected me to fail, but their low expectations spurred me to persevere. I had learned how to push through other people's perceptions. I wasn't going to let anyone prevent me from doing this job.

My new position involved selling small telephone systems to our customers in Rockford, along with customers in McHenry and the Crystal Lake area, about an hour east of Rockford. I also provided support to account executives who sold the larger telephone systems. Once a large system was sold, I met with customers to design the system, place orders, monitor the installation process, help train customers to use the system, and implement the system.

It was 1975, and I still had to battle bigotry. I worked in many business sectors—transportation, professional, government, education, and medical—and I encountered more racism among the so-called professionals than I ever did among blue-collar workers.

Once, when I called on a small law firm to take their order for a telephone system, I walked in and introduced myself to the receptionist, who stood up without a word and ran to the back offices. A well-dressed attorney came out and asked, "Can I help you?"

"I'm Carolynn from Illinois Bell," I said, "and I'm here to discuss the kind of telephone system that would be optimal for your business."

The man slid a small notepad and pen across the counter to me. "Why don't you write down your boss's name and your office number," he suggested.

I politely restated my reason for being there, but the man insisted on calling my manager, Bill. He dialed the number I'd written down and exchanged a few words with Bill, who asked to speak with me.

Bill sounded embarrassed and worried. "Carolynn, I'm sorry," he said. "Just come back to the office."

The attorney walked me out of his office to the parking lot. When he saw my company-issued car with the Bell logo on its door, I heard him say, "Well, I guess she wasn't lying."

On my drive back to the office, I was furious. I found Bill in his office, pacing and running his hand over his face. He apologized to me, and he kept saying, "I don't know what to do about this."

"Bill, let me go back," I pleaded. The Bell system had a monopoly on phone service at the time, so I knew the attorney couldn't go anywhere else. "The guy can't open his business without phone service. Either he orders it through me, or he doesn't have service!"

Bill hesitated. "Maybe I should send one of the guys," he said.

"Send me back," I said again, insistent.

Three days later, I returned to the law office, and the receptionist gave me the information I needed to set up the office's telephone system. I never saw the attorney again.

A different time, when I introduced myself to a customer, he refused my handshake and declared, "I'm not doing business with niggers."

I smiled at him. "You can call me what you want," I said, "but you won't get phone service unless you deal with me." I left with my head held high.

At times things weren't any better with my own people. When we went to statewide meetings, I was explicitly warned by another black manager not to congregate with the other few black salespeople, because it could appear that I didn't know how to get along with white people. This manager told me, "Three or more blacks together is a workplace ghetto." I quickly developed my workplace rules for survival. I learned to steer clear of the white men after they'd had a few drinks—once the alcohol loosened their inhibitions, I'd hear their deepest sexual desires. I learned to make an appearance, mingle just long enough to be sure I'd been seen, and make a quick exit.

I confided in just a couple of friends at IBT, telling them what I was enduring at home, although my cousin Evelyn was the only person who knew everything I was facing. It was difficult exposing myself to pity and judgment, but it was impossible to hold it all in. The people who knew some of what was happening tried to persuade me to leave, but where would I go? I had to have a plan. The time wasn't right yet.

More than once, I left my husband. Each time he wore me down with his persistence and his promises.

After a while I learned to keep my keys and my purse in a strategic location for a fast getaway. After one especially bad beating, I grabbed my survival kit and escaped—but I had to leave Preston at home until I could get my bearings. I had a friend from Dixon living in Rockford who allowed me to stay with her until I could decide my next steps. I would call at night to speak to Preston, and Greg would have him beg me to return home. I took time off from work because my face was so bruised and swollen. I was gone about a week before going back, unable to come up with a plan, needing to be with my son.

Twice I left with Preston and got an apartment. Each time, Greg found us.

The first time, he showed up outside the sliding patio door. How had he tracked us down? He kept coming over until I agreed to come home.

The second time, I went out to my car to discover it had been disabled. I knew Greg had done it. He'd found me again. I called him, and he promised to put the distributor cap back in if I would return home. Now that he knew where we were, I knew we'd have no peace. I moved back.

I took more time off work from the abuse than from any personal illness. He always went for my face, leaving me bruised and swollen with handprints on my neck. I quickly learned to remove my glasses when a fight was inevitable so they wouldn't be broken or add to my injuries.

During this time, I was praying for solutions. I attended several different Baptist churches in Rockford, but I never found one I could spiritually connect with. Church attendance seemed like a religious formality, not a commitment. Every sermon sounded like it was made of platitudes. What I really needed was a way to survive what was happening in my day-to-day life, not a highway to heaven.

I knew it was by the grace of God that I'd been blessed with my budding career. I saw the hand of God opening doors and lighting the way. I didn't take those blessings for granted.

But when it came to my marriage, I called out to God again and again, and I received only deathly silence. I didn't understand what God wanted me to do or how I was supposed to survive.

I was living on the fumes of religion I'd inhaled as a child. Nothing significant was being poured into my spirit. My life at home was hell, and Greg always seemed to have the upper hand. How long could I keep running on fumes?

I was living a crazy, torturous existence—but I was still living life according to my abiding plan, the plan I couldn't abandon. I had never wanted just one child. I always hated the loneliness of that. No, I wanted at least one more child, and all my children would be by the same man. This I was sure about. I was determined there would be no patchwork quilt family for me.

In March of 1977, we had another baby, a boy we named Canthon after my Uncle Kent. I planned to take six months off from work to be with him. I'd had an easy pregnancy and delivery with Preston, but Canthon's entrance into the world was difficult. Preston was quiet and easygoing, but Canthon was the complete opposite, demanding attention. This was my last baby, so I decided I would breastfeed—but he never seemed to get enough to eat, and he wouldn't sleep longer than a few hours at a time.

Canthon required more attention than Preston, but he was much more of a momma's baby. I remember thinking, before Canthon was born, *How could I ever love another child as much as I love Preston?* But my heart immediately made room for Canthon with no effort.

After Canthon's birth, I felt in some ways Greg was jealous of the complete and unconditional love I had for my sons. He demanded that his needs come before the needs of his crying children.

In the months when I was home with Canthon, Greg's tyranny and womanizing were taking a toll. Women were so bold as to call the house asking to speak to my husband. He would come home covered in "love bites" and attack me if I said anything.

I had to begin formulating my plans to escape this prison I'd been living in for far too long. I prayed for change and plotted how I could leave for good. I had held on long enough. I was done trying. I was only twenty-five years old, but I felt I'd lived a lifetime.

When I had left before, Greg always found a way to bring me back, always making threats about what he would do to me if I got away. Each time I hoped my love would finally soften the rage within him, but I finally realized this was his demon to fight, and no amount of love was going to hold it at bay.

I was living out the same life I'd led with my mother: trying to perform to get the prize of love and acceptance. I finally wanted more for my own life. I was ready to stand up and live out a life that didn't include abuse or fear. It was time for life on my terms. My husband was threatened by everything about me, and I couldn't keep reducing myself and my ambitions so that he could be whole.

I worked with my finances to determine what I needed to earn in order to support myself and the boys. I was nearly there—I could make it, although it would be tight. With child support added to my income once I returned to work, we could survive.

During this time, satisfying Greg's sexual urges was as much a requirement as keeping the house clean. I was breastfeeding the baby, so I thought I was safe, but four months after Canthon's birth I became pregnant again.

I was shocked—and while I knew another baby would stop me from leaving, a part of me couldn't help but be joyful at the idea of another child.

I loved my children more than anything, I'd always wanted more, and I wondered whether this baby was my long-hoped-for little girl.

But Greg was furious. He was adamant that he didn't want any more children. Of course he didn't acknowledge his role in the situation. Another child would be a heavy burden on our finances, he argued. He said it would also jeopardize my job—they wouldn't stand for another maternity leave so soon. "They're going to fire your ass," he said.

Every day he returned home from work and tried to convince me to get an abortion. The thought of ending my child's life was unimaginable to me, and I hated Greg all the more for pressuring me so hard, as if it was a simple decision to make. He didn't understand that from the moment I became pregnant, I lived and breathed for the life inside of me. He didn't understand.

Every day, home by myself, I fought with my conscience and struggled under the burden of it all. What finally tipped the scales was the deepest fear I'd ever felt in my life: I was terrified to bring a child into the world whose father didn't want it.

I prayed every day, but my faith wasn't strong enough to carry me through this dilemma. By giving me this baby, was God telling me to stay in my abusive marriage? If I had an abortion, would I be making a selfish decision? I heard nothing from Him that I could use for guidance. I knew what His Word said, and I understood God already had a plan for this child, but my fear of what *I* couldn't control overrode everything.

At last I allowed fear to bring me to a justifiable conclusion. It would take me some time to understand that faith isn't justifiable.

The day of the abortion, Greg went to work rather than accompanying me to the clinic, showing no concern for what I was about to do. I had confided in just one friend, who'd promised to support me no matter what I chose. She offered to go with me, but I didn't want her to miss a day of work, so she agreed to meet me for lunch after the procedure.

I went by myself. As I looked across the waiting room, I saw many different women. Some of them sat with the men who'd likely planted the seeds of the children they were there to uproot. I wondered how they had arrived at their decisions.

I had no idea what to expect. When the nurse came to get me prepped for the procedure, I felt like I was walking into a death chamber.

Once I had my legs in the stirrups, the doctor came in. He stood over me with kind eyes, gently put his hand on my stomach, and sat down on a stool beside me. He asked, "Why are you here today?"

I gave him the same response I'd given when I registered: "I was breastfeeding and thought I couldn't get pregnant. Obviously I was wrong."

"Are you aware that this procedure is not a recommended form of birth control?"

By this time I was crying. I felt so humiliated, so stupid. I nodded. I kept my eyes on the ceiling, wishing it could just be over.

"Do you have a reliable form of birth control, or would you like to discuss that after the procedure?"

"I'm not ignorant," I said. "I was just careless. Could we please get this over with?"

The doctor prepared the room and the instruments and spoke softly to the nurse. When they were ready to begin, he said, "This procedure is tough to listen to. Would you like headphones?"

"No," I said, "I want to be aware of everything I'm doing."

He was right—it was a horrendous sound of sucking, knowing the pulling and twisting going on inside my uterus was the tearing away and destruction of a life, my baby's life.

Finally it was over. I needed to know what I had done.

"May I please see it?" I asked.

The doctor nodded to the nurse, who pulled the covering from the jar. I saw the human soup, the blood and membranes floating together. I was appalled that this was what I had chosen.

I was taken to a private recovery room to wait in order to ensure there were no complications. To me this felt like a purgatory where I'd been sent to consider the terrible act I had committed. Sitting there, I thought about my husband. He wasn't there. He hadn't shown any accountability for his role in all of this, and he had not and would not demonstrate any compassion for my grief. It was over—that was all he cared about.

Soon after this, Greg went on a two-day bender, leaving on a Friday night and returning Sunday afternoon, reeking of alcohol and perfume. He went straight into Canthon's nursery to lift him from his nap. I rushed in, trying to prevent him from holding our son while smelling like another woman.

Greg turned on me and attacked. He knocked me to the floor next to Canthon's crib. Greg sat on my chest, slamming my head against the floor.

I heard Greg saying, "You can't stop me—I'm going to beat you like my daddy beat my mother!" This was his first and only reference to the abuse he had seen as a child. Canthon woke up and began to wail. I looked up to see him leaning over the crib railing, reaching for me and watching us.

Canthon's crying finally made Greg stop, get up, and flee. I heard the door slam as he left the house. I stayed on the floor for a few minutes, dazed, my head throbbing. I struggled to my feet to comfort Canthon, and then I went looking for Preston.

I found my five-year-old son hiding in the farthest corner of his bedroom closet. He reached out to me, his face crumpled. "Mommy," he said, "I thought he was going to get me too."

This was it. Suddenly, my will to provide a better life for my sons was stronger than my plan—stronger even than my fear that Greg would kill me if I left.

I hired an attorney and filed for a divorce. Greg showed up at the hearing, and he pleaded with me for one last chance. His voice was bursting with emotion. "Everything she says is true," he told the judge.

The judge looked at me and said, "It's your decision."

Yet again I wavered. Yet again I thought, *This time he finally knows I mean business.* I decided not to go through with it.

For a few months, things were pretty calm. But one Saturday, Greg went out with a promise he'd be back home at a reasonable hour. It was well past two a.m. when he called me, telling me a friend was having car trouble and he had to lend a hand. He promised to be home as quickly as he could.

After a couple more hours, the phone rang again. It was the wife of one of Greg's buddies, saying she'd caught Greg and her husband in Greg's van with two women.

After I hung up the phone, I stood at our front door, gazing through the window for a long time, just staring out into the darkness. Nothing ever changed for long, and I was just so weary from it all. I had been made a fool of for the last time. A quote I'd heard many times before floated into my thoughts and gave me the resolve to end my own suffering. At that time, I thought it was a Bible verse—it would be a long time before I learned it wasn't from the Bible at all. It didn't matter where it came from. It was just the message I needed.

God helps those who help themselves.

chapter 12

BREAKING FREE

It was time. I had lived with enough physical, verbal, and emotional abuse. I had nearly lost my own life, two babies' lives had been lost, and now it was time to give my living sons a life free of violence.

I ended my six-month maternity leave a month early so I could put my new plan into action. I gave myself a makeover: I got rid of my Afro, got contact lenses, and learned how to apply makeup. I was determined to be a new woman, a stronger woman.

Greg always took my paycheck and doled out meager amounts for me to buy what I needed. When I got tired of living under his scrutiny, I convinced him to split the bills. I paid the bills he assigned to me, and any remaining money was mine to use as I saw fit—which Greg made sure wasn't much. I secretly joined my Illinois Bell credit union and started having money drawn from each paycheck to build up funds for my escape.

When I had saved enough for an apartment deposit and first month's rent, I began looking for a new home for me and my sons. I was ready.

Now I just had to plot all the details of my escape. Greg's threats screamed in my mind, his words replaying in my head: "You can never leave me, and if you do, I'll find you and I'll kill you." But I was acting on the instincts of a mother protecting her young. No devil in hell could stop me!

One day in May of 1978, I went to work like it was any other day. Greg didn't know I came home after just a few hours. I'd arranged for a moving van to meet me at the house at noon, and my friend Jenelle—Leon and Regina's daughter—agreed to help me with my great escape. The movers, Jenelle, and I got everything packed and loaded in less than three hours.

I took the things that I deserved: Canthon's crib, my childhood twin bed for Preston, the washer and dryer, which had been a Christmas present, the piano, which had been an anniversary present, our bedroom set, and all the dishes, pots, and pans. I didn't touch the furniture in the kitchen, the living room, the family room, or the guest room.

Our new home was a brick duplex at the end of a quiet cul-de-sac. It was five or ten minutes from his house—*not our house anymore*, I had to keep reminding myself, *just Greg's house now*. The boys shared a bedroom, and mine was across the hall. I had a basement for storage and the washer and dryer. If Greg came, I'd be able to see him coming. The front entrance of the duplex faced a large driveway, and the duplex next to us was empty. This meant I could park my car at the back of the driveway, where nobody could see it from the street. The living room had sliding glass doors that opened to a deck, and through these doors I could watch the comings and goings on the street. My bedroom window looked out on the driveway.

I'd confided in my cousin Evelyn and enlisted Jenelle's help, but aside from that I hadn't breathed a word of my plan to anyone. I'd had too many false starts in the past. Once I'd settled in that first evening, I went to a payphone and called my mother to tell her what I'd done and how to reach me.

She already knew I'd gone. My husband had already called her, and she was terrified. "Greg called saying I better tell you to bring his furniture back, or he'll kick your head in!"

She begged me to let him have his furniture, but I was operating from a new place of determination. I wasn't going back, and I wasn't returning anything. Greg wasn't even demanding that I return his sons, I pointed out to my mother—just his things.

If Greg wanted to kick my head in over a bedroom set and some dishes, I was ready for him. I had finally climbed the hill I was willing to die on.

For the next several nights, I remained awake all night. I sat in the middle of the bed, wide awake, clutching a hammer and a butcher knife. If I went down, it wouldn't be without a good fight.

I was exhausted at work those first few days, barely keeping my eyes open after spending all night keeping watch. When I could, I spent my lunch break napping in my car.

Greg called me at work and harassed me, but he never showed up at the apartment. I began to feel like I had made a pretty good escape. I started sleeping again, though not very soundly.

No one at work knew what was happening in my life. The kids went to daycare as usual, and we settled into our quiet new life. I had no living room furniture, but Mom brought me some TV trays, an old drop-leaf table, and some folding chairs. Canthon ate at his high chair, and Preston used a TV tray. They ate lots of SpaghettiOs with hotdogs, and my main meal became popcorn with no butter and a large glass of water, which filled me up.

As the weeks turned into months, Greg didn't give up. He knew how badly, even after everything, I still wanted us to be a family. I was right to leave, he said, but this time he had learned his lesson and wanted us back.

He began coming by the apartment—he'd instructed one of the women he was seeing to tail us home from the boys' daycare to find out where we were living. He appealed to me through our boys, asking them to spend time with him. He bought Big Wheel racer bikes for Preston and Canthon. He was certain my resolve would weaken if he could convince me he was ready to be a real father.

He was starting to wear me down even though I could see what he was doing. I wanted to believe he had learned his lesson. I still wanted my sons to have both of their parents. I wanted to go home and be a family.

The winter of 1978–1979, Rockford received a record-setting amount of snow. In this kind of weather, getting Preston and Canthon in and out of the house took ten times longer than usual. More than once, Preston walked right out of his boots when they got stuck in the ice-topped snow. During a two-week snowstorm, snow piled up all the way to the doors, freezing them shut. I couldn't get out or use the phone, and I started to really worry once I ran out of diapers and bare essentials. Right on time, Greg got worried about us, came by in his work truck, dug us out, and took us to the grocery store.

I felt like God was testing my faith on every side—or Satan was trying to prove I couldn't do this on my own.

As Christmas approached, my husband's campaign intensified. He lobbied using Preston and Canthon, he sweet-talked me, and he wouldn't let up. Christmas was his favorite time, and spending the holiday as a family was important to him. I bombarded God with prayers. I needed Him to show me the way, but I couldn't hear an answer.

Finally, when I'd been on my own for six long months, when the only voice I could hear was my husband's, I concluded God would want me to make a decision for my marriage. I was convinced I was right in my conviction to return to my husband, the father of my sons.

I wanted to take things slowly, rather than falling back into the same old routine. I agreed we would celebrate Christmas together at Greg's house.

Then, on a Saturday ten days before Christmas, I received a phone call from a woman who claimed to be my husband's mistress. I didn't know how she had gotten my number, which was unlisted. She pleaded for me to hear her story, and something in her voice made me listen.

The woman seemed nervous. She knew my name and wanted to confirm she was talking to the right person. I tested her to be sure she was talking about my husband; she knew the car he drove and where he worked, and she said they'd met at a bar I knew Greg frequented. Then she rushed into her story, which hit me in the gut as hard as one of Greg's punches.

"I know he's trying to get you back home, and now he doesn't want anything to do with me," she said. "But did you know I have his daughter?"

My heart stopped, but I didn't say a word.

"He wants to push us into the background so he can get you back. He told me never to call the house again. I asked for money to buy diapers, and he refused to give me a dime. He wants to act like we don't exist. He never wanted her—he tried to convince me to get rid of her. I just thought you should know."

"How old is your daughter?" I asked.

The woman said the child was just a baby, born early that past summer. I asked her how she was supporting the baby—was she working?

"I'm on welfare," she said.

I knew this woman wasn't the one I should be angry at, but I burned with rage. I said coldly, "Then I'm paying your child support every time I go to work." I hung up.

I couldn't know for sure, but my instincts said this woman was telling the truth. After speaking with her, I spent hours thinking over what she'd said. I thought about how old her daughter was, and I counted backward. What had been happening in our home while she was pregnant with Greg's child?

I'd been pregnant too, I realized with a chill. Greg had known another woman was carrying his child. He tried to convince us both to end our pregnancies. She'd refused and had a daughter, and I had lost my child.

Some people believe in coincidences, but I believe in God's perfect timing. Just when I stood on the brink of making another bad choice for myself and my sons, God gave me an answer I couldn't misinterpret—a phone call that served as the final fracture to our marriage, a phone call that catapulted me and Greg into separate lives.

One of my unbreakable rules had been broken. It had been done in the dark, but God brought it to light.

It is difficult to admit the degree of mental and physical abuse I took from my husband over our seven years of marriage, but through all his betrayals, the one thing I thought set me apart from his flings was being the mother of his children. Now there was no honor in that either. He had taken that from me as well.

God had delivered my answer.

That Monday morning, I left the apartment early and went to Greg's house. I rang the doorbell. As I waited for him to come to the door, I spotted one of the boy's hard plastic snow shovels resting against the side of the house. I picked it up in case Greg tried to overpower me. I took a deep breath. I was filled with a calm rage.

Greg was surprised to see me—I hadn't been back to the house since moving out. I began telling him about the phone call I'd received, and when I mentioned the young woman's name, his expression told me once and for all she'd been telling the truth. Greg began trying to deny everything, saying that the woman was lying, that she meant nothing to him, that he wasn't even sure the baby was his.

All the past hurts rose up in me.

I drew the hard plastic shovel over my head and began pummeling him with it. He backed farther into the kitchen, and I followed him, beating him into the same corner where he'd kicked my stomach and killed our baby boy. He didn't say a word or raise a hand to me. I beat him until I was tired, and then I dropped the shovel and left.

Two months later, on February 8, 1979, I walked out of the Winnebago County Courthouse a twenty-seven-year-old single mother with two small sons to raise. Greg didn't show up—his arrogance, along with my previous false starts, made him believe I'd never go through with it.

I was entitled to half of everything, but all I asked for was full custody of my sons, child support, and half the money from the sale of the house. I wanted to take away his house, the one thing he held precious. My blood had been shed there, and my child's life had been lost there. I wanted Greg to lose something he loved.

I knew I'd done the best I could to be a good wife to my husband. I gave him my love and held out for a change to the incorrigible evil in him until I finally realized if I didn't get out of that devil's way, his demons would kill me. Even if he never killed my body, the war being waged was definitely aimed at my spirit. If I'd stayed until he killed my spirit, I really would be dead.

He allowed the demons of his past to kill, steal, and destroy everything in their path. I could feel him trying to suck everything out of me so he could feel whole. He was fighting me for total control, and I don't believe he would have stopped until I was a mindless programmed robot, moving only as he told me to move, thinking only as he wanted me to think. He wanted to be my god.

The Bible says we fight not against flesh and blood, but against the dark spirit forces of evil. When I fought Greg, I was battling the evil within him that threatened to kill my spirit. I could not allow my purpose to die in his hands. I believe I fought a valiant fight against a dark and evil force.

My whole life up to this point had been a fight for survival, and now I was exhausted. I wanted to pull the covers over my head, go to sleep, and wake up in a different reality than the one I was facing, but I had a five-year-old son and a twenty-three-month-old son, and they were counting on me to make things right for them. They were my reason for everything, and I had no intentions of failing them.

Life was not measuring up to the plans I had set for myself. When I had thrown those thirteen rocks into the water on my thirteenth birthday, this was not the future I had envisioned.

I gathered my strength. I remembered the resources I had. The past November—when I was on my own, but before my husband's most painful betrayal was revealed, God had allowed the means of my escape to be spoken by my Uncle Narvell.

Mom had given a surprise birthday party for Aunt Kathleen and me in Dixon. While I was catching up with Uncle Narvell, he'd said, "You and those boys shouldn't have to live like this. You need to come on back home." The warmth of his invitation had touched my heart and planted a seed I would cling to.

Once the divorce was final, I called my uncle to see if the invitation still stood. He let me know we were welcome to stay with him and my aunt. I felt like someone struggling to stay afloat who'd just been tossed a life preserver.

I spoke confidentially with my manager, explaining my plight and asking for his assistance transferring to the Southwestern Bell sales office, located outside of Kansas City.

Every day I kept pushing forward. I knew if I stopped to analyze everything, the way I liked to do, I might stop moving. Instead I put together my plan and a to-do list and checked things off as I accomplished them.

Everything I was doing was a giant leap into the unknown. I had never been on my own before. I had gone straight from one controlled environment to another.

As much fear as I felt, I felt the same amount of determination. I felt like an eaglet about to step out of the nest to take its first flight into independence. The divorce was final in February, and soon after that my transfer was approved.

But then the challenges started piling up before me.

I had asked for a June start date so Preston could finish kindergarten, but a position opened in April, and there was no promise it would be there in June.

My divorce attorney told me I had to request permission from the court to take the boys out of state—he'd known all along I planned to leave the area, but now he wanted more money to secure the court's approval, and I didn't have a cent to spare.

When the final paperwork came through for my transfer, I discovered that my salary would be 10 percent lower, a piece of news that stopped me cold. I was already struggling to make it. When I called the transfer department, they explained that the difference was due to cost of living variation.

Fear began to creep in. Were these signs I wasn't supposed to leave? Was God telling me I shouldn't go? Or was God telling me to trust Him, step out of the nest, and spread my wings?

I was filled with doubts, but I pushed through them. I stepped out on faith. I brushed aside the distractions and my fear and kept on moving forward.

My mother would keep the boys until Preston finished school and I could find a place for us to live. I gave the court my mother's address so it wouldn't appear the boys had left the state. When it came to violating court orders, I decided to cross that bridge if I came to it, guessing that Greg might not seek to exercise his visitation rights.

I pushed back my departure date so I could be with Preston for his sixth birthday. On Friday, April 27, 1979, I packed up my car with my clothes and everything I would need until I found a place for us to live. My mother was at work, so I took the boys over to the neighbors, who'd agreed to babysit. The hardest thing I had to do was leave behind the only two things that were truly mine—my sons.

I wrote my mother a letter begging her to love my babies for me until I could be with them again. I confessed my fear of the unknown, and I asked for her prayers. Tears rolled down my face as I scrawled the letter. I wished she would come and wrap her arms around me, offering reassurance, but that was not my mother.

An eight-hour drive lay ahead of me, but before I left I wanted to say goodbye to Aunt Tutta. She was my rock; I could always talk to her. She listened and could give me the emotional boost my mother couldn't.

We sat in the kitchen as she ate her brick toast, cooked in the oven broiler until it was hard as a rock, and her overcooked mushy oatmeal. Sitting in my aunt's familiar chair at her familiar table, I thought of everything unfamiliar awaiting me in Kansas City.

"Well," Aunt Tutta said, "you got your divorce, but you got those babies to take care of. What you gonna do now?"

"I've had enough," I declared. "I'm never getting married again."

"Girl, hush up!" my aunt said. "You don't know what you're talking about. You're too young and pretty to be talking like that. You need a man to take care of you and those boys—don't worry, you won't stay single for long."

Greg's own words came to my lips: "No one will want a woman with two small kids."

My aunt just laughed. "When you get to be my age, then you can give up on marriage, but 'til then stop talking foolishness. You just need some time."

I asked Aunt Tutta to help my mother when her patience with my boys wore thin. I didn't want her to be sharp with them or attack their self-esteem.

"Those boys will probably be down here as much as they'll be with her, you know that," Aunt Tutta said. "They'll be fine, and you'll be back before you know it. You're a good momma."

She paused a moment before saying, "Girl, you're something else, you know that. You always did know how to survive. You know, there has always been something about you. Zee never understood it, called it crazy, but you're so determined and oh, you're so stubborn."

We laughed. I said wistfully, "I wish Mom could see me in the same light you do."

She shook her head. "Foot! That Zee . . . she's always gathering up somebody's child, and she ain't got no business being a mother herself."

It was the first time I'd heard anyone in my family say a word against my mother.

"Now you hear me," Aunt Tutta continued. "You're special. You were just meant to be, that's just all there is to it. God has something He wants you to do. So go on out there and do it, and don't let nothin' stop you!"

I was stunned by her prophecy. My aunt's words seemed to come out of her like a well-kept secret that she had been holding onto for a long time, waiting for just the right time to be told.

Her words hit my spirit like an electrical jolt. I felt a spark of excitement, and foreboding filled my stomach with butterflies.

"What is it?" I begged. "What is it that He wants me to do?"

Aunt Tutta said, "Just keep on living. He'll show you."

I doubt Aunt Tutta knew how strongly her words had affected me. But I knew that God had used my aunt to speak to my spirit. Her prophecy was the seed that would take root in my soul. It became the message compelling me to dream again, to pursue a greater purpose for my life. I felt excited now. I was certain this explained the pulling I felt as a young child. I was eager for my dreams to intersect with God's will for my life. Thanks to Aunt Tutta, as I began my journey to Kansas City, I knew for the first time what it felt like to be validated.

On the eight-hour drive, I listened to Gloria Gaynor's "I Will Survive" on repeat. I remembered Aunt Tutta's words. A host of emotions washed over me: fear, excitement, doubt, and certainty. It was finally time to see who I was and discover my own power. It was time to find some peace and try to laugh again.

My childhood innocence was gone. I would never again relinquish my power, trusting somebody else to take care of me. I would never again allow other people to impose their limitations on me.

I wasn't just going to survive—I was going to thrive and learn what God had placed inside me. For the first time I understood there was a call on my life, and it was worth fighting for.

Eight hours after leaving my hometown, I saw the sign that read, "Welcome To Kansas City." I had passed that sign hundreds of times over the years when we visited, but this time I saw it as my own personal welcome mat, speaking directly to me. It was at that moment that the enormity of what I was stepping into really hit me.

I pulled over to the side of the highway and finally exhaled. I dropped my head onto my hands as I clenched the steering wheel and had a hard, emotional, cathartic cry. My sense of fear poured out of me, as though the tears were washing my fear from my body. I had escaped, I was alive, and I was starting a new life. I felt as though I had bled out the old me, and the emotional transfusion running through my veins was powerful. I straightened up, wiped the tears off my face, and spoke out loud what my spirit was thinking:

"Kansas City, you're going to know my name!" I steered the car back onto the freeway and yelled out loud to God, "Okay, let's go—if I can do this, I can do anything!"

Here I was, standing at the threshold of my new life. I was alive.

I was meant to be.

chapter 13

POWER

I was like a phoenix rising from the ashes of my childhood and marriage. I knew I had a very complicated journey ahead of me, but change always excites me, because it tells me God is up to something. Aunt Tutta's prophecy echoed in my ears, and I understood that everything I was going through was part of how God would shape and use me. I had to push through the fear and prepare myself for the lessons.

During this time, it seemed obvious to me that God was leading me to trust Him and only Him. Everything was falling into place, and I kept moving forward past the obstacles placed before me. The more I trusted God, the more I could see that He was restoring to me the years the locusts had eaten.

Coming back to Kansas City was like coming home. Uncle Narvell and Aunt Kathleen greeted me as though I was their prodigal child returning. I lived with them for nearly three months while I got adjusted to my new job and acquainted myself with the area.

It was during this time that I learned much of what I know about the first four years of my life. I asked questions of my aunt and uncle about when I'd stayed with them and where my mother had been. They were very protective of my mother's secrets, so I often pretended I already knew the facts to get them to elaborate further. I explored Kansas City, making a point to visit Union Station, trying to imagine my mother and father together there.

I knew my father lived only a few hours from Kansas City, and I planned to look him up again soon, hoping he could have a relationship with his grandsons. I thought of my sons constantly while I was separated from them, and I ached to have them with me. Every other week, I made the long drive to see them, getting in a quick nap after work on Friday afternoons before setting out for Dixon.

I grew to understand more fully the sacrifice that Uncle Narvell and Aunt Kathleen had made for me and my mother, and my love and affection for them deepened. Even now, they gave me the emotional support I so badly needed in this time of dramatic change.

One day, Uncle Narvell and I were walking in his garden, and he said, "I know you still love him."

I was moved by my uncle's kindness. No one else in my family ever talked to me about Greg. "I'm afraid I always will," I answered sadly.

"Give it time," Uncle Narvell said.

I quickly adjusted to my new job. The Southwestern Bell offices were located in Overland Park, Kansas, a large suburb twenty minutes southwest of Kansas City. The company occupied several floors in a high rise above a bank, with large oak trees all around. In Rockford, I'd seen very few professional black people, but here I was no longer the only fly in the buttermilk.

The Friday after my first week of work, my coworkers took me out for some welcome drinks. When I got home, Uncle Narvell was sitting in the kitchen, a cigarette in one hand and drinking his ever-present Coca-Cola, waiting for me. He'd been afraid something had happened to me. I was touched by his concern, but I hated feeling like a child again. I knew then that I had to double my efforts to find my own place. I spent most of my evenings and weekends looking.

My uncle and I had many discussions about where the boys and I should live. He tried to persuade me to move into a property he owned, but I was unimpressed by Kansas City's neighborhoods, houses, and school systems, and I certainly didn't want to get locked into someone else's plans for my life. My need for independence dominated my thoughts and plans.

I didn't want any limitations placed on me. I started focusing my search in Overland Park. I looked for housing, daycare for Canthon, and after-school care for Preston. I had a specific idea of the kind of home I wanted: I couldn't afford a house, but I wanted something that felt like one, so the boys could walk in the front door and feel like they were in *their* house.

One day while I was out on a sales call, I saw a "For Rent" sign on the lawn of a duplex that looked perfect for us. I pulled into the driveway, got out, and looked around, even peering into the window. This place had a garage and a big yard, and it would have been perfect, except it was right on Metcalf Avenue, Overland Park's main thoroughfare. I knew I'd never rest easy with a two-year-old and a six-year-old riding their Big Wheels so close to a busy street.

I decided to keep looking, but I couldn't find anything else I liked as much. I called the duplex's landlord, who showed me the inside of the place. I liked it even more after that, but still I hesitated because of the busy street. Plus, the rent was slightly out of my budget.

I started growing desperate. The clock was ticking. Preston had completed kindergarten, and I needed to have my boys with me. Uncle Narvell and Aunt Kathleen had a large home, and they offered their upstairs apartment. It would have been a good financial decision, but I had sworn to achieve independence, and I wasn't backing down.

Just as I was starting to doubt my plan, the duplex's landlord called me. He said, "I just got another place identical to the one you liked, but one block over. Have you found a place yet?"

I was thrilled. I arranged to meet him right away to look the place over. When I walked in, I felt I'd found the place my sons could call home. The place was set back from the street and had a long driveway where the boys could ride their Big Wheels. The main level had a large living room that opened to a patio and backyard. The kitchen had an eat-in nook that overlooked the front yard and a half bath right off the kitchen. Upstairs, it had two bedrooms and a full bath.

The rent was still high for my budget, but I filled out the application and prayed my credit would allow me to get the place. I'd worry about the details of affording it later. I felt sure that this was another door opened by God's hand—and He wasn't finished.

A week later, I was told I'd been approved for the duplex. When I went to sign the lease, the landlord said, "I see from your application you have two children. If you need a babysitter, I know the woman two doors down does babysitting."

While I was at work the next day, I called the number he'd given me, for a woman named Linda. I explained how I'd heard about her, and we interviewed each other. I liked her immediately. We scheduled a visit for me to meet her and see her home. After I hung up the phone, one of the guys in my cube pod whispered to me, "I heard you making all those arrangements. Did you happen to tell her you're black? You know, you're not in Illinois anymore, and not everyone here is as accepting as you may be used to. You should tell her you're black before you get your feelings hurt."

These words nagged at me. At the end of the day, I called Linda again. "I thought you should know I'm black," I told her, "just in case that might be an issue."

There was an awkward silence. Then Linda said, "Okay . . . is that a problem?"

I laughed. "If it's not for you, it isn't for me."

"I tell you what," she said, "I'll contact the parents of the other kids to let them know I'll be watching two black children. And if they have a problem, I'll let them know they need to find another babysitter. Will that work?"

God was making all things possible for me and my boys. Before my first month's rent was due, I got a raise that enabled me to afford to live in the new place. It would still be a struggle, but at least I could keep my chin above water. Again and again I witnessed God opening doors for me.

My cousin drove a U-Haul from Dixon to Overland Park with the household possessions Greg had allowed me to have, thinking he was being generous. He kept the bedroom set I had originally taken when I left him and sent the cheap bed and dresser from our guest room. He sent the boys' bunk beds and furniture, my piano, and the washer and dryer. I had no living room furniture, no kitchen furniture. The heat inside the U-Haul ended up melting the cheap furniture glue holding my bed and dresser together, so I just put my mattress and box spring on the floor. Uncle Narvell and Aunt Kathleen bought me a TV as a housewarming gift.

I arranged the few pieces of furniture I had, and then I walked through the duplex, praising God. "We did it!" I screamed. "Thank you, God, we did it!"

I spent the first night in my home all by myself. The next morning, I awoke with a sense of euphoria. I had my life back. At twenty-seven years old, I was officially on my own. I felt as if I'd been reborn.

After a couple of weeks, I returned to Dixon for the Fourth of July to get Preston and Canthon. As I drove to pick them up, I spoke with God, thanking Him for the new life we were about to embark on. I asked God never to allow me and my boys to be separated again. I hadn't realized how much strength and purpose I drew from them until they weren't with me.

In our new home, finally at peace, I started learning who I really was. By now I understood that when I'd married Greg, I hadn't truly known how I wanted to live my life—I just planned to be the opposite of my mother. After I escaped my marriage, I saw how much I'd given up.

I'd had enough. I had spent my childhood crying out for someone to stand up and fight for me, and now I realized I was going to have to fight for myself. No one was going to rob me again, whether it was my property, my self-esteem, or my peace of mind. I resolved that if someone pushed me into a corner, I was going to come out fighting. Anybody who tested me would know that I was a worthy opponent, and they would know my name.

I soon had to make my first major purchase as a single woman—a new car. I viewed this as a declaration of my independence. I went to a Buick dealership near my house and began the negotiations. I found a car I liked, a Buick Skylark, but I had to wait for my income tax refund to make a down payment. The salesman persuaded me to give him $150 to hold the car while he ran my credit report, saying this money would count toward my down payment. He promised to return the money if I found another model with another dealership.

"I won't even cash the check," the salesman promised.

After I shared this with Uncle Narvell, he said he knew a man he trusted at a dealership in North Kansas City who'd give me a better deal. He offered to come with me, but I said, "I need to handle this on my own. Please don't even call him—I'll let him know I'm your niece."

My uncle laughed. "I'm here if you need me," he said, reaching for his cigarette. "Otherwise I'm staying out of it."

When I met with my uncle's friend, he showed me how I could get a Buick Skylark in the color I wanted without using my income tax refund as a down payment. I decided he was the salesman I would do business with—I liked the way he operated.

After I returned to the other dealership to reclaim my $150, however, I learned that the salesman I'd spoken with had brought my check to the bank and cashed it. That much money meant a lot to me and my boys, and I didn't intend to walk away quietly.

I took them to small claims court to get the money back, but nobody from the dealership showed up. The judge explained the hollow win I had just been awarded. He said, "You won this round, but there's no way you'll be able to collect your money unless you're willing to wait until the dealership is sold, and then you can put a lien on the property for the $150."

I think he thought I would resign myself to the loss, but he didn't know who I was and what I'd been through. I was in a fighting mood, and I wasn't going to allow anyone to walk away with money I desperately needed.

A coworker of mine happened to be dating an attorney, and she told him what I was dealing with. The attorney told me how to bring the dealership to their knees. I followed his instructions, putting a lien on the dealership's checking account so that they couldn't do business without dealing with me. Then I waited.

One sunny Saturday morning while the boys and I were having breakfast, we heard a knock at the door. It was a dealership representative offering me a check for $150.

"That's not enough," I said flatly.

"Well," he said, in a condescending tone, "what is it you want?"

I closed the door in his face, leaving him to wait while I found the piece of paper on which I'd itemized my expenses. I returned to hand it to him, and I said, "I'll sign the release once you reimburse me for *everything* I lost when you stole my $150. And I won't accept your check. I want cash or a bank certified check."

He looked at me as if he was about to laugh, but I didn't flinch, and he quickly retreated to his car. He returned a few hours later with a certified check.

I got back not only my original deposit, but also reimbursement for court costs, wages for the time I took off work, mileage expenses for my drives to and from the courthouse, and interest on my initial payment. Now I felt like David after slaying Goliath.

When I told Uncle Narvell what had happened, he was shocked. "If you needed $150 so badly, I'd have given it to you!" he said.

"I needed it, but it was also a matter of principle," I said. "They thought they could get away with stealing from me. I'm not letting anyone else take advantage of me ever again!"

"Girl, remind me not to mess with you," my uncle said with a laugh.

I liked who I was becoming. I was learning how to fight back without crying.

Even so, our adjustment was far from easy. I was raising my two sons on my own, and it was hard. I carried a good amount of guilt for marrying a man who did not want to be a husband or father. This was not the life I had planned for myself or my children. They were my reason for living, and I vowed to do everything I could to give them some portion of what their father and I had promised we would. They deserved a life of love, peace, and acceptance.

Nighttime was the most difficult time for me to be alone. I would put the boys to bed, and then pity and self-condemnation would fill my thoughts. I would light candles, cry, and pray that God would equip me to raise my sons by myself. Some nights I would sit in the dark asking God to reveal Aunt Tutta's prophecy. All I heard was the sound of my breathing.

The pain of my failed marriage was still so raw. The divorce had been granted, but it would take more than a court document to dissolve the feelings I had for Greg. We were still tied together by our sons, and even though every promise he had made to me had been a lie, I'd walked away still loving him, still wanting him to be the father he had said he would be. I didn't regret the divorce, but I was struggling in the aftermath.

I was also very angry. Greg had proven all the naysayers right. He had taken so much from me, had never lived up to his promises, and had broken the vows we'd said before God at our wedding. I had married a man who, rather than giving me the love I'd wanted, turned out to be as bitter and cold as my mother. I would need time to forgive him and myself.

As always, I created plans, establishing new rules to live by as a single mother. I never dated on Friday night, which I established as family night. This was our time when we would go out to eat, and at bedtime the boys would make their pallets in my room. Then I would stay up late deep cleaning the house so that on Saturdays, we could wake up together in a clean house and run errands, go shopping, see a movie, or go visit with Aunt Kathleen and Uncle Narvell. Those visits often resulted in doing some work in Uncle Narvell's print business.

My coworkers were always trying to fix me up with someone, but I resisted until about six months after moving to Kansas City, when I finally stepped back into the dating game. Once I made that step, Saturday was my date night. I never allowed a man to pick me up at my home until I was comfortable with him. I didn't want men to know where I lived or have my sons exposed to casual dates, and I needed to be able to get away in my own car if something didn't feel right, so I always met my date at an agreed-upon location. On Sundays we attended Ward Chapel AME church with Uncle Narvell and Aunt Kathleen. After church, we often joined them for dinner at Uncle Narvell's favorite smorgasbord.

I began to organize my workdays to give myself some much-needed quiet time. I would often come home from work and just sit in the quiet of the house for thirty or forty-five minutes, sipping a cup of tea and enjoying the silence, before calling Linda to send the boys home from her house two doors down. I would stand in the yard and happily receive them into my arms, delighted by their joy in seeing me. Then I'd spend the evening listening to Preston tell me about his day at school, and helping him with homework, while Canthon shared stories about his friends at Linda's.

When I fell into self-pity, I would promise myself and God, "I'll wallow today, but tomorrow I'll get back up and start pushing myself forward."

I was getting stronger, learning new things about life, and figuring out how to manage. It felt good to know I could fall down and get back up again, with no one to beat me up for my failures. It was all about facing my fears and pushing forward.

Every time I walked into my home, I felt such a sense of peace. I didn't have to readjust my personality to accommodate someone else or walk on eggshells to keep the peace. I decided then that I would protect that sense of peace forever; maintaining my peace became my barometer to determine what got a front-row seat in my life. Anything or anyone that disrupted or threatened the peace in my home had to go.

• • •

One Friday a couple of months after we'd moved in, as the boys and I were coming home from dinner, Preston put his face up to the car window.

He shouted, "Look, it's Dad!"

There was Greg, luggage in hand, walking down the street just a couple of houses away from our duplex. A grin spread across his face when he saw us. I felt my hands tighten around the steering wheel, and panic rose in my chest, but I tried to stay calm.

We reached the house at the same time. *Why is he here?* I thought. *How did he find us? What does he want? Why can't he leave us alone?*

The boys swarmed Greg, ecstatic to see him. "I wanted to see my boys," he said.

I knew better. He was checking up on me. "How did you find us?" I asked.

He handed me a receipt from the post office. "I paid a dollar for your forwarding address," he said proudly.

The fear that tightened my stomach threatened to cut off my ability to breathe: *I will never be safe.*

He expected to stay with us, and I couldn't say no. Even with all my newfound strength, I discovered that I was still powerless against him. It may seem impossible, and it pains me to admit, but part of me still loved him and held fierce to the idea that he could be a father to my boys, if nothing else.

We never knew when he was going to show up. He would fly in, make his way to the duplex, and make himself at home. I once got home and found him standing in my garage, waiting for us—he'd been rifling through my garbage, snooping for clues about my activities. Each visit was more awkward than the last, and once I knew he could suddenly appear and disrupt our lives, I never relaxed.

I was also frustrated by the lack of interest Greg showed his sons. He would ignore their birthdays, or call late at night when he knew they'd be in bed. Rather than allow the boys to feel their father didn't care about them, I would buy birthday cards, forge his signature, and put them in the mail. I tried to encourage him and the boys to bond when he visited, always hoping for him to play a more active role in their lives. Yet it was difficult for my boys, especially Preston. He was the most attached to Greg, and he often asked, "Who's taking care of my dad?"

Whatever Greg said about wanting to see the boys, it was never about them—he just wanted an excuse to control me. When Canthon had the flu and was hospitalized for three days, Greg never made an appearance, but when I had a health scare, he was immediately at my side. He showed up a few times when I had a date and intentionally created embarrassing scenes for me. I often got a vague sense of being watched, though I didn't see him. His presence unsettled me and put me on edge. I felt that no matter where I went or how much I changed, I couldn't escape this one debilitating force in my life.

He acted as though the divorce decree and settlement didn't apply to him. He'd made no effort whatsoever to honor any of the rulings of the decree: hadn't paid a dime of child support, hadn't put the house on the market. I talked to him several times about paying child support, and he kept making promises and breaking them. On one of his surprise visits, he convinced me to buy some living room furniture, promising he'd start paying child support right away. So I did, and ended up with a nice recliner, a new bill, and no child support.

When I tried to force the child support issue, my attorney back in Illinois said I'd have to return to Illinois to pursue the fight. I couldn't afford to do that, so for the time being, Greg would continue running my life as he liked.

• • •

I knew firsthand what it felt like to grow up with a father who didn't want to be in your life. But even after my own father had refused to acknowledge me, I felt compelled to try to connect with him, wanting my sons to know their grandfather. Family connection was so important to me. After living in Overland Park for a year, I decided it was time to reach out to my father again.

I was in Springfield, Missouri, for a meeting, so I called the phone number I had for him, and a man answered. I asked, "May I speak to Harold?"

The man answered, "This is Harold.

I knew he had a son, so I said, "Harold Junior, or Harold Senior?"

The voice on the on the other end of the phone was growing impatient. "This is Harold Junior. Who is this?"

Nervously, I plowed ahead, saying, "I'm Harold Senior's daughter. I'm in town, so I thought I'd stop by and say hello."

A beat passed, and then he said, "Oh, *wow*, that makes you my sister. I guess you didn't know—I'm afraid he passed away a couple of months ago."

I was stunned. I struggled to keep my composure as my brother, a stranger to me, asked me to come over so we could meet. I agreed.

When I hung up the phone, I collapsed against the wall, surprisingly devastated over the death of my father, a man I had never gotten to know—and now never would.

When I showed up at my father's house in Springfield, my half-brother greeted me enthusiastically. For our entire visit, he was warm, accepting, and conversational. I was surprised to learn he already knew about me. Our father had told him about me, had even mentioned all the letters I'd sent him as a child. I suppressed an impulse to ask for them back. He was a fast talker, and as he talked my head swam. I was still processing the fact that my father was dead, and he was talking about history I had no part in.

I was grateful to have Harold Jr. in my life. He always said that any time we needed him, he'd be there. My father, though, represented a part of myself I would never know, a missing part of my life. It's like baking a cake and leaving out a secret ingredient that might have given the cake a special flavor. You wish you'd added that special ingredient, even though the cake is still good without it. I'll never know what my life would have been like if I'd had a relationship with my biological father. He'll always be a missing ingredient in my total story.

My mother, for her part, did a fair amount to show her support for me during this time. For my first birthday after my divorce, I met her, Candy, and Brenda in St. Louis, and we celebrated my birthday on a riverboat. For a birthday gift, my mother gave me the ring she'd bought herself as a college graduation present—a ring I'd always admired. She had always told me I could have it when she died. It was the best gift ever, with so much sentimental value. I stood up and gave her a hug and a kiss on the cheek.

As we prepared to go our own ways from St. Louis, Mom asked, "How are you doing?"

Not wanting to share much, I simply said, "We're making it."

She said, "Listen, make a list of all of your bills, and I'll pay off the biggest one for your Christmas gift."

Mom was the last person I would have turned to—I was too prideful to ask her for anything again—but I was happy to get whatever assistance I could. The list of bills totaled a little over $2,500; among them were the bills for the recliner I'd bought at Greg's urging and a new sofa I'd just bought for the living room.

I sent Mom the list in early December. Then, on Christmas Eve, she handed me an envelope. I opened it to find a Christmas card enclosing a check for not just the largest of my bills, but the full pay-off of *all* my bills. I knew this was my mother's way of showing me she was proud I had made it through my nightmare of a marriage. I controlled my urge to cry, but my sense of relief was evident as I hugged and thanked her.

"Mm-hmm," she said with a sly smile. "Now just make sure you stay out of debt."

Throughout all of this upheaval, I was continuously seeking to understand the purpose of my life. I could feel the presence of God, and I saw

His hand in many areas of my life, but I still felt compelled to dig deeper into Aunt Tutta's words, "God's got something for you to do." I wanted to know what it was!

The pastor of the church I attended was a tall, stately man in his fifties with a booming voice. Canthon sometimes covered his ears during the sermon and whispered, "Mommie, can you tell God not to talk so loud?" It felt good to immerse myself in church again, to be a part of a church community.

After about four months of attending services, I decided to pursue answers to Aunt Tutta's mysterious decree. Knowing it was the pastor's birthday, I got him a card and put a note inside, along with my business card, asking to speak to him about a religious question. I dropped the card in the offering plate.

A few days later, I got a call from his secretary asking to schedule a meeting, which we set for my lunch hour one weekday afternoon.

When I got to the church, the secretary buzzed me in, met me in the sanctuary, and walked me to the pastor's office area. He came out to greet me and showed me into his office, closing the door behind us.

"Thank you for the card," he said. "What brings you in?"

I described to him what my aunt had said to me, those words that echoed in my mind so often.

The pastor was quiet for a moment, and then he stood, walked around his desk, and leaned against it.

"You know," he said, "we all have a calling on our lives. I think someone who looks as good as you do shouldn't be worried about that right now."

He reached for my arm and pulled me up into his arms, moving swiftly and powerfully. As he grabbed me and kissed me, I could feel his full erection.

I slapped his chest and ran out of his office. I didn't see his secretary as I left. I rushed to my car and sat behind the wheel for a few minutes in a state of shock, trying to figure out what had just happened and panicking over this man of God's behavior.

That night I got a call from the pastor, who begged me not to say anything. He apologized and then claimed to have misunderstood my intentions. I wanted nothing more to do with him or with the church.

I was still deeply devoted to God, but my experience with the pastor shook my faith and confidence in men of God. My church attendance became sporadic—it would be a long time before I was ready to attend church seriously again. I even grew resentful, feeling like this man had derailed my destiny for a time.

I often felt overwhelmed, but I had no choice but to be strong—my children were depending on me. When I felt fear creeping up, I pushed it back down, fiercely determined to give my sons the life they deserved.

At work, I carried myself very confidently. One Friday there was a bake sale in the lobby of the office building where I worked, so I bought three cupcakes, one to have with my cup of coffee and two to bring home for the boys' dessert. I ate mine, wrapped the other two up in cellophane, and left them on my desk while I went on my sales calls.

When I returned, I saw that someone had unwrapped the cupcakes and taken one. When my cube buddy got back to his desk, I asked if he knew who had taken it. He pointed toward the office of our manager, Jim.

I took the remaining cupcake into Jim's office and put it on his desk. "I understand you ate one of my cupcakes," I said. "You might as well eat that one too, because I can't take one cupcake home for two little boys."

Jim stared back at me. "Do you see any crumbs in my mustache? Then I didn't take your cupcake!"

I knew it was just a fifty-cent cupcake, so I went home and tried to forget about it, but it just wouldn't rest in my spirit. Jim's arrogance and lack of accountability bothered me. His lie had been so unnecessary.

By Monday, I had decided to stand on my principles and push for a resolution. I went to Jim's boss and asked to be assigned a different manager.

I think he could see the resolve in my eyes. He said, "You want to tell me what's going on?"

I described the incident, and then I said, "I see my relationship with my manager like a marriage. There has to be a bond of trust there. Jim is responsible for my performance reviews and my career. If he'll lie to me about a cupcake, I can't trust him with my career."

"I'll look into it and get back to you," he said.

The next day, Jim called me into his office. He handed me a bakery box of a dozen chocolate cupcakes. "I hope you're happy," he said sarcastically. "You've just succeeded in crashing my career."

"Thank you," I said, taking the box from him. "And if this hurts your career, you did it to yourself."

Shortly after that, I was promoted to phone power specialist and moved to a different floor. In my new role, I analyzed customers' long distance telephone usage, proposed and sold solutions for their businesses, and provided training on how to optimize their usage.

While I was in the ladies' room one day, washing my hands, a white coworker turned to me at the sink and said, "You know the only reason you got this job is because of affirmative action. You're just a guinea pig."

I shook the water off my hands, hoping to spray her skirt, and told her, "I don't care what caused the door to open. It did, and I came through it, and I'm doing my job. You better believe if I can't do this job, they won't have any trouble pushing me out the back door."

I wasn't the only one in my family dealing with racism—my oldest son was also the target of prejudiced attitudes and behaviors. Preston was the only black student in his grade school. I'd been well aware of the school's demographics when I enrolled him, so I'd decided to take precautions to ensure my son would be okay. I met with the principal and didn't mince words, saying, "If anyone here has a problem with my son being black, I expect you to be there for him, or else I will be up here."

It wasn't long before Preston started coming home complaining about how other kids rubbed his head, saying his little Afro felt like a carpet—it irritated him.

The school's third grade teacher was black, so I reached out to her and asked her to please keep an eye out for Preston, even though he wasn't her student. A few weeks later, she called me suggesting that I come to the school. There had been some name-calling, and Preston's teacher didn't know how to handle it.

When I got to the school, Preston's teacher was in tears—one of his classmates had called him a "nigger."

"I don't know what to do," the teacher fretted. "I've never had to deal with this before."

I tried not to get angry. I thought for a moment. I said, "I'm taking Preston home. Do you mind if I come back tomorrow to have a conversation with the class?"

She agreed, so the next day I spent a half hour speaking with Preston's classmates. Protecting my son's self-esteem was my first priority, but just as important was helping those young kids understand how their behavior affected others. We talked about name-calling, which names hurt their feelings, and how it felt to be different.

Then I sat down with the kids and pointed out the three blonde children in the class. I asked them to stand up, and I suggested that we all go over to them and rub their heads.

"Ouch, don't touch my hair," one girl yelped.

"Do you see how that makes Preston feel?" I said.

At the end of the period, one little boy came up to Preston and gave him a hug. "I'm sorry," he said. This tense situation had turned into a great teachable moment for students as well as for Preston's teacher.

Life was going well. I felt confident and capable. I could take care of myself, address the issues my kids faced, and provide for my family. It was a pretty good feeling. My job was to provide support to the account executives, who sold and managed large accounts. Ultimately, account executives called the shots, and I wanted to be in that position.

One day our sales team gathered in a conference room for an account review. The account executives delivered their business reviews, followed by our supporting proposals. After I finished my presentation, the sales director asked me to stay behind for a few minutes.

The regional sales director sat across the long conference table from me, rocking back and forth in his chair, his fingers locked across his middle. Had I done or said something wrong?

Then he scooted his chair to the table and began to talk. "Carolynn," he said, "you have quite a presence. The minute you walk into a room, you're in control. I've heard you aren't afraid to hold people accountable, either, and I like that."

I smiled, feeling reassured, but I wondered where this was headed.

"I've been watching you," he continued, "and I think you'd make a damn good account executive, but there's one problem. I checked your file, and I see you don't have your degree. We like to hire people with a business degree."

I stayed quiet for a moment, thinking. I decided this was my chance. I needed to convince him I could do the job. I said, "You and I both know a business degree teaches you the book side of business, and that's great. But I know how to connect with people, and people buy because of relationships. I've proven I understand how to sell to people. You can teach me the rest of it."

A month later, I got the promotion and a new territory that covered all of Kansas, Missouri, and Oklahoma.

That director will probably never know how empowering his words were for me to hear: "Carolynn, you have quite a presence." I didn't know how others saw me, but I held my mother's words in my mind, determined to hold my head erect and command all men's respect.

I felt like I was walking in my own power. Preston and Canthon were thriving—Preston was on a soccer team and had joined a Boy Scout troop, and Canthon busied himself caring for a pet turtle our neighbor had given him—and I had a good social life. I'd learned to play backgammon and often went to games hosted at clubs. I had a couple of romantic relationships. But what I enjoyed most were my friendships with other young black professionals. My duplex was often where these friends would gather to vent, plan a cookout, or exchange ideas about relationships. I could always ask one of the guys to take my sons for haircuts, no strings attached. It was such a normal life.

Yet just when I was starting to feel at ease, the storms of change began to rumble. The divestiture of the Bell System, which courts had decided was a monopoly, was becoming increasingly certain. For years we had thought a breakup would never happen, but now it appeared inevitable.

Over Memorial Day weekend in 1981, I went home to Dixon for the long weekend. I went to a cookout with some of my former coworkers from Illinois Bell. All we talked about was what would happen once Bell was broken up. Upper management at Southwestern Bell were running around like rats on a sinking ship, trying to save themselves.

A former colleague of mine named Bob, who had become the sales director in the Rockford office, suggested that I come back and work for him. He promised that if I returned, he'd be my sponsor as I worked to become a certified account executive and support me throughout the certification process; getting my certification would mean higher pay, larger clients, and more job security.

"I'll think about it," I told Bob. "I'm always glad to have a backup plan."

Then, just a few weeks later, my sales director at Southwestern Bell scheduled a breakfast meeting to discuss my midyear sales strategy. I knew something was up—these discussions usually involved the whole team. He wanted to discuss the proposed layout of the business once the divestiture was approved.

"Other people have more seniority than you," he said, "and territories will be assigned according to seniority."

"What does that mean for me?" I asked.

"I can't promise how things are going to fall out here," he said. "You might have your territory moved under someone else—or you might lose your position."

I was wary of not being in control of my job. After my children, my career was my top priority. I had to manage it carefully so I could support my family. I didn't have the luxury of waiting to see what someone else was going to do. I had a choice—either let the chips fall where they may, or call Bob to see if his offer still stood.

I made the call to Bob, who was excited that I was ready to return. We closed the deal over the phone.

It was settled: I was returning to Rockford.

The timing of everything seemed perfect. I would have to move quickly before the school year started, but this time I wasn't operating alone. I had friends from my office who helped me pack up and move, and I had friends in Illinois awaiting my return.

I told myself that by moving back to Rockford, I would also be giving Greg a chance to prove himself as a parent. Even after everything that had happened, I believed there was a chance he could grow into a better father for our children if we lived close by.

He kept calling to tell me how much he had changed and matured. He wanted to show me how he'd evolved. When he came to visit, he told me how much he'd learned from me and from the divorce. He had an appreciation for the finer things in life now, he said, and he didn't want to share those things with anybody but me.

He said, "I have a right to have my children close so I can see them grow and play a role in their lives." Of course this was what I'd always wanted, too, and he knew it.

For the two years I lived in Overland Park, I had grown more confident. I was determined not to fall back into my dysfunctional cycle with him. I had evolved, too, and it was time for him to know the new me, the stronger me, the woman who was in control.

I believed that I was stronger than I really was. I'd escaped for a while—but the new me was about to face the same old devil.

chapter 14

A PRAYER

I didn't return to Rockford with a plan to lie dormant. I was determined to use my power to regain what rightfully belonged to me and our sons. I wanted Greg to know I wasn't the same Carolynn who had left him two years before.

As usual, Greg wanted to set the conditions of how he would prove himself. He wanted for us to move back into the house with him, but I flatly refused. I needed the chance to see if he really had changed and the freedom to escape if he hadn't.

Instead, the boys and I moved into a townhouse a few miles away from him. The townhouse didn't offer the amenities of our duplex in Overland Park, but it was nice. In front there was a common yard with sidewalks, and the back consisted of the common parking lot. We all quickly adjusted to our new home. I got them a Sheltie—they named him Buddy. I was sure we could maintain the peace and harmony we had cultivated in Kansas.

Instead, my decision to return to Rockford on my own terms was the beginning of a wild, unpredictable, nightmarish existence. In some ways, this time in our lives felt worse than when Greg and I were married, because it was so messy and confusing. I often wished that I'd simply stayed in Overland Park, but now I understand that this time, I had to truly purge this relationship from my system.

As strong as I had become, I was still no match for the power Greg was able to wield over me. Even two years after our divorce, I was still fearful of completely standing up to him—and because of this, the control games began immediately after we returned.

I wanted to be free, but freedom is the absence of repression from external domination. I didn't know how to be free. Greg and I both lied to each other and sent mixed messages. I was still, in some ways, trying to please him while I struggled to find my true voice with him. When he said he wanted us, what he really wanted was his property back so he could still have control over us.

Greg kept insisting that he'd changed. Yet it didn't take long for him to show he was the same old Greg. Once when I had an overnight meeting in Chicago, he agreed to watch the boys. When I went to pick them up, I rang the doorbell, only to see a woman sneaking out the back door, trying not to be seen.

"I see nothing has changed," I said to Greg when he finally opened the door.

"That's what you get for not moving in with me," he responded.

Greg acted like a drone, hovering over our lives but never getting too involved. He and I went to a movie or dinner occasionally, and he would come over at night after the boys were already asleep. We resumed a physical relationship, even though it was clear he had no intentions of being exclusive. Yet that is what he expected of me.

This was a different kind of abuse—a kind that caused paralysis, fear, and self-loathing, a kind of abuse that is difficult to comprehend unless you have been there yourself. I was functioning publicly, but privately I was in a constant state of depression, berating myself for stepping back into this cycle. He skirted around the edges of our lives, putting just enough pressure on me to prevent me from having a life of my own.

Greg didn't want to be more involved in the boys' lives than he had to be. If I asked him to take them to get their hair cut, he'd demand money for the barber. I orchestrated their birthday parties and told Greg when to show up. Most of the time he complied. I kept trying to cover for him with the boys, always wanting to protect them.

He still wasn't paying child support—he was more than $10,000 in arrears. He didn't buy them school supplies, not a single pencil or notebook, and never offered to help buy school clothes.

About a year after we moved back to Rockford, a year of unfulfilled promises of support and of living in this terrible limbo with my ex-husband, I decided that things had to change. I had to take charge of my life. At the time of the divorce, I'd just wanted to get out alive. Greg wouldn't have fought for our sons, but if I had pursued the financial settlement I was entitled to, he would have spent every cent he had to prevent me from getting anything.

Now, three years later, I was ready for the fight. I hadn't had these children by myself, and I was determined that even if Greg offered our sons no emotional support, he would at least support them financially.

The original divorce settlement only required Greg to pay the minimum child support demanded by law. I had no life insurance provisions for the boys in the event of Greg's death. If the boys were hospitalized, I had no medical coverage outside of what my job provided. Greg hadn't had to give me any portion of the stock he'd acquired through his job during our marriage. Finally, our settlement had required him to sell the house and split the proceeds with me, but he'd never made an effort to put the house on the market.

I got a new lawyer, who was appalled at my original attorney's pitiful settlement. "The guy must have been paid by your ex," my lawyer said, "because he sure didn't do you any favors!"

With my lawyer's guidance, I decided to demand that Greg's child support match his income—and I was going to take the house or he could buy me out. I wasn't willing to ask for my share of Greg's stock, even though I had a legal claim to it. I wasn't crazy. I knew how far I could push this man.

It was risky enough to make a move on the house, but I needed help. The house note was a lot less than what I was paying in rent. I was trusting that I was on the side of right and that God would protect me.

My lawyer was like a coach, encouraging me and convincing me that this was a game we could win.

Greg could have sold his stock to buy me out, but he wasn't willing to do that. Instead, he counteroffered, saying he would add extra money to the new child support order until he'd paid off his arrearages, but that would have taken years. I believed the boys and I should be able to return to the house, as Greg had never even attempted to sell it.

I wasn't backing down. I wasn't willing to shoulder the financial burden of raising our sons on my own any longer. We took him to court, and he was ordered to sign a quitclaim deed for the house for his back child support.

The only person who tried to talk me out of going after Greg was Aunt Tutta. Before the judge could review and approve the quitclaim deed, Aunt Tutta spoke with me privately, frightened for me and how Greg would respond to all this.

"Why are you doing this?" she asked. "You don't need that house, and it's not going to do anything but bring you a whole lot of mess. Let that man have that house he's so in love with!"

I disagreed. I was sick of being passive and letting Greg push me around and ignore our children. This was the only way I knew to fight back. I told Aunt Tutta, "I am fighting for what rightfully belongs to me and my sons!"

Aunt Tutta pounded the kitchen table. "You are one stubborn child," she exclaimed. "You know how crazy that boy is. If God wants you to have a house, let Him give it to you, but leave this one alone. I'm just afraid this isn't going to turn out like you think it is."

I tried to reassure my aunt, saying, "God has never given me anything I didn't first fight for."

Mom stayed quiet on the subject—at least with me. I think she was glad to see me standing up to him.

The court sided in my favor. Greg's child support payments were increased, he signed over ownership of the house to me, and he was given thirty days to move out.

Even after that he didn't take me seriously. On the date he was supposed to vacate the house, he hadn't yet found another place to live. I insisted that he couldn't stay, so he made arrangements to move in with some friends of his. He asked if I could keep his furniture until he found a place, and I almost laughed—this was the furniture he had refused to give me when I left. I refused him again. Finally, he asked if he could keep his art supplies in the smallest bedroom and use it as a studio. Yet again I refused him. I didn't want him having that kind of access to me.

At long last, Greg moved out, and the boys and I moved in.

And then things got much worse.

One day after returning from a weekend visit to Dixon, we walked into the house and a foul stench engulfed us—someone had dropped a stink bomb or decaying animal down the chimney.

Another day, we woke up to discover that the vinyl awnings on the living room windows had been slashed.

One evening the boys put their dog out on his runner, and when they went to let him back in, they found only a leash—Buddy was gone. I assumed Greg was responsible; he didn't care who he hurt. I had the locks changed.

Greg found an apartment just blocks from the house. About a month later, we returned home from a cookout at our neighbor's house and found Greg sitting at the kitchen table in the dark. I screamed. His head was down, and he reeked of alcohol.

He got to his feet. "You sleeping with the neighbor now?" he said.

"That's preposterous," I said. "You're crazy."

He slapped me hard across my mouth. He grabbed me by my shirt collar and pulled me close to his face. "Just because the *man* told you that you could have this house doesn't mean you deserve it. You know you don't deserve it!"

The boys and I were frozen in fear, knowing how quickly his rage could turn into more violence. Greg pushed me backward against the refrigerator and left through the garage door.

I sat the boys down, just eight and four years old, and laid out an escape plan. They were not ever to allow their father in the house, and if he made it in, they were to run next door to the neighbors' house and call the police. I started keeping the front screen door locked, the curtains drawn, and the garage door down so he wouldn't know when we were home.

A couple of weeks later, the boys were playing in the backyard, and I was on the phone in my bedroom. I looked up, and Greg was standing there. He must have gotten in through the back door.

He mouthed, "I want to talk."

I tried to keep the caller on the line. When the call ended, Greg grabbed the phone from my hand and began hitting me with it across my face.

I screamed out, hoping the boys would remember the plan, run next door, and call the police. Instead, they ran into my bedroom.

"Get out!" Greg screamed, but they didn't.

Canthon, four years old, looked up at his father with his little fists clenched at his sides. He said, "One of these days I'm going to get a gun and shoot you."

Preston remembered the plan and ran out of the bedroom and to the neighbors' house to call the police.

Canthon held Greg's stare until he left.

I got an order of protection against him, but I soon learned an order of protection only works when someone obeys it. Greg was arrested, but he never went to trial. I was told I would be contacted when it came time for me to testify. I waited and waited and heard nothing. I made several requests for an update and heard nothing.

The courts tried to get me to move into a shelter for abused women. I went to see the one they'd suggested; the women living there appeared to be homeless and seemed defeated. Everyone was living together, dormitory style, and the place was not well maintained. I knew this wasn't the life for us.

At this point I decided there were worse things than death, and living in fear was one of them. If Greg wanted to get me, he could get me. I wasn't going to live in fear, and I wasn't going to act defeated. I was determined to push through the fear.

Greg's arrest may not have had any consequences, but the threat of spending time in jail had scared him. For a few months, things calmed down, and I even began to relax.

After closing some big accounts, I decided the boys and I needed to take my bonus check and get away to have some fun. I'd always loved the summer vacations we took when I was growing up, so I planned a ten-day family road trip with my boys. I invited my mother to go with us. "There's one condition," I told her. "You're not allowed to talk about my personal life—nothing about Greg, none of that."

"Yes, ma'am," she responded.

We left Rockford in my new car, a Chevy Celebrity. We drove to Columbus, Ohio, to visit with relatives there for a few days before driving to Washington, D.C. We had the adventure of our lives visiting all the monuments and museums Washington had to offer. We stayed in the nicest downtown hotel I could afford. The boys went swimming, and one night I let them order room service. The hotel had a revolving restaurant on the top floor with a great view of the city, and on our last night there I told the boys they could order whatever they wanted, but no hamburgers. Preston ordered a steak, and Canthon ordered pancakes. We couldn't talk him out of his selection.

"You said we could have whatever we wanted except hamburgers," he said. So the waiter brought him pancakes for his fancy dinner.

We left Washington and drove to New York City to visit another cousin, who treated me and Mom to tickets for *Dreamgirls* on Broadway. We laughed so much, just relaxing and enjoying our night out together. Finally, we headed to our last destination—Niagara Falls. We stayed in Rochester with my cousin Evelyn and her family.

When our vacation was over, we were exhausted, but we'd had so much fun and created so many family memories. Mom had proved to be a great travel companion, and she'd kept her promise and stayed away from any conversation about my personal life. I promised the boys we would take a family vacation every other year. I loved seeing them laughing and enjoying themselves.

Then it was back to reality. When we got back Greg started asking to pick up the boys. They always wanted to see him—it didn't matter what he had done. They wanted their father.

One day Greg called about taking the boys to a movie, and he asked if I wanted to join them. I declined, but I said I would get them ready to go with him.

When he came to the door, he said, "You sure you don't want to come with us?"

"No, I'm good here," I said. I was hoping to enjoy a couple of hours of quiet time.

I took a hot bubble bath, put on my big chenille robe, and made myself a cup of tea. Then I heard the boys ringing the doorbell. It hadn't been very long, I thought—Greg hadn't wasted any time bringing them home.

I opened the door, and the boys ran straight into the family room to watch TV. Greg lingered in the foyer next to the door.

He whispered, "You should have come with us."

I turned to go back to my bedroom, believing he was leaving, but he violently grabbed the collar of my robe and yanked me back. He pulled my hair until I fell to my knees.

He was on top of me with one hand around my neck, so I couldn't scream. He lowered his face so it was directly next to my face.

He spoke in a whisper and spat, "You think you're too good to go with us? Don't tell me no." I tried to buck him off me but couldn't. "Don't you *ever* tell me no!"

He ripped open my robe and viciously raped me, right there in the hallway. He had so much dark rage in his face. When he was done, he grabbed my jaw hard and squeezed a kiss onto my mouth, as if what he had done had been an act of love. "Don't you *ever* tell me no," he repeated. Then he got up off me, straightened his clothes, and walked out the front door.

I pulled my robe back over my body, and looked toward the family room. Had Preston and Canthon heard anything, or was the TV loud enough? I went into the bathroom and cleaned myself up, washing the saliva and tears from my face. I didn't call the police. I had no confidence in the police doing anything, and I wasn't sure how it would play out in court.

I decided the boys shouldn't find out what had happened. I collapsed on my bed and shook with silent sobs. I thought, *Will this ever end?*

My career was flourishing, but my personal life was still an exercise in survival. The only person I confided in was my cousin Evelyn; otherwise I kept to myself. I didn't have the energy to maintain friendships. I was embarrassed and ashamed that our life was so full of chaos and drama. I hated that I couldn't control my life. My public facade was that of an organized, well-put-together woman with two adorable, well-behaved sons.

Six or seven weeks after the attack, I began having sharp pains in my right side. My doctor gave me a full exam but couldn't find the problem, so he gave me blood tests, urine tests, and even a pregnancy test. Still he couldn't see what was wrong, and the pain persisted. Finally, he gave me an ultrasound. It showed I had an ovarian cyst. He immediately scheduled surgery to remove it.

Cysts were no stranger to me; I'd had several removed from different parts of my body at various times in my life—my arms, my finger, my stomach, and even the front gum in my upper jaw. They were all removed without incident.

But my doctor also asked me to sign papers giving my consent for the ovary to be removed if it proved to be cancer. I signed the papers.

I was frightened. I considered my own mortality: I'd always told Brenda she'd have to raise the boys if anything happened to me, because my mother was too old, and Greg was unfit. I called Greg and told him about my surgery and shared my concerns about the boys' future. He said nothing about raising our sons, but he did admonish me for being afraid I would die. I had my mother on standby in case I needed more than outpatient surgery. I just needed a ride to and from the hospital, and Greg offered to do that.

On May 1, 1984, the morning was crisp and cool. I walked into the outpatient section of Swedish American Hospital praying my cyst wasn't cancer. Greg walked me in and sat a while before leaving for work, promising he would return later to take me home.

When I awakened from surgery, I was surprised to see Greg sitting by the bed, looking concerned. "The doctor wants to talk to us," he said. I realized I hadn't told my doctor about my divorce—he planned to break the news to us together.

I prepared myself to learn that I had cancer. I got ready to hear what treatment I would need and what my prognosis was.

The doctor came in with a smile on his face. "It turns out you don't have a cyst at all," he said happily. "You're pregnant."

I stared at him, incredulous. "Are you sure?" I asked.

He nodded.

I said, "But you did blood tests, urine tests, and an ultrasound, and nothing showed I was pregnant?"

He nodded. "Sometimes we miss it," he said.

I was furious, and then I had a thought that made me shift abruptly to concern. "Did the surgery or anesthesia hurt the baby?"

As the doctor explained that I wasn't far enough along for the fetus to be harmed by the procedure, my feelings shifted again, from concern to fear, which grew to panic.

What was I supposed to do? I was thirty-two years old, I'd been divorced for five years, and here I was pregnant with a child I couldn't afford and certainly hadn't planned for, by a man who was already an absentee father. I had sworn I'd never be an unwed mother. Why me? Why now?

The doctor left to write up my discharge papers, and Greg turned to me. "What are you going to do?" he asked. He knew this was the result of his attack. He kept very close watch on me, so he knew I was seeing no one.

My head was swimming. "I need some time to think," I said.

He took me home. After a few weeks, he started pestering me for an answer, and when I said I was still thinking things through, he started insisting that I get an abortion. He knew how much I cared about my reputation and my career, so that's what he appealed to.

"How are you going to be this big-shot career woman walking around pregnant and not married?" he said. "How's that gonna look?"

Nothing in my life was going according to my plans. I prayed constantly, but I heard no answer. When I was around eight weeks pregnant, I was beginning to show. I blamed this on bloating from my surgery. I had to make a decision.

Greg was right—I hated the idea of telling people at work that I was pregnant and unwed. I was finally a certified account executive, having gone through the eighteen-month certification process in just a year. I was the only African American outside of Chicago, male or female, to hold that role, and my image was important to me. I felt there was a lot resting on how I did my job, and to me, this was such a stereotypical situation for a black woman to be in.

During Canthon's piano lesson one afternoon, as I was listening to him stumble through a song with his teacher, I allowed my thoughts to drift to my quandary. I became overwhelmed and couldn't hold back the tears. Then the flood of emotions came pouring out. I couldn't stop crying.

Canthon's teacher stopped his lesson and sent him outside. She came to sit next to me on the sofa, trying to console me and understand what I was so distressed about. I barely knew her, but without hesitating, I told her everything.

With a comforting hand on my back, she asked the same question I'd been asking myself constantly: "What do you *want* to do?"

I just shook my head, overcome by my emotions, without an answer for her.

She put her hand under my chin and lifted my face so I was looking into her eyes.

"Can I pray with you?" she asked. I nodded. She placed her hand on my stomach and closed her eyes, saying, "God, give Carolynn the courage to give life to this child that you have ordained, regardless of the circumstances of its creation." She opened her eyes and said, "Every day I want you to touch your stomach and say, 'Blessed be the fruit of my womb.'" I knew this was divine intervention. You never know who God will send to speak to you when you call out to Him. It was through this woman that I heard the voice of God.

At this point I considered myself a "disenfranchised Christian," disillusioned by the church and cynical about its place in my life. Even so, I could feel the sincerity of another believer's prayer. I heard her—but I wasn't quite as certain as she was that I would bring this baby into the world.

I wanted to have the baby, but I just couldn't figure out how I'd afford it. Also, the seed for this child had been planted in violence. I would have to work hard to ensure it grew in love. The worst thought for me was having a child I knew its father didn't want. I knew what it felt like to be unwanted. I sometimes thought I could save this child my pain of abandonment by sending it to an early place in Heaven. Yet I also hadn't forgotten the hell I went through following my first abortion. A storm of conflict raged within me.

I was approaching the date when it would be too late to have an abortion. Still uncertain, I erred on the side of caution and scheduled an appointment for the abortion.

A few days before the appointment, I began bleeding—not spotting, but bleeding heavily. I wondered if God was sparing me the agony of going through another abortion. I called the doctor, concerned at the steady flow of blood, and he told me to stay in bed the next three days.

I did as he said, arranging for my mom to come and get the boys to their activities when Greg refused. I hadn't told her yet that I was pregnant. I just said I was sick. As long as I remained in bed, the bleeding slowed to slight spotting, but on the third day, when I was sitting on the toilet, I looked down to see the stool was completely filled with blood.

At that moment, I cried out loud to God, begging, "*Please* don't let me lose my baby!" I knew then this child was mine to keep and love.

He heard me. The next day, the bleeding had stopped. That morning as I drove into the office, and every day after that, I touched my swelling stomach and prayed, "God, please bless the fruit of my womb."

My other two pregnancies had been easy, but this one brought endless strange symptoms as it progressed. It was also difficult for me to face other people's judgment, though I refused to portray any weakness or doubt.

I told my mother first. She was disgusted, shaking her head. "I supposed this is that fool's baby? Why would you have another child of his?" I didn't tell my mother, or anyone else, the circumstances of the baby's conception. It felt ironic to be living out a scene from my mother's life.

When I told Greg of my decision, he told me without question that he wanted nothing to do with another child. After that I didn't ask him for anything, determining in my heart that this child was mine alone.

I summoned my resolve and bravery and told my boss, "I'm pregnant. I'm having the baby, and I'm not getting married."

I'm sure he didn't know what to say, but he gave the perfect response. He threw his hands up and said, "You'll get no argument from me!"

When it was time to tell the boys about my pregnancy, I bought an age-appropriate book that would explain things to them and asked them to read it. After a few days, I sat them down so we could discuss what they had read. Eleven-year-old Preston, who'd never liked to read, confessed he had given the book to Canthon and asked him to let him know what it said. Seven-year-old Canthon pointed at my stomach. "Okay, I understand how the baby got in there," he said. "But what I can't figure out is how it's going to get *out*." We all laughed.

Once I knew I was keeping the baby, I focused on closing sales at my highest rate ever. I was on a mission to get as many commission checks as I could before I went on maternity leave. I had gotten rid of all the baby things I'd ever had, so I was starting from the beginning. I needed to be able to afford to buy the things I would need for my child and take at least a three-month maternity leave.

When I was seven and a half months pregnant, a large account I'd been working hard on for a very long time finally agreed to sign a long-term contract with me. I got the call telling me they had signed their contract and I could come pick it up. When I hung up, I was so excited that I jumped in the air.

As I came down, I felt warm liquid filling my panties. I rushed to the restroom. I realized something was happening that could not be good.

I cleaned myself up and stuffed my underwear with toilet paper, and returned to my office to call my obstetrician. He sounded concerned and instructed me to come straight to his office, so I got in my car and drove there—stopping quickly on my way so I could pick up the hard-earned signed contract.

The liquid was amniotic fluid, my doctor said; I had a tear in my amniotic sac, and I was in labor. He predicted I would deliver within twenty-four hours. He described what I would face with such a premature baby: a long, tough medical fight if the baby lived at all. He suggested I get my insurance in order, because the medical bills would be exorbitant. I was devastated at the news that my baby may not survive.

I came home and waited. I had strong labor pains throughout the evening and into the night. I rubbed my stomach and assured my baby that I loved it and prayed without stopping, "Blessed be the fruit of my womb." Amazingly, I fell asleep and woke up the next morning feeling fine. God had heard my prayers. I got dressed and went to work.

I got a call from my doctor, who'd gotten no response when he called my house. Shocked that I was at work, he insisted that I come in again for another examination. After he examined me, he said the fetus was fine for now, but fluid would continue to leak from the tear in the amniotic sac.

"I'm concerned about an infection," he said. "I think you should be hospitalized until the baby is born."

"That's not possible," I told him. I couldn't afford to be off work. I had nobody's income to count on but my own. We compromised: I would continue to work, but I would take my temperature every hour to detect any fever that could indicate an infection.

I continued to close more sales. My boss teased that I should get pregnant all the time. I had a plan for every commission check. I intended to work right up until my due date—the doctor had set it for January 4, but I said December 30, so I could get a tax break.

My doctor had told me to stay in bed as much as possible. He said no climbing, no hot baths, and no sex; the only one of these I stuck to was "no sex."

Soon after Thanksgiving, I knew I couldn't go on much longer. I was having Braxton-Hicks contractions to the point where I could barely walk from my car to my office, and the leaking amniotic fluid had made my inner thighs raw and painful.

On December 7, 1984, when I got up to go to work, the thought of putting on pantyhose and leaving my house was just too much to bear. I called my boss and told him I'd be back three months after the baby was born.

I tried to finish Christmas shopping, but with my contractions and raw skin, I couldn't even walk through the mall. Mom came and finished my shopping for me. Greg took the boys to get a Christmas tree. The pregnancy, bed rest, and chocolate malt cravings had caused me to balloon from 118 to 178 pounds. I had to buy shoes with Velcro straps and have the boys put them on me because I couldn't bend over. I taught Preston to do laundry so I wouldn't have to get out of bed. When I did have to get up, the boys had to help pull me out of my waterbed.

Christmas came and passed and I was still pregnant, still leaking, and still praying for God to bless the fruit of my womb.

Then, in the early morning hours of December 29, something began to happen. I called my neighbor, Roberta, who'd agreed to watch the boys until my mother arrived, and I called my mother. I sat at the kitchen table to let a contraction roll through my back and down my legs.

I realized I was going to have to drive myself to the hospital. At that moment, I was gripped by the fear of going through all this alone. My life was about to change dramatically.

My contractions were now about ten minutes apart. I threw my bag in the back of my car and prayed I could make it to the hospital without having a contraction. I started out, but suddenly I pulled the wheel, changing course to head to Greg's apartment. It was four a.m.—I didn't even know if he'd be home.

He finally came to the door, looking like he'd awoken from a deep sleep.

"The baby's coming," I cried, "and I don't know if I can get to the hospital!"

"Why didn't you just call me?" he said. He rushed to dress and drove me to the hospital.

I spent an entire day in the hospital hooked up to machines. My contractions began to get not closer together, but further apart. After seven hours, my doctor decided to induce labor. But after he added the labor-inducing drug to my IV, my contractions stopped altogether. I literally felt the baby move up in my womb, rather than out toward the world.

My doctor was baffled. "I tell you what. I don't think this baby wants to come today. Why don't you go out and have a nice dinner," he said. "We'll let nature take its course."

The boys were so disappointed when I returned without their new sibling. But Canthon was also a little triumphant, crowing, "See, the doctor couldn't figure out how to get the baby out, either!" I spoke with my mother about the day's mysteries, and then I fell into bed, exhausted.

On Sunday, December 30—the day I'd chosen for my due date—I awoke to the smell of frying bacon. I put on my robe and joined my sons and my mother in the kitchen.

I yawned and wrapped my robe around myself. "I can't believe I'm still pregnant," I said.

I laughed and felt a warm gush between my legs. I rushed to the bathroom and pulled down my underwear to see it filled with a thick black slime that looked like caviar.

When I called the doctor and described what had happened, he was immediately concerned. "The baby has had its first stool and is in distress. Come to the hospital as quickly as you can, and I'll have a surgical team ready once you arrive."

I called Greg, who picked me up and drove me to the emergency room. Two nurses rushed me to a gurney and took me in while Greg filled out my papers. The doctor came in and explained that he wanted to do an emergency C-section to prevent the baby from inhaling the toxins from its stool.

He wanted to completely anesthetize me, but I refused. "I don't want to wait to wake up to know if my baby's okay," I said.

They gave me a spinal block and started the surgery.

As the doctor and nurses worked to free my child from my body, I suddenly realized I was unable to swallow or breathe. I screamed, "I can't breathe!"

Everyone moved into action. I heard someone say, "Dammit, you must have given the epidural too high!"

Then I heard the baby cry, and then they rushed my baby away from me. I've never been so frightened in my life. I struggled to breathe. I thought I was dying. I knew I needed help, but instead I faded into darkness.

I woke up in a dark hospital room. I didn't know how much time had passed, where my baby was, whether it was a girl or boy, or whether it was all right. I was nauseated from the anesthesia, and the pain of the afterbirth contractions continued to tear through my body. I thought I was alone, but then I saw Greg sitting quietly in the corner. He smiled proudly and said, "It's another boy."

My doctor came in and explained everything that had happened. My son was in neonatal care being monitored. I wouldn't be able to see him for at least a day. The epidural had been given too high, affecting my breathing. Before my doctor left, he patted my shoulder and said, "Well, you did it. You made the due date you've been saying all along. If I didn't know better, I would swear you did it on purpose."

As I lay there thinking about all that had occurred, I could see God's hand of grace and mercy in both our lives: my life and the baby's. I could have died on the delivery table, and even the tear in my amniotic sac had been for a purpose: I wouldn't have known the baby had had his first stool otherwise, and, as the doctor explained, he probably would have died.

On New Year's Day of 1985, I laid eyes on my son for the first time. He was beautiful. Everything about him was perfect. My eyes were instantly drawn to the ring of pure white hair around his head like a crown. It was amazing to see. I truly believed his white hair was a signal from God, showing me He had blessed the fruit of my womb.

All the love I had felt for this baby as I carried him came pouring out. I hugged him and cried. Here, at last, was the fruit of my womb.

I kept gazing at the ring of platinum hair circling my baby's head. When Greg came to visit, I said, "Don't you see something miraculous about this baby?"

Greg looked at me like I was high on the pain pills I was receiving. "Not really," he said.

But I had a feeling about my son. He felt very special to me. I knew he was meant to be—he was God's idea.

It took a long time to decide on a name that fit this baby. Greg insisted on having a say in the matter, and together we finally settled on Clinton Jared. It had a strong sound to it, I thought.

When my youngest son had been given his name, I rocked him in my arms and lifted him in prayer to God, saying, "Thank you for blessing the fruit of my womb. Thank you for bringing him safely to my heart and to my arms. Please bless his life and be his father." I thanked God for giving me the strength to allow him to come into our family.

Yet I felt the heavy weight of the burden of trying to raise yet another man-child alone, without a male image he could look to for emotional and physical development. Everything I had to offer him would come from my female perspective. I prayed for this child, and my other two, that what I gave them would be enough to make them feel whole in the world. I prayed that I was up for the challenge this third child would bring and that he wouldn't hate me for knowingly bringing him into a life in which his father had chosen not to participate.

This child's birth changed the balance of our family and had a great impact on the course of my faith. I watched a new pecking order evolve among my sons. Preston stepped right up and took over as the big brother, the little man of the house. He would often race me to the nursery to get Clinton when he awoke.

Canthon didn't warm up to the baby as easily; he was warier of this little one who was taking his place as my lap baby. Even so, he asked to bring the baby into school for show and tell after the holiday break. His teacher agreed, so I went to the classroom with Clinton swaddled in my arms, allowing Canthon to proudly walk his little brother around the classroom to show his curious classmates.

My maternity leave was peaceful. Greg came by every few days, and he helped out occasionally by putting baby furniture together, but he wasn't in our life to lay down rules or leave notes about what chores I had to complete before he arrived home. I appreciated his assistance, though he made no effort to be anything more than a drive-by father. I just enjoyed the peace in my life. There was no wrath to face each day.

I enjoyed my time home with the boys, taking my time to acclimate everyone to our new family dynamic. We had always been close, but during that time in our lives, it felt like a deeper bond was being forged. I developed the sense that it was us against the world. I decided I was all they had, and God would make that enough.

During my maternity leave, I began to feel restlessness, a feeling that change was on the horizon. When the house was quiet, I would pace, trying to figure out what was troubling my spirit. I felt edgy, ready for a complete overhaul of my whole life.

I was tired of my job, which had felt different since the Bell divestiture. We didn't do business the same way or deal with clients like we had, and I didn't take the same satisfaction in my work anymore.

I wanted complete freedom from Greg. It was clear that if something didn't change, I would be stuck forever in this limbo of being nothing to anyone. I wouldn't be married, and I wouldn't be free. This man had been in my life since I was fifteen years old. I had given him all of my twenties, and I didn't want to waste any more years on this relationship. I knew I could never get the life I wanted for myself or my sons as long as I gave him permission to control us, but I still didn't know how to break his grip.

I was also yearning for a new beginning in my spiritual life. In those quiet times of the day, I felt God calling me back to him. I wanted to have a closer personal relationship with God. I hadn't forgotten Aunt Tutta's prophesy, but it still seemed evasive, always nagging me.

As my restlessness grew, I decided to start nagging God right back. I needed help. It was obvious that if He didn't show me the way, I couldn't find it on my own. It seemed like every move I made by myself was sending me in circles instead of moving me forward. I was thirty-three years old, and I was sick of my life!

In early April, I returned to my job, still full of restless feelings. Leaving Clinton was the hardest thing I'd ever done. I wanted more time off with him.

For a little while, I was fine. But I wasn't really ready to be separated from my baby. And then Clinton's home caregiver proved unreliable, and I had to put him into daycare. To make matters worse, Clinton was a poor sleeper, so I was chronically exhausted. The financial pressures of a third child proved to be heavier than I had imagined, and as promised, Greg offered no financial assistance.

One day I got to the office, settled in at my desk, and burst into tears. My coworkers hadn't come into work yet—I hurried to the restroom and I locked myself inside, trying to bring my emotions under control. I literally couldn't stop crying.

This episode was the beginning of a slide into deep darkness, a frightening depression. It went on and on for weeks, me fighting to pull myself out of a dark, swirling vortex of uncontrollable emotions, trying to go into work and focus while acting like everything was fine. I would be on my way to see a customer, and I would have to pull over and cry. It was nothing I could control. I was completely debilitated, and I had no one to lean on, no one to help me get through it. It's hard to know you are falling apart and yet have to use all your mental effort trying to portray an image of normalcy.

One evening after picking Clinton up from daycare, I pulled into the garage and closed the garage door without cutting off the ignition. I had a terrible thought: *I just could not get out of the car. This would be the easy way out of this deep, dark hole I've fallen into.*

Suddenly Preston opened the door into the kitchen and yelled, "Mom, are you coming in?"

I cut the engine, pretending I'd been listening to the radio, and went inside.

Later that night after everyone had gotten to bed, I looked in on the boys and started thinking again: *If there was a way I could get all of us in the car and leave this world together, I would.*

I knew I was in a crisis, but I didn't know what to do. I was screaming in my head, "I'm strong, I can't fall apart now!" But I *was* falling apart, and I couldn't stop it. I was afraid if I said anything to my mother, she would just think I was acting crazy. I had to figure this out; my boys were counting on me.

I lay on my bed in the dark, crying tears of deep pain, total exhaustion, and despair. I knew I was in the middle of a storm I couldn't weather. I felt I had no will. I had been stripped barren.

Suddenly I clenched my fist and pounded the mattress again and again, screaming through clenched teeth into the darkness at God. "Okay, God," I said, "if you want me, you better come get me, 'cause I don't know how much more I can take!"

I have grown to understand the tremendous power of the spoken word. Proverbs 18:21 (KJV) teaches, "Death and life are in the power of the tongue." I'm certain it was my outcry in the night to my God that saved me.

When you call out to God, you'd better be ready for Him to answer.

chapter 15

OUR HOUSE

Amazingly, after that night when I called out to God, my dark cloud of depression began to lift away. Several days afterward, our temporary receptionist stopped me as I headed out of the office to go on my sales calls. Out of nowhere, she asked, "Do you believe in God?"

The question stopped me. "I do," I said, a little guarded.

"What church do you go to?" she asked.

"I don't have a church. Besides, I don't need to go to church so some folks I don't know can judge me and tell me how to live my life," I told the receptionist. "And I certainly don't want them telling me how I'm supposed to act!"

She smiled calmly and responded, "When you go to church, it's not people correcting you. It's God's Word that will correct you, if you'll receive it."

Zealot, I thought. *Who is she, anyway?* But I just smiled and walked away.

As I drove to Crystal Lake to meet with customers, the receptionist's words kept running through my mind. I thought of the timing of her message, delivered so soon after I'd begged God for His help.

I laughed as I felt something happening in my spirit. It felt like sparks, like camera flashes popping off in my head. All at once I knew who had sent the receptionist.

Then, as I drove the back road to Crystal Lake, I saw three white doves swoop down in front of my car, causing me to slow to avoid hitting them. I pulled over to the side of the road and watched the doves as they disappeared over the cornfield. I knew this was symbolic somehow—I got out of my car and walked around it several times, just laughing and praising God.

He was responding to my cry for help. He was letting me know He had heard me and had come to show me the way. In recent years, God had become my distant friend. I thought about Him all the time and called on Him when I needed some assistance, and I believed we could always pick up where we'd left off. I knew I had lost the innocence, passion, and curiosity I'd had as a child. But now I was ready to reopen my soul and reconnect to His love, power, and plans.

Once I'd opened my spirit to receive God, He continued to send angels to show me the way. One day during one of Preston's soccer games, a lovely, soft-spoken black woman walked up to me and struck up a conversation. I quickly learned that her name was Sharon Malone—she was friendly and had a great smile. After we'd chatted a while, she asked where we went to church.

"Well," I admitted, "I've actually been looking for a church home for a while."

She said her husband, coincidentally, was the pastor of a church on the same street where we lived, just about four blocks away: St. Luke's Missionary Baptist Church. I'd driven past it but never taken much notice of it. They were having a revival, and she invited me to join them. I told her I would come.

Privately, though, I wasn't sure I would. I talked myself out of going on Monday, and then again on Tuesday, but Wednesday came, and I felt compelled to keep my word and give this church a try.

I left Preston to babysit the younger boys and went to the church alone. I figured I could remain anonymous enough if I slipped in, heard the sermon, and slipped back out again. I immediately liked the atmosphere and how the Word was delivered. The minister, Reverend Malone, wasn't a very tall man, and he had wavy black hair, a dark complexion, a mustache, and glasses. He had a friendly, open demeanor and plenty of charisma. What appealed to me about Reverend Malone was how relatable his preaching was.

I went back on Thursday and again on Friday. I went that Sunday, too, and for the next several Sundays after that, never speaking to anyone. It was easy enough to put in my offering before the Benediction and march right out the door.

One Sunday, I was attempting to slip out unnoticed when one of the ushers whispered to me, "If you want a friend, you have to first show yourself friendly." I smiled and kept walking, but I heard her. She was calling me to the human connection I needed but always shied away from.

It didn't take me long to know I'd finally found a church home for me and the boys. We began to attend regularly, and Reverend Malone became the Shepherd who led me and my sons to the Word of God.

One Sunday Reverend Malone preached from Psalm 110:1. I fixated on what he was saying about God's promise to "make my enemies my footstool." I envisioned me stepping on Greg's back and walking away from him in victory. I claimed that his reign of terror in our lives was over. I closed my eyes to seal the image in my mind. Later in the service, when Reverend Malone did the altar call, I went forward with my eight-month-old son in my arms and rededicated my life to Christ.

After that, everything started to change. I was again filled with an insatiable hunger to fully understand the Word of God and how it applied to me. I'd finally found a church where I could learn not just how to get to Heaven, but how to grow in Christ and walk out my life. I had some catching up to do, and this time I knew I wouldn't let anyone or anything stop my progress.

Reverend Malone proved to be the perfect pastor to guide me into my adult Christian experience, as well as to draw Preston and Canthon into receiving Jesus Christ as their personal Saviors. He took my questions seriously, and he patiently guided me into trusting relationships within the church. The members of St. Luke's Missionary Baptist Church reached out to me and my sons and made us feel like we were joining their family.

My desire to understand God's plans for my life gave me an unquenchable thirst to hear what "thus saith the Lord." The Bible says faith comes by hearing and hearing by the Word of God, and Reverend Malone was the one who had been sent to deliver that word. If he was preaching or teaching anywhere in the city, I'd be there.

On Sundays, we went to Sunday School and morning services, and if there was an afternoon service, I often went to that also. On Wednesdays we all went to Bible study. Each Friday evening, the black Baptist churches of Rockford held a Minister's Fellowship at a different church, and I was there for that as well. During church services, Clinton was distracting, babbling to his brothers and asking for his bottle—so I began bringing a little handheld audio recorder to church to record the sermons and listen to them later in my car while I drove to sales calls. I was like a sponge, trying to soak up every bit of the Word I could.

I'd found the answer to my prayers: a supportive church community, and a spiritual mentor who would talk with me and guide me through the ugly issues of my life. I had spiritual questions, and Reverend Malone always gave me thoughtful, insightful answers.

I asked questions about God's will and how we could tell we were really hearing from God. And of course, I asked the big question: "How will I know what God has for me to do?" He suggested that I continue developing my relationship with God, and he challenged me to grow beyond just coming to church by studying His Word.

Then he told me something I had never heard before. He said, "Just pay attention to what you are naturally gifted at doing, because that's usually what God will tap into." This advice exhilarated me—it was more tangible than Aunt Tutta's "Just keep on living."

Not only did I appreciate Reverend Malone's wisdom and delivery of the Word, but I also trusted him as a person and as a spiritual advisor. I told him about my experience with the minister back in Overland Park, and other stories about my disillusionment with the church. He promised me he'd never meet with me alone or with his study door closed, and he always kept his word. He knew Greg—they would talk sometimes when Reverend Malone passed by the house—and I confided in him about my and Greg's tumultuous relationship and even about how Clinton had been conceived.

I told Reverend Malone of the piano teacher's words that I'd repeated throughout my pregnancy. Then I described the day I walked into Clint's nursery, when he was just three months old, and saw a circle of light above his crib.

Reverend Malone said, "You just don't know the power you were speaking into your child's life when you spoke those words. I believe God was showing Himself to you, to let you know He was watching over Clinton." Reverend Malone's counsel reassured me, and I grew to trust his sincerity as a spiritual leader.

He encouraged all members of the congregation to find our talents and use them for the building of God's kingdom. I liked this challenge and began thinking about my spiritual gifts and how I could contribute them to growing the kingdom.

Every Sunday when it was time to collect the offering, Reverend Malone gave a plea about supporting the building fund. I grew weary of hearing about this building fund—I am about the purpose of things, and I'd never heard any details about what we would build with all the money we were collecting.

There was an empty lot on my daily drive home from work. For months I saw a sign posted on the lot saying it was the future home of a church, and then one day without my noticing it, a church had replaced the sign. I pulled into the church parking lot and stared at it.

Ideas started taking shape, bursting like popcorn in my head—the way I had learned God often spoke to me. I pulled out a notebook and began writing down my ideas, and after the boys went to bed that night, I pulled out my notes and kept writing.

The following Sunday, I stayed after the service to talk to Rev. Malone. I told him, "I'd like to join the building fund committee." He seemed a little skeptical, but he gave me the names of the men on the committee, all of whom had been on the committee for a while. I called a meeting.

Everyone showed up, and Reverend Malone asked me to take notes.

I said, "I don't mind taking notes, but I didn't join this committee to become its secretary!"

Reverend Malone laughed, but he got my point. As the meeting progressed, I began to ask questions: "How long has this building campaign been going? What is the desired outcome? How much has been raised to date? How long do you anticipate it will take you to reach your goal? How have you gotten the congregation committed to the project?"

Nobody had answers to my questions. They knew they needed to build a larger building, but that was as far as the planning had gone.

I shared the ideas I'd written down and the strategy I'd created. As a committee, we needed to know what we were looking to accomplish, determine how much it would cost to do it, and set a goal for when it would be accomplished. Then Reverend Malone should lay out his vision for the congregation; after that, the building fund committee should create a campaign that would engage and excite the congregation members to lend their financial support. I suggested that someone should draw up sketches or build a small model so everyone could envision what we were working toward.

A few men tried to enlighten me on the high cost of construction. I answered that we could do the project in stages. We should get an estimate on the cost to completely remodel the building we were in and compare that to the cost of constructing a whole new building. Then I would develop a business plan we would submit to the bank for financing.

We all got busy and worked on the campaign while I worked on the business proposal to present to lending agencies. I broke it into stages, each of which could be financed separately. We determined that our first stage would be to get the existing building into shape to support the growing membership. After that, we could use that building as collateral for the purchase of land we'd eventually build on. When the proposal was completed, Reverend Malone and the trustees took it to the bank, and we got approved to begin moving forward.

Reverend Malone was the first to point out how my job had given me transferrable gifts and skills that I could use in the church. My résumé suddenly had a purpose. God was beginning to use my gifts for kingdom building.

The more involved I became with church, the more I felt the spirit of God grow in me. The more I heard the Word, the hungrier I became for more. As my spiritual growth progressed, Greg's influence in my life began to fade. I wanted to be free, released from the weights that were anchoring me to the past.

The biggest of those weights was the house. It represented a bond between Greg and me—it represented the past, and I could never build a new future as long as I lived in it. I decided to put the house on the market.

Once Greg heard what I was planning to do, he started talking about us getting back together and buying a larger house. His motives were as transparent as glass. He wanted to recoup the investment he'd made in the house. He didn't want us—we would just be collateral damage.

I was miserable with Greg in our lives. He hadn't changed. He was as controlling and mean as before, but still just as charming when it suited him. Every day I fought myself to keep him at bay, and yet I gave as many mixed messages as he did, trying not to set off an explosion. I was struggling to take control of my life and stand for the woman I was on the inside.

I prayed every day for the strength to be free of the hell and turmoil Greg represented in my life. It was a delicate dance. How do you break out of prison and not get captured again? When he talked about getting back together, I still didn't have the nerve to say flat out I didn't want him. I acted skeptical, saying things I hoped would put him off. Finally I told him, "I want a Christian man in my life!"

No one can tell me I wasn't fighting an addiction as powerful as any drug.

But privately, I made and pursued a plan of my own, and I never let him know I was moving on without him. I wrote down the amount I needed the house to sell for, the date when it needed to be sold, and what I wanted in a new home—the most important feature being a bathroom of my own. When I was done, I prayed for God to bless the plan, and I then I moved forward without any explanation to Greg.

My prayer was answered. Our house sold for the price I'd set and within the timeline I'd planned. Every barrier that came up was cleared away in time for us to move into the house before the 1985 school year started.

The new house was seven miles from the old one, on a large corner lot. It was a raised ranch house with a wide driveway that led to a three-car garage. The upstairs had a living room, dining room, kitchen, three bedrooms, and two baths—the master bedroom had the private bathroom I demanded. A large foyer separated the upstairs from the downstairs, where there was a laundry room, family room, rec room, built-in bar, bedroom, and another bathroom. It was everything I wanted. The new house was twice the size of the one we had just moved out of, and the new house payment was more than five times the old one—but I didn't care. This was what I wanted, an emblem of my independence. Every time I pulled into the driveway, I gave thanks to God for His favor.

Everything was falling into place. I was certain God was pouring out His blessings on me. Despite still feeling restless at work, I was flourishing in my job. Now I had a new house, releasing me from the ties of the old house that had held me to my past with Greg. I was once again moving forward.

Then, in quick succession, my life began to unravel.

We got our first "Welcome to the neighborhood" message in our mailbox soon after we moved in. After my boys mowed the lawn one day, I got a note in the mailbox that said, "You knew when you bought this house you couldn't afford to maintain it." I guess they thought I should have hired someone to do the lawn.

Another note I received said, "I told everybody we didn't need niggers here." Some kids egged a house, and the neighbors blamed my boys. One of my banking customers lived in the subdivision, and when he saw me he refused to acknowledge me. Once, after our schnauzer got loose and was urinating in the neighbor's yard, I heard a shrill scream: "Get that nigger dog out of my flowers!" When I went to get the mail, I did it at night, without looking to either side.

Also, even after carefully planning my budget, I faced daunting financial challenges after buying the new house. Canthon was precocious but needed structure to thrive. He was in a private school where he was learning French and Bible studies in the second grade. This school gave him what he wanted and needed, but I struggled to afford the tuition. I stood on my faith, expecting God to open a door that would allow Canthon to remain in the school, and I kept on sending him. Eventually, my finances were stretched so thin that my electricity was cut off and I could barely afford enough food. When I had to pull him out, I was heartbroken.

Adding to my worries, all of my boys faced health issues during this time. Canthon already had asthma and allergies that had to be monitored, and now Clinton's health began to suffer. He was normally such a happy baby, but there was something wrong. His sleep pattern became even more erratic than usual, and his crying became more intense, making it obvious he was in pain. He rarely had a solid stool, and his dirty diapers were so acidic that they would burn his skin if I didn't remove them immediately. I took him to doctor after doctor, and despite my constantly giving him Gatorade and Jell-O water—their recommendation—he had to be hospitalized for dehydration several times. At last he was diagnosed with pediatric lactose intolerance that would require permanent changes to his diet. I also had to make changes to our lives to respond to his frequent and messy stools. The doctors told me I could expect he'd be in a diaper until he was three or four.

Preston was skateboarding with friends one day and came rushing in the house. He was sweating and his face was contorted in pain. He kept clutching his chest.

Canthon ran in behind him, screaming, "Mom, Preston can't breathe!"

Preston's heart was racing—I got him to lie down and put cold towels on him. I gave him some ice chips to suck on, and eventually he calmed down and fell asleep. I assumed he'd overheated and overexerted himself.

But at a soccer game a month later, as Preston ran down the field toward the goal, he collapsed on the field. He was out cold—when I rushed over to him, I found his heart racing again. He was rushed to the emergency room, where they tested him. This was the start of a difficult journey to diagnose his symptoms that spanned more than a decade. Doctors thought it could be mitral valve prolapse, sickle cell anemia, and Marfan syndrome before finally diagnosing Preston with Wolff-Parkinson-White syndrome. He was out of school for so long he needed a tutor. He endured three surgeries and numerous hospitalizations.

There was an urgency to keep Clinton's diaper dry, so I had to pull him out of daycare and find a personal childcare provider again. Thankfully, one of Greg's younger sisters agreed to help. I monitored Canthon's asthma and allergies. I cared for Preston, transporting him to specialists, keeping him on his medication, and trying to help him manage the changes brought on by adolescence.

I was overwhelmed by the responsibilities resting on my shoulders, yet I had to keep all the balls in the air and make everything as normal as possible. When I felt overwhelmed I sometimes went into my bathroom and turned on the shower while I broke down so the boys wouldn't hear me crying.

I tried asking Greg for help one time. I begged him to stay with Clint just so I could get a full night's sleep. He said coldly, "I'm sorry, I can't help you. I told you not to have that baby." Greg never made a sacrifice that benefited his children—he sacrificed neither time nor money. They were pawns he used to gain access to me. He would stop over when I was at work and act as if he lived in the house, giving the boys chores to do. He wasn't trying to father them—he was trying to regain control of them. He lived to dominate everything within his sphere. I always told the boys not to let their father in when I wasn't home, but they were afraid not to. I eventually put locks on my bedroom door and hid everything in there so that when he came over, he couldn't gain access to my personal life.

Because of Clinton's medical issues, I started staying home from church. After missing several Sunday services, I got a call from Reverend Malone asking where we'd been. I told him about what I was facing, especially

Clinton's issues, which made it difficult to sit through a service. Reverend Malone encouraged me to return to church and bring Clinton so he could pray for him and lay hands on him.

The Sunday of our return, Reverend Malone called me and Clinton up to the altar, along with the church deacons. I stood in the center holding Clinton, and they laid their hands on his head while Reverend Malone prayed for Clinton's health and complete recovery. During the prayer, Clinton didn't make a sound. It was an emotional moment, and I was filled with gratitude and faith. In the months following that, Clinton still had some trouble, but I watched his health make a remarkable improvement. He ended up being potty trained far earlier than the doctors had predicted—even earlier than both his brothers.

Things began getting more manageable again. I began dating a man from church, who served on the building fund committee with me and sang in the choir. His name was Henry. He was quiet, kind, and soft-spoken. He was a family-oriented divorcé who didn't mind trying to help me out with the boys. He would drive to our house before church and pick up Preston and Canthon to take them to Sunday School, giving me extra time to get ready with Clint.

And then one Sunday Greg showed up at church.

I saw him sitting in the front pew, and I watched him from my usual spot in the back. After the service, Henry usually came down from the choir stand to help me get Clinton bundled up and out to the car. On this Sunday, though, Greg came to us before Henry, took Clinton from my arms, and carried him out to the car. I lingered so I could talk to Henry.

When I started to explain the situation, Henry said, "I understand. I'll call you later."

I walked over to the car. It was a messy, strange moment, an intrusion on my privacy masked as a conciliatory gesture, nice and nasty at the same time. "What are you doing here?" I asked Greg.

He smirked and said, "You said you wanted a Christian man in your life. That's what I'm trying to give you."

"Just coming to church doesn't make you a Christian," I said.

It seemed like every time I started building my life up, Greg came by to try to tear it apart again. He became a regular attendee at St. Luke's, and he even became active in the building fund efforts. He assisted in remodeling projects, put in ceiling fans, and installed a programmable thermostat.

On Sundays, I wanted to scream as I saw him marching past us, carrying his Bible in a briefcase, never acknowledging me or the kids on his way in or his way out. Everyone knew he was my ex-husband, and everyone knew I was dating Henry. I hated how complicated everything felt.

After a month of coming to St. Luke's, Greg accepted the altar call and officially joined the church as a candidate for baptism. The Sunday of his baptism, the boys, Henry, and I attended church in Dixon and then had dinner at Mom's. I didn't want my sons being exposed to Greg's mind games and hypocrisy, and I refused to be a witness to whatever he was doing. If his religious conversion was sincere, he didn't need us there to witness it. He called the house later, demanding an explanation as to why we hadn't come to witness his baptism. I hung up on him.

Still the conflicting images warred in my spirit: I'd told him I wanted a Christian man in my life. Was he truly trying to be that man?

I took a day off work to fast and pray, seeking to understand my situation. I prayed to have either his conversion confirmed or his evil revealed. God answered me, saying to my spirit, "Judge his conversion by how he treats his children."

Soon afterward, Henry called to tell me someone had followed him home from his job at the Chrysler assembly plant. He described a car I knew was Greg's. After that, Henry saw Greg frequently—parked outside my house, peeking into my garage.

One night, Henry and I were coming home from seeing *Cats* in Chicago. Mom had come to stay with the boys, but as soon as we walked in, I realized my sons weren't at home.

I found my mother doing dishes in the kitchen. "Where are the boys?" I asked her.

"Greg called and asked to pick them up for the day," she said.

"Why would you let him take them?" I said, livid. "Don't you think I would have told you he was coming if he was scheduled to have them?" Somehow, I was sure, Greg had learned that Henry and I would be out.

"How was I supposed to know?" my mother said. "The boys wanted to see him. He said he would have them home by seven."

Not long after we'd arrived home, Greg pulled into the driveway. Preston and Canthon bounded up the stairs into the kitchen, and Greg followed, carrying Clint. He handed Clint to Preston.

Then, without any provocation, he exploded with anger, yelling at

Henry and moving toward him aggressively. The rest of us stood frozen, shocked and afraid of what might happen.

Greg backed Henry up against the kitchen cabinets. Henry was bigger and taller than Greg, but Greg's rage seemed to give him the advantage, and Henry simply stood his ground, pushing Greg out of his face when he got too close.

Greg ripped a gold chain I'd given him from his neck, yelling, "Did she give you one of these, too? You may as well have this one, because she's playing both of us!"

Then Greg stormed out. Henry came and held me, saying, "I'm not a passive man, but I didn't want to fight in your house in front of the boys and your mother. That is one crazy man!"

After Henry left, Mom said, "I was hoping he would deck Greg, but he just stood there and took it. He's not worth two cents!" I disagreed, seeing Henry's behavior as quiet valor. I needed someone like that, patient and steady.

Unfortunately, though, Greg got what he wanted. Soon after that incident, Henry concluded we should take a break. Maybe things would be different in six months—but I knew my baggage was too much to burden him with.

Having successfully eliminated his competition, Greg came by the house to talk. I can still see him sitting on the foyer steps leading up to the kitchen. He said, "I've come to the conclusion we just can't work this out." He dropped his head and sounded like he might be crying. Then he said the strangest thing. "It's these kids," he said. "I just can't live with these kids!" Greg said the boys had been out of his control for too long, that they didn't even feel like they were his anymore. He suggested putting them through his self-designed boot camp to regain control of them and break them of the habits I had taught them.

I sat on the step next to him, staring back at him in shock. These children were his flesh and blood, the sons he had wanted, and he spoke about them—these boys who feared and loved him—as if they were strangers. How do you dismiss your own children as misfits in your life?

Looking at this cold, heartless man, my thoughts traveled back to all the talks we'd had before we married, about never abandoning our children the way our parents had abandoned us. Even when the marriage ended, I never dreamed he wouldn't remain in his sons' lives. Our children were what bound us together in my mind, the tie that had kept me from really leaving. It was always his promise to be a better father that kept me from losing hope.

At the close of this sad speech, Greg said, "Maybe when the two older ones are out of the house, we can get together and try again." I remained silent.

When God told me to judge Greg's conversion by how he treated his sons, I'd never dreamed my answer would be so blatant—but here it was. It was hard to hear Greg reject our children, but his words also filled me with a sense of deep relief. I was thirty-five years old, and I had been under one man's complete control since I was nineteen years old. I prayed that finally it was over.

One day I woke up and felt a sense of peace and joy. I called my cousin Evelyn and said, "It's finally over. I'm free."

"What are you talking about?" she said.

"I don't love him anymore," I told her. "Nothing he can say is going to bother me anymore. I'm done."

But this didn't mean that Greg was moving on. He was still angry, still controlling, still trying to run my life.

I tried dating again. One evening, my date walked me to my front door and gave me a farewell hug. Over his shoulder, I saw Greg sitting in his Bronco across the street, watching us. I wondered when this would ever end.

About six months after joining St. Luke's, I was asked to deliver a speech at the Friday night kickoff banquet for the Pastor's Anniversary celebration, a week's worth of activities to celebrate Reverend and Sharon Malone. I was honored. I felt indebted to both of them for giving me my growing faith.

At the banquet, I spoke about how I'd met the Malones and what they and the St. Luke's community had done for me and my sons. "Because of you," I finished, "it's no longer me and my boys against the world."

A few weeks later, the telephone rang and Canthon answered it. He handed me the receiver, saying, "He says his name is Reverend Nelson. He sounds nice!" He saw every male as his potential father.

My guard was up. Who was this man, why was he calling me, and how had he gotten my unlisted number?

I'm sure my tone made him nervous—he stammered and sounded

defensive. "I hope you don't think I'm crazy for calling you," he began. "I hope I'm not disturbing you. Is this a good time?"

I got right to the point. "I'm sorry, but do I know you? How'd you get my number?"

"I saw you speak at Reverend Malone's banquet," he said. "What you had to say sounded real good. I told Reverend Malone I'd like to meet you, and he gave me a church bulletin and said your number was in it." He paused and said nervously, "You don't mind, do you?"

I laughed—this was about the crudest introduction I had ever gotten. "You don't even know me, and all I know about you is your name. This is too weird!"

I was about to hang up when he hurriedly said, "Talk to Reverend Malone, he'll tell you I'm a good guy. Just ask me what you want to know, and I'll tell you. I'm recently divorced," he continued. "I have five kids, and my wife ran off with four of my kids. My oldest daughter lives with me. I'm forty-two years old, and you already know I'm a pastor. Does any of that bother you? I'm not too old for ya, am I?"

He had an extremely unsophisticated style about him, and based on our brief conversation, I wasn't very interested in pursuing any sort of relationship with him.

But when he asked if he could call again, I said yes.

Looking back, I realize I was emotionally bankrupt by then, desperate to make a change that would help me escape Greg's clutches. I had devoted my spirit to God—but when it came to my personal life, if Satan himself had promised me freedom from the hell I was living in, I might have considered him.

chapter 16

DÉJÀ VU

Over the next couple of weeks, Reverend Nelson—Eric—called me often. He had a simple, unthreatening attitude and style, so even though he wasn't at all my type, I found myself relaxing during our conversations. By the time he invited me out to dinner, I felt comfortable being with him.

When we met for our first date, I recognized him from various church events. He was the pastor of a very small church, and he was also a friend of Reverend Malone's, which made it easier for me to trust him. He was a nice-looking man, about six feet tall with a full frame and a short Jheri curl.

He wore ill-fitting clothes and drove a tan Chevy Impala—his clothing, car, and demeanor made him seem much older than his forty-two years. He was from Tennessee, and his flat country dialect made him seem even more unsophisticated in person.

As we looked over our menus, Eric seemed flustered by all the choices. He kept saying, "I know I'm out of my league, trying to spend time with you." I found this irritating—I've never been the type to hold myself up as better than anybody else—but there was no denying that we were ill-matched. Our first date should have been our last.

But after that first date, he began a relentless pursuit of me, maintaining a simple and uncomplicated nature that I found refreshing. So I kept on seeing him.

Eric's ministry wasn't his full-time job; he also worked at the Chrysler assembly plant. He had been married three times before, he told me. His daughter from his first marriage, Barbara, lived with him—she was fourteen years old, the same age as Preston. He'd had four children with his second wife, three boys and a girl, but she'd taken them with her when she left him. His third marriage had been very brief. Now it was just Eric and Barbara.

Fairly quickly, I began to trust Eric. We kept talking on the phone, and we started seeing each other almost every day. Eric would pick me up from work to go to lunch. He often brought gifts for the boys or offered to take them to their practices and games. He was working hard to endear himself to the boys and me.

He was eager to please. When he asked what I thought of him, I told him frankly that his style could use an update. I said, "I love a well-dressed, good-smelling man." I suggested he update his wardrobe with a few new suits, some more stylish shoes, and casual slacks. I even went shopping with him.

One morning I woke to the buzzing sound of the lawnmower close outside my bedroom window. It couldn't be the boys—it was too early. When I looked out the window, there was Eric, mowing the grass in new dress slacks and loafers I'd persuaded him to buy. He ruined the shoes and slacks, but he was so happy that he was doing something to help me.

Meanwhile, things with Greg were getting worse and worse. After I demanded child support for Clinton, Greg pursued a court-ordered visitation schedule, but this was just to wreak havoc in my life. Greg was supposed to have the boys every other weekend, but he wanted no real responsibility or accountability. He didn't want to take them to extracurricular events or buy them anything, and he complained about how much they ate. I asked the judge if Greg could be *made* to visit the boys, but he shrugged and said, "I can order him to pay child support, but I can't order him to be a decent dad."

Greg did whatever he could to cause confusion and stress. He stopped sending me his child support checks, instead making them out directly to the boys and dropping them off when I wasn't home. Each pay period, I had to get permission from the bank to endorse the checks. When I stopped picking up the slack for Greg when it came to the boys—sending birthday cards on his behalf, going overboard to involve him—he blamed me for their bad relationships.

He started playing sick mind games with our sons. He told them they had to call him every night at seven if they wanted to go fishing, whether he picked up the phone or not. Preston quickly tired of this, but Canthon always did just what his dad asked him to do, even though his dad never answered the phone. Greg reneged—it seemed he'd never really planned for them to go—and instead they found out he'd taken his girlfriend's sons with him. Later, when Greg wanted Preston and Canthon to come to his family reunion, they refused. I was tired of playing referee. I told Greg, "They're old enough to make the decision for themselves." After this, Greg wanted nothing to do with Preston and Canthon.

Yet Greg insisted that Clinton come to the reunion even if his brothers wouldn't. I couldn't help seeing the irony in this. The child he didn't want me to have was the child he was insisting go to his family reunion. When we went to drop off Clinton, he turned, looked up at us, and asked in his high little toddler voice, "Isn't anybody gonna go wiff me?"

Preston, Canthon, and I got back in the car and cried.

It was a horrible time, and I often felt alone, trying to be all things for my kids. Until now, I'd had nobody to lean on—but Eric kept urging me to lean on him. He became completely indispensable.

I was honest with Eric about my feelings. "I'm emotionally bankrupt," I told him. "I just don't have the inner strength to pour out to anyone."

"That's okay," he said. "Just let me pour into you." And he did. When I had a problem, he tried to find the answer. When I faced a difficult situation, he faced it with me.

I was struggling to pay Canthon's private school tuition and my property taxes, and Eric loaned me $1,000. When I tried to pay him back a few weeks later, he wouldn't accept the money.

I revealed my history with Greg and the battle we were waging, but Eric wasn't intimidated by Greg's behavior.

Instead, he seemed like someone who'd stand up for me. I began to feel myself relax because someone was willing to fight for me. Not only was I vulnerable, but I was also yearning to depend on someone—to have someone take care of me. I was exhausted, and Eric represented an island where I could go to rest and rebuild.

After we'd been dating for just six weeks, Eric said to me, "God has shown me you are going to be my wife. Will you marry me?"

I was surprised. "I'm not *in* love with you," I said, "but if I can just rest in the love you offer me, and if everything you're showing me is true, I believe my love will grow."

"But do you love me?" Eric asked.

I nodded yes, and that was all he needed.

This hadn't been part of my plan, but I'd realized by now that you can't plan for everything, and sometimes your plans don't work out the way you want. When I married Greg, I'd been crazy in love, and look where that got me. This foundation of kindness and gentleness, I thought, was a safer way to enter a marriage.

We picked out the rings and announced the news to close friends. Eric sat down with my mother after I'd accepted his proposal to outline how he would help out with the boys and shoulder some of the housework. She wasn't one to be impressed—but she did seem relieved, and she later made a nice contribution to Eric's church for the purchase of hymnals.

Still, I planned to have a long engagement. I was in no rush to set a date. I'd just started seeing this man six weeks ago, after all. There was plenty of time for a wedding.

I don't know how Greg found out. Once he did, though, he became relentless in his efforts to dissuade me from marrying Eric. He would come by the house and say to the boys, "Tell your mom I have something very important to tell her about her boyfriend." The boys begged me to call him, but I refused. I wasn't going to let him ruin another relationship.

One day my lawyer called me, shaken. He told me Greg had come to his office building and trapped him in an elevator to discuss his concerns about Eric. "I know you've been through hell with this guy," my lawyer said, "but he made some valid points." Greg had sworn his concern was for his sons, my lawyer said. I knew better. Greg was like the little boy who'd cried wolf one time too many. Nothing he said was worth listening to.

I didn't want to hear any more. My lawyer hesitated. "Are you sure you know what you're getting into?" he asked. I assured him I did. "Well, slow down and get to know this guy better," he said. "And whatever you decide, don't do anything without a prenup!"

That seemed ridiculous—prenuptial agreements were for movie stars. And when I asked Eric if there was anything I needed to know, he promised he'd already told me everything. I trusted him and decided to just continue to keep my distance from Greg.

One night when I came home, I couldn't find the house keys to lock the deadbolt. After I'd looked everywhere for them, Preston told me casually, "Oh yeah, Dad came by."

I stopped in my tracks. "You didn't let him in the house, did you?"

After a long pause, Canthon said, "He knew we were home. We were scared *not* to."

I gave them the same reminder as always: "I can't go into his house when he's not home, so he doesn't get to come into our house when I'm not home. Okay?"

He'd taken the deadbolt keys, but he didn't have the key for the bottom lock, thank goodness. I would go to the locksmith the next day.

At three a.m., in the dead of night, I woke up and found Greg standing over me.

I gasped, flooded with adrenaline, and scooted away.

"You haven't been returning my calls," he said in a low voice. I didn't move. "I just want to talk to you. If what I have to say doesn't change your mind, I'll leave it alone."

He sat down on the edge of the bed. I remained silent and still.

Greg started talking, sad and resigned. "If you're really going to get married," he began, "I would rather see you with ole Henry, not this slick preacher. This man doesn't own a thing. He's renting a broken-down old house. He doesn't have a pot to piss in or a window to throw it out of. He just wants you for what he sees you've got. He's using you!"

With this he dropped his head onto his chest and started to cry. I really believe he was feeling the conflict of his emotions. He knew he didn't want me back in his life, but he wanted to find a way to stop someone else from getting in.

Or maybe he truly wanted to protect me, but it was too late. His voice had no sound.

For hours I lay on my back while he rambled. He talked and talked, blaming himself that I was in the arms of this man he thought was no good.

I lay there with my eyes on the ceiling, wishing he would leave. His words had no power over me. He kept talking until Clinton woke up, stumbled into my room, and crawled into bed next to me. As Greg left, he said, "I'm sorry. For everything."

Every day I wondered when this terrorism would end. I'd lived through my marriage to Greg, and then I'd finally worked up the courage to leave him, divorce him, and even leave town. Yet again and again he tracked me down and reeled me in. Eight years after leaving him, here I stood, still living in a world of his making. I couldn't keep going like this.

It was Aunt Tutta who urged me to make a move. We were on the phone one day, talking about Greg's aggressive and bewildering behavior, and she said, "Are you going to marry that preacher?"

"Eventually, I guess," I said.

"Well, I don't know what you're waiting for," she said. "You better not be planning a big wedding, because I'm not coming to some big affair for Greg to show up and go crazy on everyone. You know that boy scares me. He's liable to do anything!"

This was true, and I knew it.

Aunt Tutta continued, "You need to go on and have a quiet wedding somewhere when no one knows, and shut his mouth—the sooner the better."

"But we're not ready for that yet," I protested. "I'm not even sure I'm in love with Eric."

"I don't care," Aunt Tutta responded. "He's got a good job, and he can take care of you and those boys. He's a preacher! You told him you were going to marry him, so just do it—get it over with and shut Greg's mouth!" She hung up.

My aunt's words set my mind to racing. I sat on the edge of my bed and tried to think it all through. I was exhausted and sick of the confusion and stress.

I finally decided that getting married again would end the cycle of terror I was caught up in. I allowed myself to believe that Eric could solve my problems and save me from this hell.

I called him and said, "You still want to get married?" That was all it took.

We planned to marry two weeks later. We kept everything secret, telling only a few family members and close friends. I bought a wedding outfit: a skirt and top in ivory silk. Eric asked Reverend Malone to perform the ceremony, which we planned to hold in my mother's living room. I asked Mrs. Malone to be my matron of honor.

Mom surprised me with the details she managed to pull together on such short notice. I took it as evidence of how badly she wanted me to leave Greg behind for good. She got my old organ teacher, Mrs. Hughes, to play the wedding march, and she invited a family friend to sing a wedding song. Preston walked me from the back bedroom out into the living room. Mom rented a flowered trellis for us to stand under as we said our vows.

On June 6, 1987, just three months after he and I first met, I became Eric's wife.

We spent our wedding night in the nicest hotel Dixon had to offer. At breakfast the next morning, Eric reminded me he had to go to Indianapolis to pick up his four young children from his second wife. They were set to visit for a month.

"Couldn't we postpone the kids' visit by just two weeks?" I asked. Already I was anxious, anticipating an adjustment period while Eric and his daughter Barbara packed up the rental house where they were living and settled in with me and the boys. Adding four additional children to the mix immediately seemed crazy—I didn't even have enough bedding for all of them.

"Nothing is going to stop me from seeing my kids," he said stubbornly. "It's my right to have my children." So the very next day, we drove five hours to get his kids.

Suddenly I found myself living in a house with eight children. Clinton was the youngest at two, and Preston and Barbara, both fourteen, were the oldest.

Eric did little, if anything, to care for all these kids. He had Barbara watch them when I was at work. I cooked, and Barbara made sure they were fed and bathed and put in bed.

Every day brought fresh disasters. In a week, Eric's children did more damage to my home and property than my children had done in their lifetime. They broke my recliner, they broke my favorite ceramic tiger, they broke Preston's glasses, they broke my sons' videogames, and worst of all, they shot a hole in my full-wall bathroom mirror with Canthon's BB gun.

I knew they were bored, and Eric barely took them outside, so I asked him to plan a daily schedule for them: going to the park, going to the pool, and so on. This was what I did for my own kids, who went to daycare and sports camps. He refused. All he did was yell at Barbara, who was a sweet girl, to take better care of them.

By this time in my life, I couldn't abide anything that disturbed my peace. Two weeks into the kids' visit, I hit my breaking point and told Eric if he wasn't going to do more to manage the little ones, they had to go. I didn't care where he took them, but if nobody was going to supervise them, they had to leave my house. He shipped them off to stay with his mother in Tennessee for the remainder of their visit. I felt sorry for the children, because they were all sweet, but I was already seeing a new dimension of the man I'd married. I wished I'd held off the wedding until I saw him managing his children. It would have told me a lot.

This was just the beginning. Eric broke all the promises he'd made. His deceit kept falling away to reveal a man I just could not respect.

Because Eric was a pastor, I had to play the role of pastor's wife—and this meant leaving St. Luke's, the church where I had finally been fed spiritually. It was hard to walk away from that community and Reverend Malone, who'd been such a patient, steady guide for me.

Now I found myself not only a member of Eric's church, but its first lady and church pianist. The congregation was so tiny, with fewer than a dozen members, that Eric would eventually ask Preston to be one of the deacons. It was a hilarious sight to see a sixteen-year-old attempting to play out the role of a deacon, especially when the pastor often had to wake him up to fulfill his responsibilities.

To my disappointment, I quickly realized that Eric's preaching was shallow and clichéd. I had hoped to gain a spiritual ally in my new husband, someone who could continue to help me grow as Reverend Malone had, but Eric wasn't well-equipped to guide me. Once after a Bible study where he talked about the power of evangelism, I suggested that we should do what he was asking his congregation to do and go around knocking on doors to bring souls to Christ. He looked at me with distaste and said, "My job is to *teach* the people to do that. I don't do it myself." He was nothing but a hypocrite, I realized—and what was more, I seemed to know more about the application of the Bible than he did.

I had formed an overly optimistic picture not only of Eric's spiritual understanding, but also of his financial situation. Just a few weeks into our marriage, I sat down and organized my bills and wrote them in a ledger, as always. I asked Eric to do the same, and I was surprised to see how much of his pay went to child support.

"How did you afford to give me that thousand dollars when I needed it?" I asked.

Eric confessed to having taken out a loan. He'd wanted to impress me.

For his part, he was indignant to discover the expenses related to living in the house. "Why are you paying so much to live here with all these white folks who don't even want you out here?" he said. "I was better off where I was. Besides, why should I pay that kind of money when my name isn't even on anything in this house?"

Then he took up another financial issue. He knew that I was a tither, but he wanted to make sure I was giving my 10 percent from every dime that came into the house. He looked at the money I was getting from Greg for child support. "Do you tithe from that?" he asked.

"That child support money is for my children," I said.

Over the next week, Eric brought this up several times. "God will punish you," he said, "for withholding that money from the church." I wouldn't budge.

A week later, Eric called a business meeting with the congregation, and I was not invited. When he returned home, he proudly informed me, "I told the members that it was only fair that I should begin receiving a salary to support my new family. They voted unanimously to pay me a weekly salary."

I was taken aback. Wasn't he being paid before?

Then, when I discovered the amount of his new salary, I felt duped and foolish. It was the amount of my weekly tithes.

The widest chasm between us was my independence: my house, my career, my opinions. Like Greg, Eric wanted to control me, but he couched this desire for control as an insistence on religious submission.

Within the first month after Eric and I got married, I got a phone call from a mom inviting Clint to her son's birthday party. I covered the receiver and asked Eric if we had anything planned for that weekend.

"No," he said.

I accepted the invitation. After I hung up, Eric said, "What was that about?"

"Oh, she was just inviting Clinton to her son's birthday."

Eric looked at me and said, "Next time before you accept those invitations, you need to ask my permission first."

Had Eric been the one I'd married at nineteen, he might have found an easy mark. But I was not about to be bullied by another man. He had the wrong woman.

I said, "Excuse me? I tell you what you can do—you just hold your breath waiting for me to ask your permission to take my child to a birthday party. I'll respect you, but I will *not* bow down to you."

Eric's biggest concern was gaining partial ownership of the house. I had never thought about how to bring in Eric as a co-owner of the house—probably because, had I moved into his home, fighting for co-ownership of his house wouldn't have been my first priority. I figured we could work out these details in due time, but Eric didn't want to wait. He felt that because he was the man, he was entitled to everything I owned, or at least a percentage.

He was unrelenting. Finally, after learning that Eric had spoken to Reverend Malone about it, I sought my former pastor's advice. Reverend Malone came to the house to speak with us. Being Eric's friend and colleague, he was clearly in a tough position. He said, "I think the only hope you two have of making this marriage work is selling the house and buying something together, closer to town." He looked at me and said, "It's hard for a man to live under his wife, and he's not used to this kind of lifestyle."

I usually had a great deal of respect for Reverend Malone's advice, but Eric wanted to reap the benefits of an investment he had no part in. "If living under his wife is the problem, we can sell this house," I said. "But what will we use to buy a new house? What sense does it make to use *my* investment to buy *him* a house with his name on it?" It wasn't my job to subsidize Eric's ego. I couldn't see the logic in it.

Reverend Malone stayed silent after that. He knew I was right, and to say anything more would have made him a co-conspirator in Eric's little plot.

I offered to add Eric's name to the title and the loan if he gave me half of my investment in the house, but he didn't have the money. He added, "I don't like living way out here with all these white folks, so why should I go into debt to stay here?"

We'd reached an impasse, and that's where we stayed. Eric paid the utilities and bought the groceries, but he refused to do anything that supported the upkeep of the home.

Now I wished I'd listened to my lawyer and had Eric sign a prenup, because it was clear to me that I had not married an honorable man. I contacted my lawyer to get his advice on how to remedy this. Without any I-told-you-so's, he explained that if Eric and I were in a fatal accident, and if it could be proved that I died before him, then his heirs would get everything I owned.

This scenario chilled me—I owed my sons a better legacy than that. My lawyer suggested we should draw up a will and have Eric agree that my sons were the heirs to all my property obtained before the marriage.

Eric was surprisingly receptive to this idea, but he had one condition. "I think Barbara should be given equal beneficiary status as your boys," he said.

I just looked at him. I said evenly, "Your daughter has a father, a natural mother, and an adopted mother. Why is she my responsibility to provide for? If I were to do that, I would be providing more for her than her own parents. Now tell me, what plans do you have to provide for my sons?" I finished, "Think again, cause that boat won't float!"

It was at this time, when we were having the new will drawn up, that I decided to use the same attorney to finally have my name legally changed. By now my name had changed so many times and been the source of so much confusion. I didn't even have a social security number associated with my name. I wanted to honor the man who had offered me his name and salute the women whose DNA made me who I was. I was thirty-five years old when I legally became Carolynn Grace Alversia Ashford.

Soon after that, one Friday evening while we were dressing for a church event, Eric turned to me. He said, "You know, Barbara needs a mother. I think it would be good for her if you adopted her."

I laughed in his face. This must have been exactly what he'd said to his second wife, who had done just as he suggested. Eric must have forgotten how he'd bragged to me about getting his child support reduced by charging his second wife with abandonment for leaving Barbara behind, even though she was unemployed and already burdened by caring for her own four children.

The final remnants of my respect for this man dissolved. I told him, "I think Barbara's been used one time too many."

Three months after our wedding, our marriage had become a façade. I was used to watching TV before bed, but this kept Eric awake, so I started rolling the bedroom TV stand out into the living room until eventually I just kept sleeping on the couch. Preston, Canthon acted fairly respectful around Eric, but they really only tolerated him.

Even after losing respect for Eric, I wanted to try to make our marriage work. In some ways, he was my bodyguard—he wouldn't put up with any of Greg's antics. Once, when Greg called the house and cursed at me about something having to do with child support, Eric got on the phone. He said, "She's my wife now, and I swear, if you threaten her again, I will get you.

No matter where you are, I'll find you. If you're taking a shit, I'll come up through the toilet and grab you by your balls." Eric may have been crass, but he was effective.

I'd heard that Greg was telling everyone who'd listen that my marriage to Eric wouldn't last a year, and I admit that a small part of my determination to make things work stemmed from a desire to prove Greg wrong.

Once Eric and I tried to go to marriage counseling. The counselor told Eric, "You are married to a professional woman, so you need to make some adjustments." Eric stood and walked out, saying he didn't need some other man telling him what to do.

The counselor said to me, "You do present yourself as a strong woman. I'd like to work with you to show you how you might be less intimidating."

I sighed and said, "You know, I wish I had the time."

That autumn, four months or so into the marriage, I made the decision to leave my thirteen-year career with the Bell System, now Ameritech. Since the Bell divestiture, I'd grown disillusioned with the company as it was run now, disliking how we dealt with customers. I wanted a fresh environment and a new challenge. So when a contact of mine offered me the opportunity to open a new sales office for Sprint in Rockford, I accepted.

From the outside looking in, my life seemed picture-perfect. I was climbing the career ladder, I had a lovely home, and I was married to a nice-looking minister. Few people knew my marriage was a false front.

But whereas with Greg I'd had to dismantle my personality when I came home, with Eric I was always myself. I refused to dilute my spirit to keep a man happy, to make him feel whole.

As Eric failed again and again to gain access to my money, I could feel his resentment and frustration building. One Sunday after church, he suggested that we take a ride alone. We drove up to Beloit, Wisconsin, through the state park. Eric pulled over to the side of the dirt road. No one else was around, no cars within eyeshot.

Eric said, "You haven't been much of a pastor's wife, and you don't have any idea what it means to be submissive. I could kill you and bury you up here, and no one would ever find you. I'll just tell everyone you ran off." He laughed, but it was a hollow laugh. He wasn't joking.

In a flash, Eric was a hundred times more frightening than Greg, because I had no idea what he was capable of. An image came into my mind: the sawed-off shotgun Eric kept under our bed, despite my fervent pleas to get rid of it. Eric said he needed it in case Greg tried to come into the house, but now I imagined myself looking up the barrel.

Eric pulled the car back onto the road and looked over at me. "Does that scare you?" he asked.

It terrified me, but I wasn't going to let him know that. My heart hammered in my chest. "No, I'm not scared of you!" I exclaimed. "You're crazy, and I'm going to let everyone know just how crazy you are." We didn't say another word to one another on the way home. My mind raced, and all I could think of was getting home safely to my boys.

The second we got back to the house, I went straight to the phone and called my cousin Evelyn to tell her about Eric's threat. I told her where I kept my journal, in case anything happened to me. Her husband got on the phone and said, "Don't let him isolate you. Don't go anywhere alone with him." Then I called one of Eric's pastor friends to tell him everything, too.

He grew very concerned. "Is everything okay?" he asked. "Should I come out there?"

"I'm fine," I said. "I just wanted you to know what Eric said to me and what he could be capable of."

Eric overheard the conversation. "Girl," he said, "can't nobody even joke with you. I'm not going to touch a hair on your head."

"I'm going to make sure of it," I said. With Greg, I had operated in the dark. I wouldn't allow that to happen again.

Eric drew his self-worth from his status as a pastor. In the black community, he enjoyed the feeling of being a respected leader, and as the pastor's wife, it was my role to uphold his status. I played my role perfectly. I wore my big hats and attended church functions. Many people were drawn to me for counseling, and I tried to give them wise counsel—yet Eric's ego got in the way of any impact I might have had. People began calling me the "assistant pastor," and he resented me for that. No one but those I confided in knew the truth about my marriage or Eric's hypocrisy.

I went to monthly meetings for pastors' wives. These meetings were held one Saturday a month, each time at a different home. We would gather to talk about whatever book we'd selected to read and discuss, and the hostess would prepare a feast.

I hated all the ceremonial grandeur and the empty ritual. I saw no real purpose to the meetings, and we weren't trying to change or accomplish anything. During one meeting I asked, "When are we going to take off our hats, get off our high horses, and get into the trenches where our young women are, to try to solve some of the issues they're facing?"

There was a long pause. "Sister Nelson," one of older women finally said, "as the first lady of the church, we are on the same level as the first lady of the United States." I stared at her in disbelief.

Another one of the women said, "You have the zeal for God without an understanding. Our job is to stand by our husbands, not take a stand on social issues."

With as much respect as I could muster, I said, "We can stand by our husbands and still use our positions to make a difference in the lives of these young girls who are getting pregnant and on drugs."

They patted my hand like I was an idiot. I knew anything else I said would not be heard.

Eric heard about how I'd challenged the pastors' wives. He was nervous and angry. He said, "Can't you just go to those meetings and be quiet? You always have to find some way to embarrass me." I wanted substance, but he wanted image.

Meanwhile, I was growing more and more dissatisfied in my work. A year into my job at Sprint, I realized that the restlessness I'd felt back when I was with Ameritech hadn't only been due to the Bell divestiture and the changes it had brought. I was simply sick of the sales game. Whereas at one time I'd gotten a buzz from closing a sale, now I was just tired of being only as good as my last sale, having to hustle constantly and worry about meeting my quotas.

But I had to keep my career doubts on the backburner for the time being—in the middle of working, parenting, church obligations, and dealing with my marriage, I injured my knee and discovered I would need arthroscopic knee surgery. I was scheduled to take six weeks off work.

This stretched into five months of rehab, two surgeries, and a 30 percent salary cut due to going on short-term disability. Eric was still only paying utilities, and my bills were piling up. I had to supplement my disability paycheck, and once I felt I had no other options, I decided to take out a loan from my 401(k).

I discovered I would need Eric's signature to do this. When he learned I was going to be coming into some money, he complained, "We're supposed to be one, but you're taking out money just to pay *your* bills."

He talked about this until at last I yielded, going against everything I was feeling in my spirit, hoping that by lending Eric the money, I'd finally make him feel we were on equal footing. I agreed to *loan* him $6,500 to get all his bills cleared up. He fully understood this would be a loan that he'd have to pay back so I could put it back into my 401(k). Eric reassured me completely and even provided me with a repayment schedule.

When the time came for him to start paying me back, I asked him where his first payment was. He acted wounded, becoming defensive. "Wait a minute," he cried, "I thought we were married! I ain't never heard of a man having to pay money back to his wife!"

That Sunday Eric preached a sermon called "The Tragedy of a Closed Mind," which included a part about it being a sin when a man had to borrow money from his wife and pay it back.

And the more I pressured Eric for the money, the more irate he became.

One day we started arguing about it again. I was propped up in bed with my bandaged knee elevated on pillows.

"I see now," Eric spat. "You deserved everything Greg ever did to you." I watched him gather up all the past hurt I'd poured out to him back when he'd had my trust, using old words to inflict fresh pain.

"I agree with your mother," he continued, his face twisted cruelly. "You're the worst thing that ever happened to her *and* me! You ain't even a good pastor's wife."

His words stung me, stirring up bile in my stomach. He'd lit a fuse inside me. I swung my legs over the side of the bed and stood up. I screamed, "Get your stuff and get out of my house *now*!"

"I'm not going anywhere," Eric shot back, "so you just sit your crippled butt back down!" He came toward me and pushed his hand against the middle of my chest, making me fall back onto the bed. He went to leave the room.

"You're getting the hell out of my house now," I yelled, "or I'll call the police!" I reached over to the phone.

Eric leaped from the bedroom door onto the bed in a single jump. Suddenly he was on top of me, wrestling me for the phone, bending my injured knee beneath me.

I yelled out in pain. He slapped me across the face and began choking me. I bit him and then kept on screaming, pain shooting through my knee.

All at once he stopped, knowing he'd gone too far. He pulled himself off of me, grabbed some clothing, and yelled, "Barbara!" He went and got his daughter, and they left together.

At that moment, I knew the marriage was over. I'd pledged never to allow any man to put his hands on me again.

An acquaintance of Eric's, a respected older minister, attempted to counsel us, but he focused on trying to get me to take Eric back. "You know what your problem is?" this minister said. "You just think you're better than him, and that's not right. You need a man to break you down so you can learn to submit. Your husband needs a place to sleep, and he needs to sleep in his own bed."

I stood up. "You want him to have a place to sleep, then you can take him home with you," I said flatly. I wasn't going to allow him to bully me either. I'd had enough of their religious machismo. After a couple of weeks, I allowed Eric to return to the house, and he came back apologetic, but it made no difference. As soon as he put his hands on me, our fate had been sealed.

I started planning a new future for myself and my sons. I went into my circle of one and prayed, and once I heard an answer in my spirit, I simply followed where it led. I didn't know where my decisions would take me. But I'd learned a long time ago that if I pushed through my fear, fueled by my faith, my actions would lead me to freedom.

First I met with a real estate agent and made plans to put the house on the market. Next my district manager at Sprint told me our Rockford office was going to be closed, and I'd report to a sales district in Rosemont, Illinois. I had no interest in commuting to Rosemont every day.

"Well," he said, "I know about a sales manager position for a company called Telecom USA." I knew about Telecom USA for its phonebook distribution, but I hadn't heard about its long distance resell business. "Let me give you the recruiter's contact info," he said, "and I'll be your reference."

I got in touch with the recruiter, and when she described the position, I was intrigued enough to agree to go to Cedar Rapids, Iowa, for an interview. What did I have to lose?

As I prepared for the interview, I evaluated what compensation package I would need in order to consider any offer that Telecom USA made. During the three-hour drive to Cedar Rapids, I thought about the path I'd taken so far in my career, and I saw God's hand in every step of my journey.

Only God could have taken me again and again into positions for which I had no experience or education. Every time it looked like I'd be knocked down, God had opened a door for me to walk through. I showed up with a bold determination to accept the opportunities and work hard, and He showed me the way. Now I prayed for the wisdom to know my next step, along with the courage to take it. If He opened a door for me, I would walk through it.

The day of the interview, I went from office to office interviewing, describing my experience, and selling them on my ability to do the job. I liked everyone I met. Over and over, I said, "I'm ready for a new career opportunity." After a while I grew tired of talking about myself, so I started asking questions, flipping my interviews around. "What's the culture like here?" I asked. "Is there any information I shared with you today that leaves you with any concerns about my qualifications or fit for this position?"

Just when I thought I was finished, I was asked to return to the senior vice president's office. I had met with Mike earlier in the day, so I hoped this callback was a good sign.

"Carolynn," Mike told me candidly, "you're a very impressive woman, and you have a great presence. Everyone who has met with you today has had very positive feedback." He paused for a moment and leaned back in his chair. "Have you ever considered going into sales training?" The question took me aback. "The way you present yourself, your sales experience—I believe you'd be a natural, and we could really use someone with your background to round out our training team. What do you think?"

I sat quietly for a moment, processing what Mike had said. I had prayed for a career change, but this was something I'd never considered or done before.

I felt a sense of certainty in my spirit that this unforeseen opportunity was my answer from God. As I allowed my spirit to fill with the positive charge, I took a moment to give my Creator a silent prayer of thanks.

Mike had seen my résumé, but I felt compelled to say, "I've never done sales training before."

He wasn't deterred. "All you need are the platform skills," he said. "Everything else is going to come naturally for you. We'll send you for training to get whatever else you need."

I asked, "Where will this position be, and who does it report to?"

"You'd have to relocate here to Cedar Rapids," Mike said, "and you'd report to Kim, our director of sales training, whom you've already met. Kim has two other training managers reporting into her, but none of them have your sales background."

I lifted my eyes and looked Mike straight in the face. Again I felt the spark in my spirit, the reassurance. I had to chuckle and shake my head.

Mike hesitated. "I hope that laugh is a yes," he said.

"I wish I could explain to you what just happened," I said. "I'd be happy to discuss the details of the position."

He stood up to shake my hand, grinning. "I was hoping you'd say that!" he said.

He brought me back to Kim's office, where he explained the situation and told her, "If you can convince Carolynn to join us, then take her down to HR and let them wrap up the offer."

I spent another hour talking with Kim. She seemed genuinely pleased that I was considering taking the position. I liked Kim, I thought I'd like having her as my supervisor, and I liked what she told me about the job. Kim took me to HR to discuss the final piece of the equation: the compensation offer.

When I'd set my terms for the salary I would need, I had figured on having a sales commission; now I'd be working with just a base salary. I did a quick mental calculation, set a new salary goal, and wrote it on a corner of paper in my notebook. This was what I would need in order to accept the position and move to Cedar Rapids.

After a long discussion with the HR rep about what I owned, relocation costs, and company benefits, she pushed a salary offer across the desk to me. She said, "I'm going to give you a few minutes alone to review all these documents and decide what you'd like to do next." She got up and walked out.

With some trepidation, I opened the paperwork. There, in black and white, was the exact dollar amount I'd written down.

I didn't even try to negotiate for more. I signed all the papers and accepted the position— manager of sales training—on the spot. Mike returned to shake my hand. "You made a great decision," he said. "We're going to get some great things done and have fun doing it."

Before I headed out of town, I took a quick tour of the downtown area, trying to get a feel for the city that would soon be our home. It was very clean, but I didn't see many black people—and there hadn't been many at the Telecom USA office either. I pushed this thought from my mind for the moment. I filled up my gas tank and headed home to Rockford.

I drove about a half-hour to Iowa City. When I got onto I-80 heading east, I pulled my car over under a viaduct. I got out of my car and walked around it in circles, laughing and lifting my hands to God in praise. I knew everything that had happened that day had been divine providence. God had given me a way to escape.

By the time I pulled into the garage, it was close to eight p.m. Eric went to bed with the chickens, so I knew he'd be asleep already. Canthon met me in the foyer, wanting to know all about how my day had gone. I called the two older boys together in the basement and told them I'd taken a new job. They sensed my joy and hugged me, glad to see me happy. I went to the bookshelf and found the "C" encyclopedia. "This is where we're moving," I said, opening the heavy volume to the entry for Cedar Rapids. "Read about it."

I went to the bedroom to change clothes before going to sleep on the couch as usual. I found Eric lying in bed awake. When I told him the boys and I would be moving to Cedar Rapids, he said, "What does that mean?"

Did he really not understand? I said slowly, "They offered me a job as a sales training manager in Cedar Rapids. I accepted their offer, so the boys and I are moving to Cedar Rapids at the beginning of September."

Eric was silent for a moment as I gathered up my bedding to head into the living room. "What about Barbara?" he asked. "Who's supposed to take care of Barbara?"

His question stopped me cold. "Barbara is your daughter," I said, "so I would assume you'll be taking care of her."

Before I moved to Cedar Rapids, I went to St. Luke's to see Reverend Malone. He was so disappointed. "I wish I'd known that Eric was like this," Reverend Malone said. "I never knew this side of him."

I didn't blame Reverend Malone, and I didn't see any point in dwelling on all that had happened. I'd based my decisions on the information I had at the time. If I'd been able to see where my choices would lead me, I would have made different ones, but as Proverbs 19:21 (NIV) says, "Many are the plans in a person's heart, but it is the Lord's purpose that prevails." All I could do was learn from my choices and keep on walking.

By this point in my life, I had little faith in men, but a deep, abiding faith in God and His plan for me. Once I decided to place my trust in Him, everything moved very quickly. I had paid heavily in my marriage to Eric, and I wasn't done paying. Yet here I stood—grateful, excited, and ready for the next leg of this adventure called life.

Faith would be my ship, and God had set my course for Cedar Rapids.

chapter 17

WATER IN THE DESERT

At thirty-seven years old, I was drained from the chaos and calamity of my life. I was trying to reach a place of peace, but I was making too many wrong choices.

What hurt the most was the knowledge that my choices were impacting my sons—I was their sole source of love, support, discipline, and spiritual guidance. I had to get my act together. Preston was sixteen, Canthon was twelve, and Clinton was four. We were all ready to put the unpleasant few years behind us, and I was looking forward to a fresh start. I was determined, with God's help, to make things right.

In mid-August of 1989, after accepting my new job, I drove with the boys to see Cedar Rapids. The city was full of smells that alternated with the way the wind blew: sugary Cap'n Crunch being made at the Quaker Oats factory, the putrid smell of cattle being slaughtered at the stockyards. We walked and drove around the city, I took them to the mall, and we went to look at the house where we would live. It was a nice ranch house on top of a small hill in a quiet neighborhood with lots of trees. We drove past the schools they'd be attending, which were close to the house.

Canthon was sociable and outgoing, always finding it easy to make friends, so he wasn't too bothered by the prospect of moving. Preston, who was beginning his sophomore year in high school, was more resistant to the move—and not afraid to say so.

He was going through puberty, he was on heart medication that had the side effect of altering his moods, and he was often surly and obstinate. I felt like someone had stolen my once-cooperative son and put a stranger in his place. Four-year-old Clinton was our little peacemaker. On the drive home, he disappointedly piped up from the backseat, "I never got to see the rapids!"

We moved just a few weeks later. It's funny: I can't even remember how Eric and I said goodbye. We simply went our separate ways, and the boys and I prepared for our new life.

Cedar Rapids was around half the size of Rockford, with a much smaller black population. Families were focused on religion and education. Our lives quickly became centered on my work, church activities, school, and sports.

There were only two major black churches in Cedar Rapids, and I chose the Baptist church, because that's what I knew. Mt. Zion Baptist Church had a much larger congregation than I'd had at Eric's church in Rockford, and it was a traditional church, as opposed to the converted gas station Eric had been renting. Mt. Zion had a congregation of about 350 people, and each Sunday the pews were filled. Well-dressed, middle-class African American men and women sat on the main floor, and young people loved to sit up in the balcony, where they could nod off or talk, out of reach of their parents. Mt. Zion didn't have a full-time pastor when we began attending. Instead, there was an aged interim pastor who gave short, to-the-point sermons, which I liked.

The boys started going to Sunday school, and during church services, Clinton would crawl into my lap and fall asleep. People knew I was married, and I made no effort to hide it. But they didn't ask me about my husband. I wondered if they'd be so friendly once I got divorced. In Rockford, if you weren't married, it was less likely you would socialize with married couples.

At work, I was in awe of the unexpected opportunity God had created for me. Telecom USA had begun in Cedar Rapids; many people there had been with the business since the start.

I was part of a small, three-person team; I worked with two seasoned trainers, Colleen and Diana, who I could learn from and emulate. Colleen, a former schoolteacher, was the most experienced in delivering training, and she seemed to think very highly of herself. I respected what she knew, but not always how she shared it. She seemed resentful of me, like I didn't deserve to share her space. I never felt as comfortable around her as I did with Diana. Diana, the youngest, was genuine, unguarded, and the most creative of all of us. Diana often prompted me to learn new skills, such as how to use the computer to develop training materials. She also proved to be the most patient and forgiving as I learned the new techniques. Kim, our director, managed our three very diverse personalities smoothly. She was always a calm sounding board and a diplomatic peacemaker with a great laugh.

We worked well together, and we brought our respective talents and experience into play to deliver effective sales training. I started out by going through the sales training myself as a new hire. Diane, Colleen, and other company leaders were the subject matter experts, teaching the company's philosophy and how to sell Telecom USA products; they had designed all the training materials themselves. I shadowed my team for several months as they gave this training to new hires. Finally, in January, I attended a ten-day training class in Sanibel Harbor, Florida, to learn the platform training skills and adult learning techniques. When I returned, I was ready and eager to lead a group of newly hired salespeople.

I loved coming to work every day, honing my skills and launching myself onto my new career path. I relished working in Telecom USA's entrepreneurial culture.

Adjustment to life in our new home was easy. In a city the size of Cedar Rapids, it didn't take long for my arrival to be noticed. I was soon sought out and invited to meet other business and community leaders, attend business luncheons, and participate in friendly networking events. I was glad to be part of this warm, accepting community, but for the time being all I wanted was some peace and quiet. My goal was to keep a low profile and remain respectable and unthreatening.

I didn't want people to get too close. I thought if I smiled publicly, mingled, and acted appropriately, no one would be able to see the turmoil going on inside me.

One Sunday the visiting minister at Mt. Zion had a special altar call asking those who needed prayer to come forward. I made my way to the front, my head bent, tears flowing down my cheeks, seeking the power of prayer to guide us on this new journey.

When the prayer ended, a woman I didn't know appeared at my side and embraced me. "God told me to tell you everything will be okay," she said with a caring smile.

I smiled and thanked her, but moved away from her, skeptical. I needed prayers, yes, but her approach made me uncomfortable—it was difficult for me to embrace strangers invading my personal space like that.

I assumed she was a religious fanatic. How could she know anything about me and all that I was dealing with? The loneliness I was feeling, the sense of regret and defeat I was trying to manage? Who was she to tell me what God was saying to me?

Later that week, I was surprised to discover that the woman was a receptionist at Telecom USA. Her name was Bonita. We became acquaintances, and she was a resource to me, advising me about where to shop and where to get my hair done. Gradually we slipped into friendship.

I'd always considered myself a loner, reluctant to allow people into my personal life. I met most people through work, and when a job ended or I relocated, I seldom maintained those relationships. I didn't want to manage too many people's expectations—acquaintances are easier to let go. Usually when I got home, I just wanted to do me, moving at my own pace, responding to life my way.

Little by little, though, I allowed Bonita in, and I found her to be accepting and respectful of the boundaries I set. I'd found a friend. When Bonita came over one Saturday, Clinton met her at the door and said, "My mom must really like you, because she lets you come to our house."

I found myself opening up to more and more people. I had such a feeling of being at home in this place. Canthon's school principal, the doctor I ended up going to, and several other Telecom USA employees attended Mt. Zion Baptist. Everyone there embraced our family and showed us kindness, inviting us to social gatherings. I always brought Clinton along—everyone called him my shadow.

For the first time since leaving Overland Park, I allowed myself to drop my guard and make friends. I attended the monthly "First Friday" events where black professionals gathered for solidarity, camaraderie, drinks, and laughs.

Bonita invited us to spend our first Thanksgiving in Cedar Rapids with her family. I told her we usually spent Thanksgiving with my mother, so Bonita told me to bring her, too. My sons, my mother, and I joined Bonita's family and some other members of Mt. Zion for a warm, welcoming meal with lots of laugher. Bonita, a woman after my own heart, even had chitlins and collard greens on the menu. This was unexpected kindness, and I received it with deep gratitude.

Even with this new sense of community and support, though, I faced daunting challenges, especially as a single mother raising three sons and managing a demanding career. It felt like an insurmountable task at times.

Six months after we arrived in Cedar Rapids, Preston's heart health took center stage. When Preston's cardiologists in Rockford had learned we'd be moving close to the University of Iowa, they were encouraged, recommending that Preston see the specialists there. When we consulted the University doctors, they ran the same tests and prescribed medication to manage his arrhythmias.

In early March of 1990, a college basketball player named Hank Gathers dropped dead while playing basketball. That changed the passive approach and treatment plan that the University of Iowa cardiologists were taking. Preston's doctors immediately scheduled him for surgery.

The week beforehand, I went before the church and told the congregation what our family was facing. I asked for their prayers. The outpouring of love and kindness we received would have made Jesus proud.

The day of the surgery, my mother came to be with me, along with Greg's oldest sister. Linda, a friend from church, showed up with her husband, Richard, at 5:30 a.m. to drive us the half-hour to the hospital in Iowa City. Another woman from Mt. Zion showed up at our house before dawn to get Canthon and Clinton up, give them breakfast, and send them to school.

My mother, Greg's sister, and I waited hours and hours as Preston received cardiac catheterization to treat his arrhythmia. The surgery lasted longer than expected—not four hours, but twelve. I wouldn't be home to pick Clinton up from daycare.

Worried, I called home, hoping Canthon could find someone else to get Clinton—but I discovered that yet another woman from church was already at the house. She'd picked Clinton up and was preparing the boys' dinner. "I'll stay here until you get home," she said.

When I checked my work voicemail, there was a message from my senior vice president, Michael. He said, "Carolynn, family comes first. Do whatever you need to do, and we'll be here when you get back." I'll never forget how much comfort his message gave me.

Linda and her husband returned to the hospital at 7:30 p.m. to bring us home. Preston remained in the ICU, where he would stay for a week.

At the end of that long, emotional day, I was overwhelmed by the unselfish and sincere love, compassion, and caring that had been extended to my family.

Even after everything we went through, Preston's heart wasn't fixed. The doctors were unable to reach the electrical current causing the problem. They put him on medication, but he eventually refused to take it because of the effect it had on his appetite, his mood, and his stamina. And once the school learned about his medical condition, there was no convincing the coach to play him more than a few seconds at the end of a quarter. Of course I wanted Preston to take his medicine and quit basketball, but some of the only times I saw my son smile were when he was on the court. What was I supposed to do? I did my best to take care of my son, and I prayed.

That spring, my financial problems threatened to overwhelm me. Preston's medical bills amounted to more than $100,000. I was spending a lot to provide for the boys while I traveled for work. My house back in Rockford wasn't selling, so I'd begun renting it, but the tenants weren't paying, and now the house stood on the brink of foreclosure. Eric never paid me back the money he'd borrowed, and to make matters worse, he'd declared bankruptcy and never paid his half of our taxes, as ordered in our divorce settlement. Eventually the IRS came after me and seized my entire paycheck. I called and worked out a payment plan. My money troubles kept mounting, but all I could do was push through.

In late spring I got a cold that wouldn't go away, accompanied by an unrelenting cough that rattled deep within my chest. Finally, once the pain in my chest became unbearable and I couldn't sleep, I sought medical advice, certain I had pneumonia.

The doctor took chest X-rays and did blood tests. "You don't have pneumonia," he told me. "What's going on in your life?"

Briefly, I told him what I'd been dealing with—my divorce, the move, Preston's heart problems, trying to sell the house, financial disasters, trying to learn my new job, traveling.

My doctor stared at me. "Can you take a week off work?" he asked. I hesitated. "I can write you a doctor's order," he said. "I'm going to give you a prescription to get rid of these symptoms, but you really have to be on bed rest for the medicine to be effective. Can you please trust me on this?"

I filled the prescription, stocked up on groceries, took the medicine, and went to bed for a week. I don't even remember waking up to eat or go to the bathroom. It was like one continuous, long, peaceful dream. When I returned to the doctor, my cough was gone and the pressure in my chest had lifted.

My doctor smiled and said, "If I'd said you were suffering from exhaustion, you wouldn't have believed me. You would have continued to push yourself. Thank you for trusting me and giving yourself some much-needed restoration." He continued, "We don't realize how stress affects the body. You've experienced all the major life stressors except death in a matter of eight months."

I was grateful to feel renewed and restored.

Meanwhile, in Telecom USA's enterprising work environment, I saw an opportunity to use my gift of identifying a need and developing a solution. The telecommunications business was an incestuous one, with many of the salespeople we hired coming from our competitors—Sprint, MCI, and AT&T. This meant they brought our competitors' sales techniques with them. I went to Mike and Kim and said, "Why don't we recruit our own sales force from college campuses and train them to sell the Telecom USA way?"

Mike and Kim liked my idea. They gave me the freedom to design a business internship and mentoring program that I named The Alpha Program. I recruited recent college graduates with the goal of hiring them and having them go through a summer program that prepared them for sales positions. During that internship, we'd coach and train them in corporate procedure, sales, life skills, and more.

I developed the concept, but it would take the full collaboration of our small training team to make it work. Together we came up with ideas and aspects of the program I hadn't thought of. Mike told me, "Some of these kids have never been on their own. You'll have to talk to them about managing their finances and renting a place to live."

I recruited from five different colleges and universities. I wanted to get a diverse group of graduates. One of them hadn't graduated at all, but I thought he showed promise and wanted to see how he'd do in the program, so I made him agree not to tell anybody he had no degree.

We arranged for different people in the company to be subject matter experts and come in to train the graduates on various aspects of Telecom USA. We had someone advise them on financial matters, I coached them on dressing for success and the psychology of selling, and I did my best to teach them the value of a dollar.

When they got their first paycheck, several of them went out and bought Movado watches, which I mocked them about. I held up my own watch and said, "I paid less than thirty dollars for this, and it tells the same time as your expensive Movado. Did you really need a Movado at this point in your career?"

At the end of the program, the training department took the interns out on a riverboat excursion to celebrate their graduation from the Alpha program. I gave them each a wooden nameplate that they could put on their first desk. Laughing, they presented me with a new watch—a black-faced Timex. It wasn't a Movado, but it looked like one.

After the program, the graduates went to work for Telecom USA's sales organizations in different parts of the country, and I decided we needed a mentoring program to support them. First I went to all the locations throughout the Midwest where our interns had been assigned to ensure that the leadership within the sales offices had structures in place to support these young employees. Then in late summer, once the interns had started their jobs, I went to each of the various locations to evaluate their assimilation into the business.

Then, less than a year after we first arrived in Cedar Rapids, Telecom USA was bought by MCI Telecommunications, casting the livelihoods of thousands into uncertainty. MCI planned to eventually close down the Cedar Rapids office and move a fraction of our workforce to Denver, Colorado.

The office was buzzing, everyone uncertain what would happen and what their futures held. I overheard some women say, "I'm drawing a line in the sand. I'm not going to relocate!" I envied them—I didn't have the options they did. I had no second income to support my family, so while they were drawing lines, I was making decisions.

The training team and I went to Washington, D.C., to the MCI headquarters to do a presentation on our sales training. At the end of our presentation, someone asked me about the Alpha Program, so I did an impromptu presentation about it. The MCI managers seemed impressed.

That evening in my hotel room, I got a call from an MCI representative.

"We've made our decision," he said. "We'd like to offer you the manager of training position."

When I hung up, I sat on the bed, completely shocked. For several minutes I sat there just quietly thanking God. Then I got up and started laughing, walking in circles around my hotel room, taking it all in.

The first person I called was my mother. She was aware of my concerns about losing my job. I explained the situation, the impossibility of what was happening to me—the magnitude of my blessing.

She understood. She simply said, "You go, girl."

When I returned to Cedar Rapids, I learned that my entire department would be let go except for me. My fate could only be attributed to God's favor and to my willingness to take a risk.

My new position was training manager for the western region. I was responsible for eight training specialists spread from Iowa to California. I was charged with evaluating the training programs' content, selecting vendors to design the training, and managing trainers as they delivered the training programs. It was a dream role for me, but the travel requirements were going to pose a problem.

I was expected to move to MCI's Denver office—but by the time final decisions for the merger had been made, the 1990 school year was about to begin. I figured I would try to put off the move as long as possible, ideally until December so the boys could change schools at the semester break.

The Cedar Rapids office was still open, so the people at MCI were okay with me traveling between Cedar Rapids and Denver. For the next five months, I worked out a schedule where I'd be in the Cedar Rapids office on Monday and Friday and fly to Denver for Tuesday, Wednesday, and Thursday—going between my office there and a hotel room. Linda and her husband came to my rescue again and agreed to keep Clinton for me during the week, and I left Preston to manage the house and Canthon and take care of our miniature Schnauzer, Spud.

This schedule was exhausting, and it made my heart ache to be away from my boys so much, having them take on the parenting role. This was the part of being a single mom I hated the most—choosing between my sons and the job that fed and clothed them. On Clinton's first day of first grade, I had to attend a mandatory management meeting in Denver. I tried to get out of the meeting to no avail.

I sat down with Clinton, trying to explain why I would be gone. My sweet, easygoing little guy put his arms around my neck, hugged me, and said, "It's okay, Mommy. Preston knows the way to my school. It'll be okay."

Monday morning before I caught my flight to Denver, I called Clinton's teacher. She wasn't there, so I left a voicemail message: "Today you'll meet my son Clinton for the first time. I have to be out of town for business and can't be there to bring him or meet you. If you could call me and let me know how his first day went . . ." By the end of the message, tears were falling.

Late that afternoon when I checked my messages, I found Clinton's teacher had called me three times. She was delighted to have him as a student, she said, and he was adjusting well. I was gone for three days, and at the end of each day she left me a progress message.

I just didn't have the energy to move to Denver. I dreaded uprooting the boys again, especially so soon after getting them settled. I sat down Preston and Canthon and explained the situation. "If we stay here," I said, "I might be able to get a job at Quaker Oats or one of the meatpacking companies, but there aren't many other options. I doubt I'd be making the income we have now, and I don't think I'd be happy working in a factory."

Clinton, who was quietly sitting at the kitchen table working on one of the big puzzles he loved putting together, yelled, "I'm going to Denver with Mom. I want to see the mountains!"

That Labor Day weekend, the two older boys were spending time with friends, so I planned a hike and picnic lunch with Clinton. When we stopped to eat, Clinton saw a couple of children he knew from school and ran off to play with them. I began to pray: "God, give me the strength to run this race you've laid before me. Help me to accept your plans for my life, and remove all fear of failure."

I heard God say in my spirit, *You just take the first step, and I will be there for the rest.*

When I traveled to Denver that Tuesday, I contacted the relocation department and started putting plans into place for the move. For the next few weeks, all my trips involved house hunting.

My mother visited in mid-November, just after I had finally signed all my real estate and school papers. While we were out to breakfast, I explained my lingering concerns about moving. I was worried about

Clinton's school situation: the transportation from school to daycare, caring for him during the time gaps, and so forth, especially in a new city with no support network.

Mom gazed at me over the rim of her coffee cup. "There is no way you can do this and do your job," she said. "The only way this can work is if you let Clinton come back to Dixon with me to finish out the school year and give you some time to figure all this out."

I knew this made sense, and I should have been grateful for her suggestion, but the thought of being separated from my baby was unimaginable.

Later that evening, I held Clinton in my lap and cried as I thought of him being so far away. I let my tears flow down my cheeks and onto his sweater. He was too young to go months without his mother and brothers. In that moment, I cried out to God, saying, "I took the first step. Now I need you to help me find a way to keep my son with me, please!"

That Monday—November 14, 1990—was my thirty-ninth birthday. I came to the office trying to be cheerful, not showing the conflict I felt inside. I was surprised to find that my team had decorated my office with red and black streamers, the favorite colors in my wardrobe. Funnier yet was how they'd decorated my desk: completely cleared off, with just a red and black mug of steaming hot coffee sitting in the center and every inch of my desktop covered in sugar packets; I was infamous for the amount of sugar I required in my daily coffee. I hadn't realized how badly I needed a laugh that day.

While I was telling some of my coworkers about the plans I'd made in Denver, my director called. "How was the trip?" he asked. "You didn't do anything permanent while you were out there, did you?"

Thinking he was being sarcastic, I said, "Yeah, I got the boys enrolled in school for the spring semester and put a down payment on a townhouse." He didn't say anything. "What's wrong?" I said.

"Keep this confidential," he said, "but I'm hearing there's about to be another reorganization. If you move to Denver, I think you'll have to move to San Francisco in less than a year."

I sat there in shock. "What do I do?" I asked.

"Just sit tight," he said. "We'll reimburse you for any money you laid out. I have a feeling you'll be staying in Cedar Rapids for now."

This was the best birthday present I could've hoped for, my answer from God. I truly believe that He turned a whole company around to prevent me from being separated from my baby boy. After I showed my obedience in taking the first step of faith, God did the rest.

During the next year, as I approached my fortieth birthday, I dug deep in the Bible for the significance of the number forty. It was a number that seemed to signify change, a time when God opened people up for transformation. I believed I stood at the threshold of some sort of change, so I tried to open my spirit to whatever God had planned for me.

I could feel God asking me to let go and trust Him, but it was still so hard to do. I knew He had carried me through the hard times and opened doors for me, but I still felt I had to fight for myself. I'd always tried to control my life and destiny. It was going to take some practice to unclench my fists and trust God to fight my battles, knowing He had a better plan for my life than I ever could. It had grown clear to me that God's plan for me in Cedar Rapids had been about much more than a new career path.

At that time, I had a deep sense of discontentment in my spirit about my life and purpose. As the noise and distraction of bad relationships quieted, I felt a transformation beginning.

For the first time since reaffirming my commitment to Christ, I had no outside forces pulling on me. At last I could think and meditate. It was just me and the Lord. I was questioning God again, wondering what He had in store.

I challenged every religious norm I had learned, seeking still greater understanding. I was growing tired of the religious rhetoric I'd listened to at church, Mt. Zion included. I was frustrated with how the spiritual high of gospel music and a moving sermon wore off. It didn't provide the spiritual fuel I needed. I wanted more—my soul ached for growth. I wanted answers, not just activity. I developed a voracious appetite for God's Word, trying to get the answers church wasn't providing.

People were living by religious rules that simply seemed ignorant and not founded in faith or Biblical truths. For instance, the women at Mt. Zion Baptist, or any Baptist church at that time, were not permitted to wear slacks in the sanctuary. We were rehearsing for a church play for Black History Month when it was announced that our next rehearsal would be in the sanctuary—so the women would have to wear skirts for that rehearsal. I normally wore skirt suits, but it was February and bitterly cold, and I just could not hold my tongue. "It's cold out there!" I told the deacon. "Why don't you men put on a skirt and let the cold air whip up your legs and see how you feel?"

He looked at me and said, "A woman is not allowed in the sanctuary dressed as a man."

If women were asked to speak at church, we weren't permitted to stand behind the pulpit. Instead, we had to stand behind the lectern. The pulpit was for the pastors, and women weren't deemed acceptable as pastors in the Baptist religion then. No one gave the scriptures to support their rules, and no one else thought to challenge them. They were just religious customs.

I began to search the Bible to see if scripture supported the church customs we practiced, and I concluded they were based in religion, rather than in faith, or they were misinterpreted. In every Baptist church I'd ever attended, the congregation was asked to lift their hands to visiting ministers. I found Psalm 134:2 (KJV), which said, "Lift up your hands in the sanctuary, and bless the Lord." I refused to lift my hands for the minister.

I'd seen behind the curtain, and I'd known too many ministers who didn't deserve that blind trust or respect.

Church gatherings were becoming less and less relevant to me and the spiritual needs I had. I began to refer to them as "religious socialization." I had reached a place in my spiritual life where I didn't want to waste my time on matters that didn't have deliberate intentions. I knew accepting Jesus Christ as my personal savior was my ticket into heaven—but what had God equipped me to accomplish while I was still here on earth?

I knew that others felt the same way I did. I was vocal about my beliefs, and many women began coming to me, telling me their stories, wanting my spiritual insight. I listened to, advised, and coached the women who came to me. They began asking me to start a home women's group, but I hesitated, not wanting to appear as a heretic pulling them from the church. Yet I remained adamant that we should be challenging the religious habits and traditions we were so blindly following. I tried to encourage them to seek the truth, but I didn't feel righteous enough to lead such a revolution. I was still asking questions and seeking answers myself.

In Cedar Rapids, I was in a quiet place where my spirit experienced a paradigm shift. I was moving away from the religion of my childhood, based on mere salvation and rituals, and toward a new agenda of kingdom faith, based on standing on the Word of God as my truth. I could feel my spirit separating from my past and moving toward a new beginning.

I was examining the past—the thoughts, the problems, the people—so

I could be fully used. Every time I released a part of the past and stopped condemning, I felt my spirit connecting to God in a way that amazed me. It felt like an awakening. I knew God was speaking to me, providing revelations about all the things I had to resolve and release.

One of these revelations was about my mother.

In many ways, my mother was helpful and supportive. She was an amazing grandmother to the boys, she was held in high esteem within the family and in the community, and she frequently came to my assistance when I needed it.

Yet in other ways she was still the same mother who lived behind the lies of my birth and humiliated me as a child. She still stung me with her harsh tongue, calling me "Fool," disparaging me with sarcasm, and ignoring me during times of illness—even once I was an adult, she always sent Aunt Tutta to care for me instead of coming herself.

The weekend of Mother's Day in May of 1991, I was asked to be the keynote speaker for our church's Woman's Day banquet. Linda was the event's organizer, and she asked if my mother would come to introduce me. I liked the idea and asked my mother, who agreed to come.

Excited, I prepared for the event. I asked a friend to record it. I even went shopping and bought my mom and myself matching dresses. My mother didn't ask for any input on what she should say, and I didn't provide any. I figured she would keep it simple.

There were around fifty women at the banquet, many of whom I barely knew. After dessert, my mother stood before the crowd and began to speak.

Instead of displaying some semblance of pride or even just making a simple family-related introduction, she took a sarcastic tone. She used her platform to air our dirty laundry. She told these women about our tumultuous relationship and spoke about my reluctance to make friends. Then she read from Kahlil Gibran's *The Prophet*—which I'd given her on my eighteenth birthday—quoting a passage about our children not belonging to us. She said that I had always tried to prove her wrong. She spoke of my career. "Carolynn has spent her entire career trying to prove to me she can make it without a college degree," my mother said. "Thank you for embracing her. I hope she can finally be happy."

The room was totally silent. I stood up slowly, wanting to scream. Once again, my mother had humiliated me in public, had laid bare my most vulnerable secrets. I didn't meet her eye. I collected my thoughts, tried to breathe, and delivered my speech. Afterward, the friend I'd asked to record it rushed over and said, "What *was* that? Are you okay?"

I couldn't even try to joke it off. On the car ride home, I exploded at my mother. "I don't know what I ever did to you for you to publicly humiliate me like that," I said, "But I can't do this anymore!"

My mother chuckled. She said, "What, you're mad because I told the truth? What did you want me to say?"

I just glared at her, afraid of what might come out if I kept going.

The next morning, I didn't come out of my room until she was gone.

I was tired of trying to figure out what kind of mother she was. I was tired of picking myself up when she knocked me down with her verbal jabs. I had reached a point in my life where I was done.

I knew I had to purge her dark influence from my life, but how do you marginalize your mother? It was painful to explore, but I cracked it open anyway. I tried to push through what I'd carried inside for so long. I had to face that I couldn't trust my mother's image of me. I couldn't be lost in how she defined me. I had to take ownership of my self-image.

My mother and I went months without talking, although she still lavished love on the boys and tried to reach me through other family members.

In the fall, Melvin called and mentioned that Mom was driving him to Minneapolis to visit his in-laws. "Would it be okay if she stayed with you on her drive back?" he asked.

"You don't need to do her work for her," I said. "If she decides to come by, I'll be here."

And so she came to stay, coming through the door, acting like nothing had happened, asking, "Where are my babies?" After the boys had gone to bed, I went to speak with her privately. She was staying in Clint's room. She was propped up in one of the twin beds, reading an issue of *Jet* magazine.

"Mom, can we talk?" I said. I didn't wait for an answer. "I can't figure you out. As I approach my fortieth birthday, I need to say something. I don't know what it is about me that you find so hard to deal with, but I know I'm a good and loving daughter, and you have no reason to treat me like you do."

I wouldn't look at her while I spoke. Instead I stared at the wall in front of me, being careful not to look at her face.

"I'm sorry if I haven't fulfilled your dreams for my life," I continued. "I didn't get my college degree, and I married a man you didn't want me to marry. I'm sorry. If it makes any difference, you were right on both counts, but I'm not sorry I was born, even though you act like *you* are.

"My career has nothing to do with you," I went on. "I'm not out to prove anything to you. I'm just taking the opportunities that help me make a living so I can provide for my children. The opportunities have nothing to do with you."

I gathered my thoughts before I finished what I had to say. "I wish you'd just celebrate my successes with me instead of being so critical," I said. "I love you, and I'd love if we could just have a normal, loving mother-daughter relationship, instead of always feeling like I'm in a battle with you. That would mean a lot to me."

At last I looked at my mother. She had her magazine lying across her chest, and her eyes were closed. I knew she wasn't asleep, but it didn't matter. I'd said what needed to be said, and I knew she had heard me. I wasn't going to let her opinion of me diminish my true self. I was standing in a new place. I shut off the light and went to bed.

Around that time, I had a gradual revelation: I could not make my mother someone she wasn't, and I couldn't try to be someone I wasn't in an effort to please her. Although I would always love, respect, and care for my mother, I let go of the image I'd always held of what our relationship should be. I shouldn't have to prove that I was worth keeping and worth loving.

• • •

God was in charge of my plan, but how I viewed myself and what steps I took on my path were up to me—and this included my job.

Following the decision not to relocate me to Denver, I'd been assigned to the Chicago training team and put under a new manager of training, Bradley. Although Bradley and I had never met and he didn't know me, it was obvious he didn't care for me, perhaps because we shared the same title—although mine was for a division that no longer existed. Bradley and I emailed and spoke on the phone, and he was always brief and curt.

Every time Bradley was scheduled to visit Cedar Rapids, something always came up that caused him to cancel. I conducted the required training sessions and sent my reports and evaluations to him, and that was the extent of our interactions. I could see the politics at play. Bradley was the well-known, respected superior working from his seat of power in Chicago. I was on the outside, in deposed Cedar Rapids, working from an office brought on through an acquisition. I knew it was in Bradley's best interest to eliminate me.

He chose his poison: the performance review. He gave me a rating of "Below Expectations" without ever sitting in on my training or providing any feedback, and he delivered it by email, like a coward. He'd scheduled a face-to-face meeting for my review, but of course he canceled it because of a snowstorm.

Bradley had chosen the wrong time, the wrong weapon, and most importantly, the wrong woman. He could have simply eliminated my position, paid me severance, and sent me on my way, but to eliminate me based on my performance was just not going to happen. I knew I was good at what I did, and I had the outstanding training evaluations to prove it. This was a battle he didn't have the power to win unless I gave up.

Around this time, we received a company-wide memo announcing the new director of human resources for the Central Division. The new director, Lester, was someone I'd met when I had an office in Denver. We'd been introduced to each other and exchanged business cards. I remembered he had an authoritative air about him. He said once I got settled, I should call him if I needed anything. I hadn't thought of Lester after my move to Denver was canceled, but now I needed something. I despised asking for help, but I decided this was my best hope.

"Of course I remember you!" Lester exclaimed when I called him. "Who could forget that smile?" As I explained my plight, Lester listened thoughtfully. "I think your personality is probably a bit too strong for Brad's," he said. "He's probably just intimidated by you, and since you have the same position, he just wants to eliminate his competition. Give me some time to look into this, and I'll get back to you," Lester said cheerfully.

"Sure," I said, wondering what choice I had. "I appreciate your assistance."

Within a week, he called me back. He explained that Brad was highly respected in the Central Division—but Lester had an alternative solution.

He said, "I've done my homework, and I've heard some good things about you. You have a reputation for knowing how to develop programs from the ground up, and I need someone with creative ideas to help me get this organization built to succeed.

"This is a new role and would have you operating as my chief of staff. Your other option is to report to Brad, but no longer as a manager—your title would be training specialist." At last he stopped talking. I didn't know what to say. I had no idea what a chief of staff even did.

"Either way," Lester finally said, "I'll need you here in Chicago as quickly as possible." With this, his tone changed from friendly to matter-of-fact. "This is a job offer," he said. "If you turn it down, there will be no severance offered. Understand?"

I was completely speechless. I'd just wanted to have my performance review looked into. I hadn't expected any of this. Flustered, I asked for some time to think about it. He had me over the proverbial barrel; I knew I had to seek God for my answer.

After hanging up, I left the office immediately to withdraw into my thoughts—I thought of my car as my prayer chamber, where I could be alone with God. I drove around Cedar Rapids, thinking and speaking out loud to God. I've always believed that when new doors are opened for me, God is giving me a new assignment and taking me to a new level of faith. This time, though, I felt some apprehension I couldn't explain. While I wasn't afraid to try something new, I had no idea what I'd be doing as Lester's chief of staff.

I knew I didn't have much choice but to move forward. I just had to trust God and go where I believed He was leading me. I recognized that God was continuously sending me into assignments where I had no training or education and raising me up, demonstrating to me that His power over my life was greater than man's opinion.

I accepted the new position and convinced Lester to allow me to wait to begin my new job until after Christmas, at the beginning of a new school semester. Preston was a senior in high school by now, and I didn't want to move him. A young professional at Mt. Zion said Preston could live with him to finish out his senior year, and after interrogating this man thoroughly and checking into his background, I was convinced Preston would be safe with him. God kept removing barriers and providing answers.

That November, on my fortieth birthday, I returned home from a work trip, exhausted. I'd had two birthday celebrations on my thirty-ninth birthday, so I was going to go quietly into my fortieth year. When I got in, the boys told me one of the older men at church had called looking for me. When I called him back, he said, "I heard you were out of town. We know you're getting ready to leave us. Could you come down to the church? We've got something for you."

I arrived at Mt. Zion to find him and one of the older church ushers waiting for me in the church basement, both smiling broadly. "Happy birthday!" they exclaimed. They escorted me to a table they'd draped with a white tablecloth and set with china for one. They pulled out the chair, put the napkin in my lap, and began to serve me. They brought out a plate heaped with chitlins and collard greens—I'd told them often how much I loved soul food. I just bent over in laughter at this sweet and thoughtful gesture. They both sat and watched me enjoy my soulful delicacies, poised to provide whatever I might need.

When I first arrived in Cedar Rapids, I never expected such sincere kindness.

I was sad to leave, but I was grateful to have lived there. God knew what I needed far better than I did. I was blessed to make lifelong friends in Cedar Rapids and experience the agape love Jesus wanted us to demonstrate to one another. I found a sense of belonging there—a degree of warmth, acceptance, and genuineness I hadn't found anywhere else. My sons and I were strangers passing through, and the people of Cedar Rapids and Mt. Zion Baptist Church opened their hearts, their homes, and their lives to us. They showed us a kind of unconditional love I hadn't seen before and haven't seen since.

An older member of the Cedar Rapids community called me before I left to say goodbye. He said, "You got something special that lights up a room. Watch out for folks who'll want to put that light out."

It was a lesson I would need to remember.

chapter 18

AT LAST

Yet again, God was leading me into new and unfamiliar terrain, and I just did my best to follow where He led. In early spring of 1992, one week after Canthon's fifteenth birthday, we settled into Streamwood, a northwest suburb of Chicago. The boys and I lived in a townhouse community, and the unit I rented had a yard where Spud could play. I was eager to begin my new job, excited to make the most of this new opportunity as Lester's chief of staff.

On my first day of work, I arrived at the office of MCI Telecommunications Central Division, located in a towering forty-four-story high-rise on Michigan Avenue, to find that no arrangements had been made for my arrival. My boxes from Cedar Rapids had arrived, but they were stacked in a hallway. I had no office, no telephone, and no desk.

I went to one of the assistants and asked, "Can you tell me where my office is?"

She responded curtly, "You managed to get the job without anyone's help. I'm sure you can figure out the rest." It seemed whenever favor opened the door, hostility was there to greet me.

I would quickly discover she wasn't the only one who felt this way. A lot of people at my new job were not happy I was there. I would hear many times, "Others were more qualified than you and would have liked to have a shot at that job." It also wouldn't be long before the gossip mill began to churn, with people speculating that something inappropriate was going on between Lester and me.

I had never worked in such a hostile environment. My lone ally was the HR senior manager, Francine, an African American woman who by all accounts should have gotten Lester's job as director. Francine explained how the process worked and why everyone was acting so hateful toward me. I'd had no idea that protocol had not been followed and the position Lester offered me was never posted—nobody else had gotten an opportunity to apply for it. She had reason to be resentful, but she was fair and patient, taking me under her watch and walking me through an informal orientation.

Francine became my unofficial mentor, which was especially valuable because I had no one else to talk to about what was happening in my new work life, no role model to help me navigate these waters. I had no outside council to consult, either, because no one in my family had ever worked in corporate America.

My coworkers' nastiness was hurtful, but I had a job to do, and I intended to do it well, regardless of others' opinions. When it came to my actual job and what it entailed, Lester hadn't even created an actual job description of my responsibilities—so I designed my own role. I spent time listening to the issues, I got the lay of the land and figured out what was needed, and I sought ways to keep Lester informed and help him do his job. This was one more opportunity to use my gift for identifying needs, providing solutions, and putting systems into place. For instance, the relocation process I'd gone through was inefficient and stressful, so I recommended ways to provide more oversight and provide reimbursement more quickly.

I immersed myself in all facets of the HR world, from compliance, to budget, to relocation management, to diversity. MCI was a federal contractor, so affirmative action compliance was paramount. Francine was responsible for our affirmative action plans, and she allowed me to shadow her to learn the process of affirmative action reporting and preparing for audits.

I went from being a big fish in a small pond in Cedar Rapids to being a small fish in a *very* big pond in Chicago. To get to work from our house in Streamwood, I would get up at 5:45 a.m., leave by seven, and drive a half-hour to catch the train into downtown Chicago, where I then took a bus or a taxi and arrived at work around nine. At the end of the day, I would usually try to catch the 5:40 or 6:10 p.m. train home. Before I left the office, I'd call to tell the boys I was on my way and see what they needed me to pick up, if fast food was on the menu that night. Once I got home, we often spent time on homework or went to one of Canthon's basketball games. I usually crawled into bed by midnight so I could wake up and do it all over again.

It wasn't long before it became apparent that Lester had an eye for me, and he didn't do a very good job of hiding it. He would call me to the executive floor for the most trifling reasons, and he would make suggestive innuendos about how nicely I always dressed, how I accessorized my clothes, how my hair was styled, or how nice my nails looked. He made me so uncomfortable.

Once at an offsite meeting, he asked me to keep his day planner in my hotel room, only to call right before I went to bed to say he needed it. "I'll just come up to your room to pick it up," he suggested.

"No," I said firmly. "I'm already dressed for bed. I'll leave it on the floor outside my door."

"No, I have some confidential papers in there," he protested.

"I won't open it," I said. "Can't you wait until the morning session?"

"No, I need to review some things tonight," he insisted. "You can just pass it to me around the door. I won't even look." But instead, he stepped around the cracked door, looked me in my face, and said, "See, that wasn't so bad."

The next morning he approached me and said, "I bet there's no one else in this room who can say they've seen you without your makeup, standing in a bathrobe."

I got up every morning dreading my workday. I never wanted to live in Chicago, yet I hated living in the suburbs and feeling so isolated. In my job, I felt like I was walking into the lion's den every day. Every day when I rode the train into Union Station, I would repeat to myself over and over, "No weapon formed against me will prosper, and every tongue that rises against me in judgment shall be condemned." That's all I had to stave off the attacks that came at me. Some days I was strong, and other days I got whipped.

Even while I was determined to succeed in my career, I was balancing the many demands of single parenthood. Fifteen-year-old Canthon made friends in Streamwood quickly—but he also started acting out, angered by the move. He skipped school sometimes, his grades slipped, and he broke a lock on the patio door so he could come and go without me knowing. I did the best I could to discipline him, but my long workdays and travel gave him the freedom to make his own rules. I was frustrated.

Seven-year-old Clinton had to demonstrate maturity beyond his years as a full-time latchkey kid. Canthon had basketball practice every single night, and Clinton was often alone. I put lots of rules into place for him to follow, and he was responsible—he didn't like to worry me. He always called me as soon as he got home. He was also smart and resourceful. He got his homework done and figured out a way to get his favorite after-school snack. He wasn't allowed to use the stove, but he loved grilled cheese sandwiches—defying his lactose intolerance—so he figured out how to make them by putting slices of bread in the toaster, buttering them, placing cheese between the warm toasted slices of bread, and then putting his sandwich in the microwave to melt the cheese.

Preston was still living in Cedar Rapids with a member of Mt. Zion Baptist while he finished his senior year, so I went back every other weekend to spend time with him, watch his basketball games, and participate in all his senior year school activities. Nothing had changed as far as his health was concerned—he was still stubbornly refusing to take his medication. He wore me down, and I just stopped trying to block him, deciding to surrender him to God's will. I gave the school a signed release, telling them if he died on the basketball court, I wouldn't sue them. At least he would have been doing what made him the happiest.

When it came time for Senior Parents' Night at Preston's school, Clinton had the flu. He was running a fever and vomiting. These were the choices of motherhood I hated. Both children needed me, and I had no backup plan and no other recourse.

On the drive to Cedar Rapids, I stopped and bought a mop bucket so Clinton had something to throw up in. By the time we got to Cedar Rapids, Clinton seemed to be doing better, and his fever was gone. We went to the game, and at halftime, I went down to the court so my oldest son—now handsome and all grown up at 6'6"—could escort me in the senior parent processional.

I glanced into the bleachers, and my breath caught as I saw Clinton leaning forward. Canthon grabbed Clinton's coat and used it to shield the spectators sitting in front of them. Once the processional was finished, I rushed back up to the bleachers. Another parent had taken Clinton to the restroom—his coat was a mess, but thanks to Canthon's quick thinking, that was the extent of the damage. I made my apologies and took Clinton back to our hotel room.

Life seemed to come at me from all sides, and I just kept finding ways to keep moving. I had so many balls in the air that I'm not sure how I managed not to drop any. We always managed to push through the difficulties and make the best of our situation.

During my hours on the train, I often slept, but I also read a lot. I was doing a lot of deep thinking and spiritual reflection during this time, asking God how I could learn to cope in a world that seemed so annoyed with me. What was I doing to generate the responses I was getting?

I was also asking God to send me my husband—my *true* husband. By this juncture in my life, I had learned many lessons about the journey I was on, yet I knew I was meant to be married. I had said my vows twice, but I had still never had a true marriage commitment. I prayed fervently for the husband God had for me, the husband who would help me fulfill His purpose. With three children, a full-time career, and a passion to serve God, I knew it would take someone special to step into my life and embrace the package I presented. While I was still in Cedar Rapids, during a period of prayer and meditation, I asked God, "Where is my husband?" I heard His response clearly in my spirit: "The one I have for you will come to you as a man." This didn't make any sense to me, but I wrote it in my journal exactly as I'd heard it, believing its meaning would one day be clear.

When June came, it was time for Preston's graduation. I was so proud of Preston for the responsible way he'd handled himself in Cedar Rapids without any parental guidance. He'd been diagnosed with ADD and early dyslexia, but he had persevered. He'd gone to school every day, he'd worked his part-time job, and now he was determined to attend college.

Yet his hopes and dreams brought me fresh heartbreak. I didn't have a dime saved for the boys' college education, and I made too much money for Preston to get any financial assistance. How could I deny Preston a college education he wanted so badly and had worked so hard for?

Again my mother showed that for all the areas where she failed me, she made up for it with my boys. She suggested that Preston move in with her and attend Sauk Valley Community College in Dixon for his first two years of school. He agreed, and with that we'd solved another problem, cleared another hurdle.

On June 10, 1992, I watched my oldest child walk across the stage to accept his high school diploma, pride pushing out my chest and tears dampening my cheeks. My mother, Candy, and Candy's family were with me, along with my half-brother, Harold. It was a gratifying day. After the ceremony, we caravanned back to Dixon, where Mom had planned a graduation party. She'd rented out the Knights of Columbus Hall, sent out the invitations, hired a DJ, and booked a caterer.

When we got to Mom's house, she had a message on her machine from Miss Ruth, the woman catering the party. It was sad news: Isabelle Brooks, Miss Ruth's niece, had died earlier that day. We all knew Isabelle, and her death came as a shock, casting a pall over the festivities. Isabelle had done my hair sometimes, and in high school I'd even dated her nephew, Ron. I'd heard that Isabelle had lung cancer, but I hadn't realized it had progressed so quickly. I said a silent prayer for her husband, Jimmie, and for their daughter. I had never known them as well as Isabelle, but I knew they must need prayers.

Because Miss Ruth could no longer cater the party, we improvised, ordering a few pizzas and some party-sized Subway sandwiches. We set everything up in the main room of the KC Hall.

The hall quickly filled with family, friends, and other well-wishers. One of the guests was George, a family friend I'd grown up knowing. George was originally from Brooklyn, New York, and he'd once been a professional boxer. He was bald and medium height, still with a boxer's build. George was known for being a jokester, full of braggadocio, and flirting with every girl from age twelve to ninety-five. He always had a cigar in his mouth. I called him "Dapper Dude" because of the snappy way he dressed—he liked the finer things in life, and he preferred to be the center of attention, entertaining everyone with his crude sense of humor. George also lived next door to Isabelle and Jimmie Brooks.

George put a card on the gift table and came over to talk to me. "Did you hear about Isabelle passing today?" he asked.

"I did," I said sadly. "I'm sure this is a difficult time for her family. How are they doing?"

"Oh, they'll be all right," he said, almost brushing my question away.

"Hey, you got yourself a boyfriend up there in Chicago yet? I know a big-time businesswoman like you wouldn't be interested in anyone from outta Dixon, wouldcha?"

I was offended and curious at the same time, which wasn't uncommon when talking to George. "What are you talking about?" I asked.

"I just wondered if you were seeing anyone up there in Chicago. If not, I got a good man for you."

"George, I'm not seeing anyone, and I'm *especially* not interested in any long-distance relationship with someone from Dixon." I paused, wondering who George could have in mind. I knew everyone he could be talking about, I figured, and none of them interested me—but I was still curious. "Who are you talking about, anyway?"

"The guy I'm talking about is a good man," George said. "He's hard-working, good-looking, and he needs a good woman like you."

I was getting impatient. "Who in the world are you talking about?"

"Jimmie Brooks, he'd be—"

"George, stop," I interrupted. "How sickening. His wife's body isn't even cold yet, and you're trying to fix him up. I'm not interested!" I walked away before he could say another word.

I was back in Dixon again for the Fourth of July. It was our custom to spend the holiday in Dixon, where we went to the Fourth of July Petunia Festival parade and then to Dixon High School, where the Petunia Festival carnival was set up. During the Petunia Festival, the city of Dixon planted petunias everywhere, especially down Galena Avenue, Dixon's main thoroughfare, and most people's homes had petunias spilling over hanging baskets or planted along sidewalks. Some of my favorite childhood memories were of the carnival and other Petunia Festival activities, so I wanted to expose my boys to these as well. Also, the boys spent a lot of time in Dixon during the summer with my mother, so they had as many friends there as they had anywhere else.

That morning, the two older boys went off with friends, and Clinton and I walked the two blocks from my childhood home on Sixth Street to Peoria Avenue to watch the parade, which was like something out of a Norman Rockwell painting. Once the parade had passed, Clinton and I began walking back to the house. I heard someone behind us yelling, "Versie, hold up."

I turned to see George, who added, "Girl, you sure got a swing on your back porch." No one could have said that to me but George. He also wasn't afraid to be nosy. "You met anyone yet? I know a girl like you is probably beating guys off."

I laughed. "I don't have time for dating," I said.

"I don't know why you won't give my boy Jimmie a chance," George said. "He'd make a good guy for you."

I hadn't given Jimmie Brooks another thought since Preston's graduation party. I laughed again, saying, "What's with you and Jimmie? Does he know you're out here campaigning for him? Give the guy a chance to grieve for his wife before you start fixing him up with women."

George persisted, saying, "I just know he needs a good woman and I think you could use a good man. Why not Jimmie?"

"George," I said firmly, "Jimmie is too old for me, and besides that, I'm *not interested*!"

George laughed and threw his hands up in defeat. As he walked away, he called back, "I know what it is—you're too uppity for a Dixon man now that you're making it in Chicago. I'm telling you, you're gonna let a good guy get away."

Later that day, Mom and I made some "popcorn visits," as she called them—popping by the homes of some other black families in Dixon to see everyone. We eventually made our way to the home where I'd heard one of my childhood friends was visiting her aunt and uncle. As we got out of the car, I saw my friend's uncle, Bobby, sitting in the back yard with none other than Jimmie Brooks. They were talking and enjoying a couple of beers together.

I'd known both of them, Bobby and Jimmie, as long as I could remember, but I'd never really had much interaction with either of them aside from passing greetings. As Mom and I approached them, though, Bobby got up and said, "Come on over and give me a hug—and Jimmie needs one too."

This has to be some sort of conspiracy, I thought.

When Jimmie stood up, we hugged, and I immediately noticed how thin and sad he looked. He was also badly in need of a haircut and a shave. We all made small talk until Jimmie got up to leave for work. Then, once it became obvious my friend wasn't coming, Mom and I left.

After watching the fireworks that evening, I returned to Streamwood alone, leaving the boys to spend a couple of weeks with their grandmother.

During the hour-and-a-half drive, now and then I saw fireworks exploding in the darkness on the horizon.

My thoughts briefly drifted to Jimmie Brooks. It had been years since I had seen him last—I'd always thought he was a good-looking man, but now he was sad and gaunt, which made sense, considering what he was going through. I wondered how he was managing with his daughter, who was around the same age as Canthon. I knew he worked at Northwestern Steel & Wire, but that's about it—he kept to himself. I laughed out loud at the coincidence of having seen him just after declaring to George that I had no interest in him whatsoever.

I dismissed any further thoughts of Jimmie Brooks, popped in a CD, and listened to music for the rest of the drive home. The next time our paths crossed was in September. My mom was running for a county board position, and she asked me to come to Dixon to help her with a campaign fundraiser party. When I got to town, there were several cars parked outside Mom's house already, as Mom had invited several of her girlfriends from Chicago to attend. I saw George's car, too, and while I was unloading, he came out. He greeted me and said he was heading home to get dressed for the party, which was being held at the KC Hall. In Dixon, nobody cared much what the occasion was, as long as it was a reason to get together and have a good time.

Mom needed me to run some errands in preparation for the fundraiser. One of those errands was to pick up the hors d'oeuvres from Miss Ruth, the same woman who was supposed to cater Preston's graduation party—who happened to live across the street from both George and Jimmie Brooks. I saw George and Jimmie talking together in Jimmie's yard as I was loading the food into my car.

As I was pulling away, I slowed the car, rolled down the window, and asked George and Jimmie if they were coming to my mother's campaign party. I knew George was, but I wanted to be sure Jimmie had heard about it. George looked expectantly at Jimmie, who said, "Oh yeah, I'll be there."

By the time I got to the KC Hall, the event was in full party mode. There was music, some dancing, some drinking, and some card playing. My cousin James was the DJ, and when I spotted him up on the corner stage, I went up to give him a hug. Right away, he pointed at a card table where some people, including Jimmie Brooks, were playing Bid Whist.

"Hey Vers," James said, "have you ever thought about going out with Jimmie Brooks?"

I bent over, shaking my head and laughing. "Did George put you up to this?" I asked. "What is it about Jimmie Brooks that everyone keeps throwing his name at me?"

James seemed genuinely surprised. "What?" he said. "No, I just think he's a nice guy, and you deserve someone nice after all you've been through. You can't go wrong with Jimmie, he's a good guy."

"I've heard that a lot now," I said. He laughed. "Thanks for looking out for me," I told him, "but as I've said before, I'm not interested."

I left the stage and joined the rest of the guests. I sat down at the table with the Bid Whist players. After a while George spoke up—and as usual, you never knew what he might say.

"Hey Versie, you picking up a little weight?"

I stood up and smoothed my hands over my hips. "Maybe I am," I came back, "but nobody wants a bone but a dog, and all he's gonna do is bury it!" I was about to leave the table when I heard Jimmie say, "I wouldn't mind being that dog." Everyone at the table laughed.

"What'd you say?" I asked, laughing.

Jimmie seemed a little embarrassed. He laughed and stood up, asking, "Anybody want a drink?"

I followed him to the bar, deciding I wanted to get to know this Jimmie Brooks everyone was talking about. I walked up behind him and said, "I'll just have a Pepsi."

He looked over his shoulder and laughed. "I hope I didn't offend you?"

"Oh, no," I said. We sat at the bar and chatted while the bartender filled his order. Then I went to another table, mingling with some other people, until the woman I was speaking with said, "I think that guy wants to dance with you."

I turned around to see Jimmie standing right behind me with his hand out. I got up and danced with him, a slow dance. I realized he was better looking than I'd noticed from a distance. I was attracted to tall, well-dressed, good-smelling men, and Jimmie was at least 6'1", a shade darker than me, and wearing a distinguished salt and pepper close-cut beard. His aftershave smelled nice, but it was mingled with the scent of cigarette smoke, a turnoff. He was an awkward dancer, but we managed to make it through the song. I was curious about what had made him ask me to dance, but once the song drew to an end, I went back to talking with my friends, and he returned to playing cards.

As the party was winding down, Jimmie approached me and asked how long I planned to be in town. I said I was heading back to Streamwood the next day, but I'd be staying the night at my mom's.

He seemed pleased. "Okay, good," he said. "Would you like to grab a bite to eat or just a cup of coffee, or is it too late?"

It was after midnight. It wasn't too late, I said. He followed me to my mother's to drop off my car, and then I rode with him to Kathy's, a little hole-in-the-wall restaurant in a virtually deserted retail strip we called "Dement Town" on the west side of Dixon.

We ordered breakfast, and after eating, we lingered for a while drinking several cups of coffee, talking and getting to know each other better. During our conversation, I learned his daughter was sixteen years old, and he and Isabelle had been married twenty-six years. We talked about my sons and my job, and he shared his frustrations with his job's crazy work shifts. He was more serious and thoughtful than I'd expected. Our conversation flowed very easily. We shared some laughs and had an easy time being together.

I asked if he was aware how many people had mentioned him to me, especially George. He seemed amused but oblivious to their efforts.

I've always been pragmatic, and I saw no reason to be evasive when it came to gauging his thoughts on dating now that we were talking. I knew I didn't want to be part of any man's midlife crisis, and if he was still grieving and wanted to be left alone, I could understand that, and in that case I would accept this as a friendly cup of coffee and move on.

"You were married for a long time, and you're just recently widowed," I said. "What are your plans now? Are you looking forward to sowing your wild oats and just playing the field for a while? Or are you hoping to find someone to develop a relationship with?"

He let out a short laugh. "Wow, I don't think anyone has ever come at me that direct before," he said. "Let me think about that."

I knew it was a bold way to come, but I didn't see the point of wasting either of our time. It was all about clarifying boundaries to protect myself.

By the time we finally decided it was time to leave, I at least liked who Jimmie seemed to be. He opened my car door for me, but he said, "This isn't even me."

I found his unfiltered remark refreshing. "Don't do it if it's not you," I said. "I'd prefer to see who you really are." I'd had my fill of men showing up phony.

When we pulled up outside of Mom's house, it was after two in the morning. Jimmie opened his car's sunroof to the warm September night and we sat there a while longer, enjoying each other's company.

During a lull in the conversation, Jimmie said, "I've got an answer to that question you asked me. I think I'd like to find someone to build a relationship with. Why'd you ask me that?"

"Because I'm not a game player," I said. "If we both want the same thing, there's less chance of either of us getting hurt."

Jimmie said, "Or you could just wait and see how things develop."

"Yeah, but what if things develop and I find I really like you?" I countered. "If all you really wanted was some fun, then we're both left dealing with a lot of emotional junk that wasn't necessary."

By now Jimmie was laughing. "I can see you're going to be something else to deal with," he said. He reached across the seat and hugged me.

Before I got out of the car, I had one more question. "By the way, how old are you?"

"Why, you trying to figure out if I'm too old for you? I'm fifty-two. You gonna tell me your age?" When I told him I was forty, he asked, "So what do you think? Am I too old?"

Instead of answering, I leaned over, kissed him on the cheek, and said goodnight.

After that evening, our relationship and our love for each other grew quickly. We talked on the phone for about a month. We talked about his marriage, his daughter, and his adjustment to being the single parent of a teenage girl. I learned about his family and his work. He wanted to know about my dating life. We talked about my previous marriages. We talked about my job. I told him about what Lester was putting me through. Occasionally he would fall asleep while I was talking. I'd hear him snoring, and I would quietly hang up the phone.

One evening, he declared, "Girl, I can't take this talking on the telephone to you anymore. I need to come see you."

I was flattered by the urgency in his voice, and I was also feeling hopeful about our relationship going forward. I wanted the boys to meet him, so I told them about his upcoming visit. Seven-year-old Clinton had one criterion: "He'd better like Spud, or he can't be your boyfriend," he said.

When Jimmie came to visit, I arranged for my boys to stay with my cousin. Jimmie and I had dinner at a popular Chicago restaurant, Portillo's.

We came back to my townhouse, and he gave me a bottle of wine, which I never drank. We sat on the floor in my living room watching TV until he nodded off. I watched him sleep for a little while and then nudged him. He said he was going to stay at a hotel, but I offered to let him stay at our house in Canthon's room.

The next morning we went out for breakfast, toured Streamwood, and went to get the boys. Jimmie took them into the yard to toss around a football, which was a great start to winning their affection.

Clint ran up to me and whispered, "Did he like Spud?"

"Yeah, Clinton," I whispered back. "He liked Spud."

Clinton said, "Good, because I think he's nice." He paused. "But how *old* is he?"

I had never met a man as genuine as Jimmie. His sincerity and unabashed affection for me took my breath away. He treated me like I was a brand-new experience in his life, which I found so refreshing. When we were together, either in Streamwood or in Dixon, we were inseparable—and when we couldn't be together, we talked on the phone for hours. If Jimmie had time off, he spent it with me. When he came to visit and the boys had games or activities, he was right there next to me cheering them on. No other man in my life, including the boys' own father, had ever stood by me or my sons like that.

A few months after we started dating, I got to my office and my telephone was ringing. It was the Streamwood High School assistant principal. Canthon had gotten into a fight at school, they were going to suspend him, and they wanted me to come get him. I was getting worn out with Canthon's antics. I closed my office door and allowed myself a few moments to cry.

My telephone rang again, and this time it was Jimmie, calling after his night shift before he went to bed. He heard the trouble in my voice and said, "Baby, what's wrong? You okay?"

I shared what I'd just learned. Without hesitation Jimmie said, "I'll meet you there."

Jimmie's voice and assurance gave me an immediate surge of relief. I backtracked my morning commute, and by the time I made it to the school parking lot, Jimmie was pulling in at the same time—he had to have been flying.

We walked into the school like a united front. Jimmie asked me to let him do the talking, which I did. When we left the school with Canthon, Jimmie told me, "You go on back to work and let me handle Canthon." So I did.

As I rode the train back into the city, I felt a sense of calm wash over me. When I got home from work that evening, Jimmie was asleep, and Canthon was in his room doing homework. Neither of them ever shared what had transpired between them, and I never asked. I was content just knowing there was someone standing with me when it came to the boys. I wasn't alone. From that point on, Jimmie would be there.

Even with Jimmie's moral support, though, I was struggling to balance my roles at work and at home. Money was tight, and my finances were often on my mind. I needed Canthon to watch Clinton whenever I was traveling, but I learned that Canthon often used my work trips as carte blanche to run wild, leaving Clinton alone in the evenings. This was unacceptable, and my threats weren't working.

Just when I was at my wit's end, my cousin Evelyn, my confidante, announced that she was getting a divorce and moving to Elgin, just a ten-minute drive from our home in Streamwood. I wasn't celebrating the demise of Evelyn's marriage, but she was my ram in the bush—she was willing to help me out, keep an eye out for Clinton, and put my mind at ease. Evelyn had five children and had been married to a Kodak executive, so she didn't have to work. After her move, she'd often pick Clinton up and keep him at her house until I got home. She had twin boys who were just a few years older than Clinton, so they became very close. Her presence was a godsend.

• • •

One of my favorite aspects of my work was helping to investigate and manage the Equal Employment Opportunity (EEO) charges that came across Lester's desk. Large companies with deep pockets, like MCI, were frequently sued. Whenever anybody filed a complaint, the EEOC would begin an investigation. I worked with our legal team to write responses and prepare for depositions.

Our DC legal team was often frustrated by the inconsistency and lack of detail in the HR investigation notes. I saw how things could be improved, and I suggested that I be the one to conduct all the high-level investigations and provide written responses. I wanted to help with these investigations and run them in order to standardize procedure and reporting. I even received training from our corporate legal team. Lester thought it was a good idea and suggested that I present the plan at his next manager's meeting.

During that meeting where I presented this new process, however, everyone was offended. They thought I was taking away learning experiences from the HR generalists. Even Francine, my mentor, joined the other HR senior managers in calling for a vote on whether or not what I was doing was fair. It was unanimous—everyone voted against me.

Lester turned to me and said, "Well, they have spoken." Then he left the room.

I was so humiliated. Lester and I had gone over my plan together, but he hadn't even attempted to support me or justify what we had discussed. I just sat there. I was devastated, but I refused to show it.

Lester may have thrown me under the bus in that meeting, but he was still being far too friendly to me in private. Things were growing more and more uncomfortable. I confided in Francine about my situation, and she said that in order to file a complaint, I would first have to be willing to confront Lester, telling him he was making me uncomfortable. This baffled me—wasn't one of the purposes of HR to protect me from being in these confrontational situations?

But one day Lester summoned me to his office to discuss some made-up issue about the relocation budget. When I arrived, Lester looked up and said, "Girl, you are always so impeccably dressed. Turn around and let me see how that dress is fitting you."

I'd had enough.

I just glared at him. "Do you want to go over the budget or not?"

"Oh yeah, but you come in here looking so good, it made me forget what I wanted. Sit down, sit down."

I remained standing. I said, "Lester, I'm sorry, but I'm not going to sit down until you stop talking to me so disrespectfully. I don't appreciate all your lewd comments. They make me uncomfortable, and if you don't stop I'm going to have to report you."

Quickly, his tone hardened. "Wait a minute. What do you mean, 'report me'?"

At this point I had very little knowledge of HR practices, but thanks to Francine, I knew how to respond. I said, "The way you talk to me and treat me has everyone assuming something is going on between us. It makes me very uncomfortable. It's sexual harassment, and it has to stop."

Lester said, "Come on, you're no spring chicken. You should know when a man is complimenting you. I do know the difference, and I am *not* sexually harassing you!"

I turned and walked out of his office. After that meeting, I only entered Lester's office if his assistant came in with me. I stopped responding to all his frivolous requests, so he began coming down to the HR floor looking for reasons to stop by my office. His assistant would call me and say, "He's on the hunt." Either I would hide in the bathroom, go to someone else's office, or have someone else be present in my office. I felt like I was being stalked.

In May of 1993, after more than a year of working under Lester, I pursued the first viable opportunity to get away from him. At Francine's encouragement, I posted for an HR generalist position in the newly created Multi-National Division. If I got the job, people would know that I'd gotten it through the regular channels, and nobody could doubt me anymore. There would be no more special appointments for me.

The person in charge of hiring for this HR generalist position was the eastern region HR director, Jonathan, who lived in Rye Brook, New York. He flew into O'Hare Airport and did interviews from the United Airlines Members Club.

Jonathan was an African American man with a stellar reputation; he was rumored to be a heartbeat away from being the head of HR for all US operations. I took the train to O'Hare to meet with him in the Members Club for my interview.

Jonathan asked me about my present responsibilities, and then he conducted a thorough line of questioning about my work history, personal interests, and career aspirations. After that, he explained what he was looking for in a candidate for the open position.

As always, I was determined to be transparent. "I want you to be fully aware," I said, "I don't have prior HR generalist experience, and I don't meet all the requirements of the position description."

He looked at me evenly and said, "Don't worry, I've done my homework on you. Your work with the legal team hasn't gone unnoticed. I need someone here in Chicago who knows how to make things happen, aggressively handles their work, and is professional and intelligent enough to know how to work with the executives here. The person in this role will only escalate issues when I need to get involved. Otherwise, I need someone who can run their business."

He stood up, extended his hand for a final handshake, and said, "I have several others to interview before I fly back. I'll be in touch."

The interview had lasted less time than my train ride to get there. Replaying our conversation in my mind, I felt certain all I would get from Jonathan would be a form email telling me he'd gone with another candidate. I figured the moment he perused my résumé and saw I had no degree, it would be over.

Two weeks following the interview, Jonathan called my office. "Are you ready to dig in and learn the HR business?"

"Absolutely!" I said. I was so excited I could barely breathe.

Jonathan began to spell out what to expect from him. The expectation was for me to remain in the Michigan Avenue office and keep Jonathan apprised of what was happening and what he needed to know.

"I hope you're ready to work. There's a lot to be accomplished, and I expect you to do this job and learn HR as you go. I believe you can do it," Jonathan said. "To help you, I'm setting up a certification class for you and a few others to take. There will be study groups and tests you'll need to pass. If you need any help, let me know. Otherwise, when it's time, you'll go into Washington for the final exam and receive your SHRM certification and membership. Are you ready? I need you to be my eyes and ears in Chicago."

"I'm definitely ready," I assured him, wondering what in the world "sherm" was.

When I told Francine about getting the position, she congratulated me and told me Jonathan had been referring to SHRM, Society for Human Resource Management.

Back when Lester had found out I was posting for the position, he'd tried to tell me, "Jonathan's a lot tougher than I am. You should probably work for me for another year, and I'll make sure you're ready for a step like this."

Now, once Lester found out I'd accepted the position, he called my office, sounding like a slighted lover. "So you went ahead and went with Jonathan. Why, because he's single and younger than me?" I hung up the phone.

Soon after I stopped reporting to Lester, he called me at home. He said, "You know, I used to be in the military, and I know how to find people even when they don't want to be found."

"What are you talking about?" I asked.

He hung up without giving an answer. As far as I was concerned, that was a threat.

Even once I was reporting to Jonathan, I sat in the same office. Lester would call me asking for details I was no longer responsible for. For three months things went on this way.

Finally, I decided to tell Jonathan the full story. I didn't know if he knew about Lester or his behavior, but I knew I needed protection. I hated bringing this baggage to my new boss, but I called Jonathan and told him everything. I asked him to please intercede for me, because Lester's behavior was becoming more possessive and frightening. Jonathan assured me he would talk to Lester and handle things for me. I trusted that would put an end to Lester's harassment.

But by the end of the week, Lester called me again, saying, "Say, there's an art festival going on outside. You want to go with me to help me pick out some artwork for my office?"

I lost it. I yelled into the phone, "Lester, leave me the fuck alone!" I slammed the phone down, grabbed my coat, and left the office for the rest of the day. When I got home, I called Jonathan and told him I was not returning to that office.

I was quickly transferred from the Michigan Avenue office to the Rosemont office, where the Multi-National sales team was housed. The Rosemont office was just a half-hour drive from home, so everything improved after that.

My new role was exciting and allowed me to thrive. As I got further into HR, I realized it was where I should have been all along. I had a sense of compassion, but I also learned how to listen to protect the company and find equitable solutions while remaining objective.

Working for Jonathan, I had a sense of autonomy. I was the HR business partner for the Multi-National Division, supporting the sales team members and the leadership team, including the president. I had full HR responsibilities for the Great Lakes region, which included Illinois, Indiana, Wisconsin, Minnesota, and Ohio.

• • •

Seasons passed—summer of 1993 brought a trip to Jamaica with Jimmie. When Jimmie had first asked me to go to Jamaica, I declined. I couldn't afford a trip to Jamaica. Jimmie quickly solved that problem, saying, "This is on me. I just want you to go with me." But I was still determined to pay my own way, despite my financial difficulties at the time, so I tried to put aside a little money every month for the vacation. Despite my best efforts, though, once we got there I had about fifty dollars. Jimmie paid for everything and simply handed me the cash I would need. I felt so reassured—not by the money itself, but by the sense of being taken care of. As independent as I was, I still wanted to be taken care of; Jimmie always stepped up and did that for me. We continued to grow even closer and more committed to each other.

That fall, Preston decided to quit school and got a full-time job with Sony in a town very close to Streamwood. To help save money, he moved in with us. I kept on balancing my work, travel, parenthood, and my relationship with Jimmie through the winter and into spring.

• • •

In March of 1994, my Uncle Narvell's year-long battle with lung cancer was advancing. Aunt Kathleen called me and said in her usual quiet manner, "Versie, Narvell needs you to come home." My heart dropped. Without question I dropped everything and responded to her call. Jimmie took vacation days and drove me to Kansas City to be with my uncle during his final time on earth as his struggle with lung cancer drew to a close. My uncle had been my first father, and I was thankful to be included as though I was really one of his children.

When we arrived, Uncle Narvell was in the hospital, so I asked to take my turn staying overnight with him so I could give Aunt Kathleen and his children a break. He asked me to read Psalm 23 for him. I read it, and I continued reading every chapter in the book of Psalms until he said it was enough.

After returning home to Streamwood, I planned a family conference call to hold a prayer vigil for Uncle Narvell's healing, but Aunt Kathleen called me the evening beforehand and asked me not to do it. "Versie," she said, "let him go. He's ready to go, and you just have to release him."

Two weeks later—on April 23, 1994—Uncle Narvell transitioned to his eternal home. Jimmie was the first person I called after I received the news. He was my rock during my grief. He took off work again and drove me back to Kansas City for the funeral services. I was unable to believe my uncle was gone. I kept saying to Jimmie, "Maybe if I don't go, he won't be dead."

When we pulled into the long driveway to their big house on Cleveland Avenue, it was so hard to walk in and not find Uncle Narvell sitting in the corner of the kitchen, smoking a cigarette and drinking his Coca-Cola. When I stepped into the kitchen, I instinctively looked to his usual sitting place, picturing him there. I immediately broke down crying.

My mother was standing at the sink, doing dishes. When I began to cry she spoke to someone else in the kitchen, her tone cold and stern. "Someone get her out of here with all that crying!" she said. Then she turned to me and said, "Just shut up! If you're going to cry, take it outside!"

I ran upstairs to Uncle Narvell and Aunt Kathleen's bedroom, trying to convince myself that he was really gone. I was still crying and hugging Uncle Narvell's pillow when Aunt Kathleen came into the room and patted me and rubbed my head.

I wanted to comfort her, but I couldn't stop crying. When I was finally spent, I said weakly, "Why couldn't it be Uncle Jesse instead of Uncle Narvell?"

Aunt Kathleen said quietly, "Oh, Versie, that's not right."

I knew that, but I couldn't help wishing I could rearrange life's pieces. I loved the way Uncle Narvell had always seen the world. There was a greatness inside of him that was never fully developed or released. He lived his dreams and accomplished a lot, but he still had dreams that were never lived. He was a self-taught small business owner, a curious intellectual with a brilliant mind. I was proud of him. I knew I would forever miss our debates, but most of all I would miss how he made me feel. I had never felt a loss so deeply. During the funeral and throughout my weeks of deep grief, Jimmie was by my side.

• • •

Shortly after Uncle Narvell's death, MCI went through another reorganization. The Multi-National Division was no longer going to be a separate entity, but would instead be collapsed back into the rest of the organization, and all the support teams were to be absorbed back into the business.

Eighty percent of the people in the Rosemont office were given severance packages. My letter gave me a reassignment: I would return to Lester's HR department. But I had no intentions of returning to the scene of that crime.

I decided I was going to fight back. I had shared the instances of Lester's sexual harassment with just a small group of people, but now it was time for a different approach. I decided that when it came to my livelihood, I was going to make some noise. I followed protocol and filed an internal complaint with HR. I also sent a letter to the CEO of MCI and the head of our legal team so that top executives would know how their keeper of the keys was behaving.

Lester had been hired in the first place in response to outcries for more racial diversity in upper management positions at MCI, so the company was reluctant to go after him. I was asked again to take the position originally offered to me, with the promise that Lester would be closely monitored.

I wasn't willing to trust anyone to look out for me, because I wasn't sure what Lester was capable of. I remembered his threatening phone calls, his lewd comments. I adamantly refused. I was appalled that he was being protected and that I was being made the sacrificial lamb. I sought outside legal advice and was told that unless I'd been raped, there was no case. This was soon after Clarence Thomas's Supreme Court confirmation hearings; one lawyer asked me, "Who do you think you are, Anita Hill?"

I sat at home for a couple of weeks, being paid while they figured out what to do with me. Finally, I was offered a position as a training manager, doing what I'd done in Cedar Rapids. The problem with this offer was that the job would be based in Atlanta, Georgia. The boys and I would have to relocate to Atlanta, and then I'd be traveling all over the Southeast region doing training. I had no support system in Atlanta. I had an eight-year-old and a seventeen-year-old who both needed some degree of supervision. Atlanta simply wasn't going to work for me. By now I was exhausted, disillusioned, and ready to get off the corporate rollercoaster.

I also had my relationship with Jimmie to consider. When we talked about the future, we envisioned Jimmie joining me in Chicago, but that couldn't happen until after he retired, which was at least two years away. Those were our plans, but I wanted to be sure God's plans were ruling our life and our future, so I prayed, "God, if this is the man you have for me, please make a way for us to come together on your schedule and not ours."

After weeks of conversations and considering my options, I took a weekend by myself to fast and pray. I cut off all outside distractions so I could be alone with my thoughts and God. I thought about what I truly felt called to do. Aunt Tutta's prophecy lingered in my mind, and I wanted to change my path to see if I could fulfill it at last.

By the end of the weekend, I had clarity. I was at complete peace. I needed to live life on my terms for a while. I was tired of corporate politics and hostility and worrying about the welfare of my sons while I traveled. I was tired of everything. While they were trying to figure out what to do with me, I had quietly and with much faith written out a new plan for my life.

I had decided to move back home to Dixon. I wanted go back to college and get my degree in preparation to become a Christian counselor. I always had women seeking me out for advice and guidance. Back in Cedar Rapids, I had coached and mentored so many individuals that Mom joked I should hang out a shingle. I realized I had a gift for strengthening and encouraging people who were wavering in their faith. As an HR generalist, my passion for helping others see their gifts in the workplace was magnified. I felt like I finally knew the career path that justified completing my college degree, and this was the perfect time to do it. Moving back to Dixon would also give me a chance to see where Jimmie and I stood.

I wrote my plan down on a piece of paper, describing in detail what housing I wanted and my budget. Then, as I'd done so many times by now, I stepped out on faith.

This time I was able to draw a line in the sand. I turned down both of MCI's offers and got a severance package. My mother and Jimmie both offered to let me live with them, and although this definitely would have lightened my financial burden, I hadn't forgotten my promise to myself, made more than two decades before, never to live with my mother—and I had no intention of living with Jimmie before he had made a commitment.

Once I made my decision, I visited Dixon to talk through my plans with my mother. We sat on the steps of her front porch, talking like two distant friends. I told her about my weekend of prayer and how I'd come to my next move.

She didn't give me much of a reaction, just saying "Mmhmm" now and then. But when I laid out my three-year plan and told her I'd decided to return to school, she was hooked. She said, "I'm so glad to hear that." From my mother, this was an ecstatic reaction. She asked just one question: "So what do you need me to do?"

"I just need you to find me a place to live." I explained what I was looking for and what I was willing to pay. "The sooner you complete your assignment, the sooner we can move," I said.

Mom took her assignment seriously. About a month and a half in, after finding two other places that weren't what I wanted, she called me and said, "A teacher friend of mine is renting out her mother's house, but I'm not sure it's in your price range, and I don't think it has a private bathroom for you. Do you want me to check on it?"

I told her I could come that weekend to see the house. It was an older, two-story home with a screened-in front porch and an unattached garage. Upstairs, it had three bedrooms and one bathroom. When my mother's friend guided me into the fourth bedroom—downstairs, off the kitchen—and showed me the small full bathroom off the bedroom, I was excited. The house had everything I had written on my piece of paper, except the necessary appliances—we would need a washer, a dryer, a refrigerator, and a TV, as I'd given Preston our television when he moved into his own apartment near Streamwood.

The rent for this house was $400 a month. Based on an income from child support, severance, and unemployment, I said honestly that I'd only budgeted $300. "Can you do $350?" the woman asked. I said I could.

Now we had a home to live in. I asked Jimmie about the best place to get appliances, and he took me to Farley's Appliance store, where I priced out what we'd need and figured the monthly payments into my budget. I figured I could decide later if I would make monthly payments or use my severance money to pay for those items. With that, I'd checked everything off my list. I was ready.

After many years, many trials, and many successes, I was heading back home to Dixon.

chapter 19

SOMETHING WORTH FIGHTING FOR

On a warm day in June 1994, Jimmie, the boys, and some of Canthon's friends loaded up the U-Haul I'd rented and headed to Dixon. Once we were in town, while our U-Haul was being unloaded, a truck from Farley's Appliance pulled up. The delivery man pulled up the truck gate to reveal a brand-new side-by-side refrigerator, a washer, a dryer, and a new TV, the kind the boys desperately wanted—with a picture-in-a-picture feature so they could watch two sports games at once. Jimmie stood in the driveway watching me, a sly smile on his face. The driver said, "Jimmie Brooks?"

Jimmie just said, "Yeah, that's me." He had already paid for everything. I was speechless. While the delivery men unloaded all my appliances, I went over and wrapped my arms around Jimmie.

Life in Dixon was peaceful, except for the rumors floating around about us moving back. We spent the summer before I began classes relaxing and enjoying time with family. The pastor of Second Baptist Church came by a few times and took Clint fishing. It was a new calm for me.

Canthon was reluctant to leave his Streamwood "posse," as Jimmie called his large group of friends—but Dixon was glad to have him. Canthon's entrance onto the Dixon High School basketball team made the front page of the sports section in the *Dixon Evening Telegraph*. He was the grandson of Zelodious Ashford, trailblazing black schoolteacher and now Lee County Board member, and godson to Dixon High School's 1960s star football player. This made him hometown royalty.

Clinton loved living in Dixon. Now he could walk to his grandmother's house whenever he wanted to and hang out with his cousins. He adored Jimmie, and Jimmie was always around. Clinton made a summer league baseball team, and Jimmie went to every game when he wasn't working. A few months after we were all settled in, Clinton crawled into bed with me to say goodnight. "I like it here, Mom," he said. "I'm finally not afraid anymore." I hugged him tight. It felt good to know I'd made the right decision for my baby boy.

Life wasn't so idyllic between Jimmie and his daughter. Kelley had lost her mother in her most vulnerable teen years, and she resented the role I was playing in her father's life. She was rebellious, creating tension between father and daughter that was thick enough to cut with a knife. Jimmie couldn't control her. He often came to my house just to get some sleep, because when she had friends over there was always a lot of noise.

In the beginning, being in Dixon was like living in a place separated from reality. For the most part, I felt as though I'd escaped all the ugliness of that other world and the weight of everything had been lifted from my shoulders. Before I could completely bask in my newfound peace, however, I had to address some lingering issues. I didn't walk quietly into the sunset when I departed MCI. I wasn't going to be another victim. My complaints to the corporate legal team and CEO triggered an internal investigation. I also filed an EEO charge of sexual harassment against Lester. His actions had impacted my ability to find a viable position within MCI.

I also had to take Greg to court. Now that I had no medical insurance, I had to be sure the boys were fully covered under his, and I needed an increase in child support. These scrimmages took up most of the summer months. As I had expected, Greg resisted, doing everything in his power not to give his sons anything. He spent the summer wreaking havoc in our life, demanding visitation with Clinton, who hadn't seen or talked to his dad in several years and had no interest in being forced to go to his house now. We went to court several times. He glowered at me in disgust and never spoke to me, but he didn't faze me anymore. And every time I had to go to court, Jimmie was by my side. The child support increase was granted, and shortly afterwards Greg stopped coming to get Clinton.

Aside from these unpleasant legal proceedings, though, I loved the peacefulness of being back home. Having family around made me realize how much I'd missed that sense of community. My mother often stopped by for a cup of tea and conversation.

I think she was happy I was close by, yet she still had her same old sharp tongue, and so I kept my guard up, knowing I could be ambushed if I relaxed. Melvin had started calling her "Mom" rather than "Aunt Zee." On a phone call with my mother, I made the mistake of asking her about it. "What's up with Melvin suddenly calling you Mom?"

She said, "Well, he's maturing and finally realizing what it means to have a mother." She was completely calm in her response, and I dropped it. I had only asked out of curiosity.

But a few weeks later, I stopped by her house with Jimmie's daughter. As we were leaving, out of nowhere, Mom lashed out at me in a nasty tone. "And you leave my other children alone! Don't you start intimidating Melvin for calling me 'Mom.' You're just so jealous!"

Why had she waited until now, rather than saying something to me in our private conversation earlier? I was embarrassed for Kelley to witness this exchange between me and my mother. I didn't say a word—I just left, feeling belittled and remembering what my mother was capable of.

That fall, I enrolled in classes at Sauk Valley Community College. I loved being back in school full time. Despite being older than the other students, I felt like I was picking up from where I'd left off twenty-three years earlier. I was planning to major in psychology and counseling, so I took the classes required for that major. The younger students and our professors often asked me to share my real-life experiences in the corporate jungle. As usual, I used my voice to speak out to college officials against unreasonable expectations for required classes. Why should I have to take an algebra class? Who decided algebra was the gateway to success? In my twenty-year career, I had never used algebra. All I'd needed was a calculator. Why did I need to take a physical education course? I was a forty-two-year-old woman.

I took a speech class, which I enjoyed, and I became close with my psychology professor. I wrote a paper for his class about diversity, and he was curious about the topic. I frequently stopped by his office so we could talk about my career goals, the diversity work I'd done in my jobs, and the psychology of diversity in the workplace. I loved being able to take morning classes and be home by early afternoon when Clint got in from school so we could do our homework together.

• • •

In early November, we got a call saying Jimmie's house was on fire. We rushed over there to find fire trucks surrounding the smoking building. His daughter was pacing and sobbing, while Jimmie was trying to get some understanding of what had caused the fire. I went over and tried to calm Kelley down. I put my arms around her and said, "Don't cry, it's just stuff that can be replaced—I'm just glad you're okay."

She pushed me away and glared at me. "What do you know about anything?" she said. "I hate you!"

The house hadn't been totally destroyed, but the bedrooms had been significantly charred, and the water from the firefighters' hoses had added water damage. Jimmie came to live with us, and his daughter stayed with her friends.

After the fire, I began to see a marked difference in Jimmie's demeanor. He wouldn't talk about what had happened. The insurance paperwork was tedious, and he didn't have the patience for it. Yet I knew that if it didn't get completed, he would never completely regain what he'd lost—so I pressured him for details while I scoured catalogs and visited stores in order to help him recoup the costs of his lost possessions. The more questions I asked, the nastier he acted. I kept reminding him, "I'm doing this for you." Sometimes you can't really know a person until you see them when trouble hits.

Still, there was a sense of family between us. He worked his crazy hours, and I made sure he could get the sleep he needed, he had clean clothes, and he ate hot meals. We shared a happy Thanksgiving and Christmas together.

I made the Dean's List my first semester, but my unemployment benefits were ending. The plan I'd laid out in my spirit had been to go to school, but I hadn't thought of running out of money. Now I was faced with a dilemma: I couldn't afford to have no income and keep going to school. I couldn't qualify for any other educational assistance until I had a 1099 showing I had no income. I could live on public aid, but I'd never done that, and I just wasn't willing to start. I sought out every scholarship and grant available, but all I qualified for was a Displaced Worker's Grant that paid for my books.

I started looking for a job. I knew my expenses, and I concluded that if I could find a job that paid at least $25K a year, I would take it and go to school part time. I found a job advertised in the paper for a training manager position at Kreider Services, a human services facility providing direct care to people with developmental disabilities. I submitted my résumé and got an interview—but then a friend from church told me the salary would be just $13K per year. I had my boundary set, and that salary just wasn't going to make it worth it to defer my education.

I was expected to create a training vignette to present as part of my interview, and I thought about just canceling the interview—it seemed like too much effort for a job I probably wouldn't accept. But then my friend Bonita called me the night before the interview and convinced me to prepare for the interview. She urged me to trust God to reveal His plan to me. We prayed together, and I stayed up all night creating my presentation.

Two weeks later I had a job offer from Kreider Services for $26K a year. They also said that I could finish out the spring semester at Sauk Valley, given that I was already enrolled. At my new job, I shared an office with another trainer in a brick office on the outskirts of Dixon. On the days I had classes, I was allowed to leave work to attend school.

My job was to develop and deliver training for the caseworkers on how to manage the staff working under them to administer care to patients; these caseworkers needed education on how to hire and manage staff members and dismiss them when necessary.

I started off by trying to get a thorough knowledge of Kreider's day-to-day operations, spending time in the individual homes trying to understand some of the issues the caseworkers and staff members were experiencing. One of the first training topics I developed was diversity training. I created a program to address awareness and sensitivity around race, physical ability, socioeconomic background, and other issues. I talked with them about biases and where they come from, along with how biases could influence their decisions. We talked about privilege and put their backgrounds in context when it came to how they treated patients.

My schedule was working out well, but I knew this was the last semester I'd be allowed to take a full-time course load. I resented having to detract from my educational goals by working at Kreider Services. I felt like I was betraying my purpose. I spoke to Jimmie about my frustration. "I really just want to be able to go to school full time and not work." He had always been so good at helping me talk through things. This time he just said, "Well, go to school full time then."

Jimmie, rather than being my anchor in the storm as usual, was growing more and more distant. In early February of 1995, I learned that one of my and Jimmie's mutual friends had died. I'd known her family my whole life, but her older sister hated my family, for reasons I was never sure of, as she was a woman I had a great deal of respect for. I thought Canthon's arrival on the Dixon basketball scene, which took some of the spotlight off her own son, might have been an issue. Jimmie suggested we should go to the family's house to bring them something to eat and offer our condolences, and I finally agreed, hoping the older sister's hard feelings wouldn't make things uncomfortable.

We stopped by with a bucket of chicken, and the moment we walked in, I felt icy stares on me. I found a seat on the couch and stayed there, speaking only when spoken to. Jimmie, on the other hand, was greeted warmly. I heard him talking to a white woman I didn't know in the kitchen, asking after the woman's mother and sister. It was obvious he knew her well, but he downplayed this when I asked him about it later. "I just know her, that's all," he said. I knew he was lying.

For the rest of the week, Jimmie went over to the house to spend time with the mourning family. He drove his car for the funeral procession, taking time off work to do so. The evening of the funeral, I went back to the house with him. I didn't stay long, but Jimmie stayed—and that night, he never came home.

I didn't sleep much all night, wondering where he was. It felt like déjà vu. The next day I stopped home around lunchtime after my morning class, and Jimmie came in. "Where have you been?" I asked.

"I just wanted to get out," he said. "I went to a bar and then went back to my house and slept on the floor because I didn't want to deal with all this."

I calmly sat down at the kitchen table and said, "I can promise you I'm not about to start living this way. If you want to be free, then do it, but don't start this shit with me."

He shook his head and said, "I just felt like going out."

I left to go to work, not truly believing his explanation. The seed of doubt was planted.

I felt Jimmie drawing further and further away from me. He didn't pull any more disappearing acts, but he wasn't the same Jimmie. He was colder, more distant. I was also growing frustrated with my life as my plans deteriorated. I knew I wasn't going to be able to continue going to school while I held a full-time job. When the spring semester ended I signed up for evening classes, but I was unable to stay focused in the three-hour night classes after a long day of work. When I considered my state of mind and looked at my financial situation, I knew I wouldn't be continuing classes that next semester.

I wasn't doing what I'd come to Dixon to do, and I was growing more frustrated about it every day. Soon I was in a perpetual state of discontent. I was angry with myself for not having the bold faith to stick to my plan, regardless of the circumstances. I had doubts, wondering whether maybe I should have swallowed my pride and gone on public assistance. I was screaming out to God for some answers. I had stepped out on faith—where was God? Why was everything, once again, falling apart?

By late April, Jimmie's house was nearly ready for him to move back into, and I was wondering where we were going in our relationship. I was totally committed to Jimmie, but I wanted to be his wife, not his shack-up.

One Sunday as I was getting ready to go to church, I started a conversation about our future. I leaned over and kissed Jimmie and told him I loved him. He was silent. I asked, "Don't you love me?"

"No," he said coldly. "No I don't."

I was floored. I asked, "Don't you want to get married?"

He responded, "You know you don't want to marry me."

"Why do you think I came here?" I asked. He mumbled something back I couldn't hear.

"*Wow*," I said. That was all I could say, but inside I felt like he'd just slammed me against the wall. I was shaken to my core. I finished getting ready and left for church. I thought about his words for the entire church service, turning them over in my mind. I felt sick.

When I got back to the house, Jimmie was watching a football game with the boys. I called him into the bedroom to talk further. I saw blankness in his expression I'd never seen before. I asked him what was going on, but he acted like nothing had happened. He brushed past me, saying, "There you go, you know I didn't mean it."

His words echoed in my head for days—I knew what he'd said had flowed from what was in his heart. When had Jimmie reached this decision? What were we all about, and what was I doing? Everything had been called into question.

I had encouraged Jimmie several times to rent out his smaller house and move in with us, but he'd always resisted. Once his house was repaired, he wanted to know if I was moving in with him. "I need to think about it," I said. I was hurt that I'd done all the work to get him reimbursed by his insurance, and yet now that it was fixed, he hadn't even invited me to see it.

And then, while I was dropping off some groceries at Uncle Jesse's house—he lived kitty-corner to Jimmie—I saw a car pull up at Jimmie's house, and two women got out.

I watched as Jimmie took the two women into his house. Under normal circumstances this wouldn't have bothered me, but with everything else going on these past few months between Jimmie, my job, and school, this was the final straw. He hadn't even invited me to see his house yet, and here he was inviting these two women in to see the place. It wasn't any sense of jealousy that was fueling my anger—it was the disrespect and the harsh words he had spoken earlier that fueled a rage that had to be released.

By the time Jimmie returned to my house, I was ready for a full-on confrontation. I push a lot down, but when I let out everything I've been holding in, it's like a volcanic explosion.

Jimmie deflected everything. He thought I was being petty, and he refused to take it. I hadn't even asked to see the house, he pointed out. I said I shouldn't have had to ask. I told him I didn't believe he could have ever taken what he'd been dishing out these last few months. He acted like he didn't know what I was talking about. He took no blame for anything, and I was sick of the pain his behavior was causing me. I told him I wasn't taking any more from him. "Anything dead should be buried. Now that you've got your house back," I yelled, "you can just get on with your life. I'm not going to be your shack-up—I know I'm better than that. Get your stuff and get out!"

Jimmie didn't flinch; he didn't try to dissuade me. He immediately moved out and moved on, like it was a relief. I had never in a million years believed this argument would take us down the path it did.

During the two and a half years Jimmie and I had been dating, we hadn't had any major disagreements. We always seemed to just flow. I thought what we had together was strong and that our love could take a licking and keep on ticking. To see our relationship fall apart so quickly and seemingly so easily called all my beliefs about what we'd shared into question. I was shocked, and when the reality of what had happened set in, I was deeply saddened. I felt like I'd been abandoned once again.

Clinton was devastated. He said to me, "Mommy, what did you do? Is Jimmie ever coming back? Go tell him it's okay, he can come back." My heart broke for myself and for my boys.

Everybody knew. Everybody in Dixon talked about us. I avoided people so I wouldn't have to have conversations about what had happened between Jimmie and me.

Life was suddenly totally different; so much stood in limbo. Jimmie and I had been planning another trip to Jamaica with several couples, and we hadn't discussed if we'd still be going ahead as planned. Jimmie still attended Clinton's softball games, although now he stayed in his car, watching from a rolled-down window.

A few weeks after Jimmie moved out, I made the Dean's List again. It was published in the paper, and Jimmie called to congratulate me and ask to take me out to a celebratory dinner. I was filled with hope, my stomach tight with nerves when he picked me up. I was sure this would be the beginning of conversation to reunite.

We went to a steakhouse in nearby Sterling, and after dinner Jimmie drove me home and we sat in my driveway and talked in the cool May evening. Jimmie finally expressed some semblance of regret for how we'd ended things, but my heart sank when I realized he didn't want to get back together. Instead, he told me, "I just need some time to myself for a while to see what I really want. Can you give me that?"

Feeling heavy with disappointment, I agreed. We'd come together very soon after his wife's death, so I could understand his feelings—I just wished he'd come to this realization a few years earlier, before I fell in love with him, or done his rebellion in a less hurtful way.

We shared a goodbye kiss, and then I started to think about a different future, one without Jimmie in it.

The coming months would prove nearly unbearable for me. I felt like a complete failure. All of the reasons I'd had for returning to Dixon had evaporated. I was no longer working toward completing my degree. I was no longer with the man I loved. Nothing was working out according to the plan I thought God had given me.

Instead of relying on others, I withdrew into my circle of one. I started a serious walking regimen. Every evening I laced up my sneakers and set out from my house to walk briskly for an hour or more, my breath rising and falling as I moved forward, trying to work through my anger. Sometimes I went to the Dixon High School entrance and ran up and down the steps, my legs burning, fueled by my frustrations and despair.

I questioned God, and I questioned myself. Why should I stay in Dixon? I felt like I had tripped and fallen into a rut I may not be able to pick myself up out of.

The summer wore on, and people kept talking, both to me and about me. Just before Independence Day, someone told me she had seen Jimmie with another woman, but I dismissed this as gossip.

Nothing made sense. I was still in a state of shock that a love I had thought so perfect had crumbled so easily, when I believed that what we had was unbreakable. And what made it even worse was being the subject of gossip and innuendos. People I wasn't even particularly close to would stop by my house and ask what had happened with me and Jimmie.

I needed to get away. I called Bonita and asked if I could spend the Fourth of July with her in Cedar Rapids to be among friendly faces. After I arrived, we went to see a movie. When we returned to her house, before I could get out of the car I dissolved into uncontrollable crying. I needed the safety of someone who truly cared about me to do a deep flush of the pain I was carrying. I was tired of standing strong. "That's the first time I realized how much you loved Jimmie," Bonita would tell me later, "and that you weren't as tough as you seemed."

On the drive back to Dixon, a sense of calm came over me. I had dismissed the rumors that Jimmie might have someone new in his life, but as I drove home, I heard a confirmation in my spirit: "Jimmie has someone in his life." I accepted the truth this time. Once I was home I called Jimmie and left a message saying I wanted to talk to him. I wanted to know the status of our plans for Jamaica, and I wanted to hear from Jimmie's own mouth that he was seeing someone else.

He came by the house several hours later, and we sat down at the kitchen table. I was direct with him.

"I hear you're seeing someone else now," I said.

"Yes I am," Jimmie said, "and there's nothing you can say or do about that to make me change my mind."

Whoa, I thought. Who was this man? "What about our plans for Jamaica?" I asked.

Jimmie acted like nothing had changed between us, saying, "You and I said we were going to go, and I still want us to go. It's already paid for."

I was naturally curious. "What's your girlfriend going to say about that?"

"I don't know," Jimmie shot back. "You want me to ask her how she feels about it?"

I just glared at him, smirked, and shook my head. He was being cocky and arrogant. I'd never seen this side of him before. Jimmie asked me to make a list of everything I would need for the trip, saying he would come by and pick it up. Then he got up to leave as though everything had been settled. When he reached the door, he turned back and asked, "We're going, right?"

I nodded, but I was seething. I had no idea what he thought would happen in Jamaica, but he clearly didn't know who he was dealing with.

The plan was for the whole group—me and Jimmie, George and Sylvia, and the others—to ride in a rented bus to O'Hare Airport, leaving at six a.m. The night before we were supposed to leave, Jimmie called the house.

Canthon picked up. He covered the receiver and told me, "Jimmie says he'll pick you up and bring you back to his house to catch the bus."

"No, tell him you'll bring me to his place in the morning," I said to Canthon. He raised his eyebrows and delivered the message. After Canthon hung up, I assured him he wouldn't need to wake up early the next morning.

Morning came, and at 5:45 a.m., the phone rang. It was Sylvia.

She said, "Versie, everyone's here. Are you on your way?"

"No, I'm not going," I said.

There was a long pause on the other end of the line. "Does Jimmie know that?" Sylvia asked.

"I doubt it," I said, "but you can tell him."

"Oh, no," she said as she hung up the phone.

A couple of minutes later, the phone rang again. "Versie, where are you?" Jimmie asked. "You want me to come pick you up?"

"No, I'm not going," I said. Then, using his same cocky words, I said, "And there is nothing you can say or do to make me change my mind about that."

"Come on, Versie, don't do this," he pleaded with me. "Get your things, and I'll come pick you up."

"I told you, I'm not going!" I said. I hung up the telephone.

Within ten minutes, Jimmie was knocking at the back kitchen door. I opened it but kept the outside screen door locked. He said, "You want me to beg? I'm begging. Don't do this. Please get your luggage and come on. Everyone is waiting for you, and we don't want to miss our flight."

"I can't get my luggage, because I never packed," I said coldly. "I told you I'm not going, and I meant it. Now you go on—have a good life, and don't darken my door again!" I shut the door and forced myself not to look out the window after him.

I had made my own vacation plans. After Jimmie left for Jamaica with the rest of them, I took Clinton with me to visit Aunt Kathleen, Candy, and Candy's family in Kansas City. I couldn't stay in Dixon and answer people's questions about why I wasn't in Jamaica.

While we were there, I formed a new resolve to leave Dixon. We would move to Kansas City, I decided. I was ready to get back to the business world. When I returned home, I put my ideas in to action and began sending out résumés for HR jobs in Kansas City. But Jimmie returned from his vacation with new plans, too. He moved his new girlfriend into his house.

I decided that until I left Dixon, I was going to carry myself in a way that would make Jimmie wish he still had me. I made a point of staying away from Jimmie's side of town until Mom took a trip to Europe with Aunt Kathleen and asked me to care for Uncle Jesse for the two weeks that she'd be gone. Every other day I took Uncle Jesse his groceries, checked his medication, and made sure he had everything he needed. I had to pass by Jimmie's house, but I never even glanced in that direction. Once I saw Jimmie mowing his yard, talking to his neighbor, but I just stared straight ahead, not acknowledging I'd seen him.

By early August, I was beginning to feel some healing. I realized I didn't have the answer to why all this was happening, so all I could do was trust God and release my anger and frustration. I was learning to be in a state of forgiveness and faith, trying to be content where I was. I was introduced to a mechanical engineer eight years my junior, and we began to date. He was just a distraction for me, a reminder that I still had it—a movie, a dinner, and friendly conversation were all I wanted from him.

One Saturday afternoon, I was taking advantage of the quiet in the house while Canthon and Clinton were hanging out with friends. I sat in the living room finishing *The Value in the Valley* by Iyanla Vanzant. The book's message—about finding the value in the most difficult times in our lives—was exactly what I had needed to hear. When I closed the book, I felt a total sense of release, like my soul smiled. My solitude no longer felt like a prison. I allowed this feeling to wash over me. I finally felt free of the anger.

Then I decided I needed to get up and get out of the house. I made plans to meet my cousin at the mall. While I was doing my hair and makeup, I heard a knock at the back door.

Instinctively, I smiled and said aloud, "It's Jimmie." When I went to the door and saw it *was* him, my stomach filled with butterflies.

He acted very formal. "I'm sorry," he said, "I hope I'm not interrupting anything. I need the rest of my clothes and my stereo."

"Oh, no problem," I said, being very formal myself. "Everything's in the basement." I stepped aside and allowed him to go down and find his things. We exchanged just a few words before he left.

I was relieved to feel at peace once he had gone—I no longer harbored any animosity toward him, even though I could tell my feelings for him weren't completely gone.

A week later, while Clinton and I were watching a movie and eating popcorn together, Spud started barking. We heard a knock on the back door. Jimmie was back. This time he was looking for some class reunion pictures he thought he might have left behind.

He couldn't keep making these unannounced visits. I needed distance to keep on healing. It didn't help to continue seeing his handsome face, the same face that had captured my heart. Rather than let him come in to look for the pictures, I said I would search for them. "How do you want me to let you know if I find them?" I asked.

"You can just call the house," he said.

"No, I'm not trying to create any trouble with you and your new lady," I said. "I'll give them to George." I walked him out and saw that he had parked not in my driveway, but across the street. "You're obviously afraid of being seen coming in my house," I said angrily, "so don't come over here anymore. I mean it! I don't mess with married men, and you might as well be married."

I found the photos he'd been looking for, and I wrote him a letter.

I reminded him that he had who he wanted to be with now, and it wasn't fair to me to keep stopping by. I asked him to leave me alone so I could get on with my life. I put the letter and the pictures into an envelope and gave them to George to deliver to Jimmie.

A few days later, on a warm August Saturday morning, I was up early, getting ready to meet my cousin to get our hair done. I got in the car and was just about to pull off when I realized I'd left my book on the kitchen table. I ran back into the house to get the book, and as I turned back toward the door to head out, I saw Jimmie coming through the open doorway.

He didn't say a word. He just grabbed me by my shoulders, leaned me against the counter, and kissed me. "Okay, now tell me to my face you don't love me anymore," he said.

My heart raced with surprise and some degree of happiness. I looked back at him and said simply, "I can't say that."

Jimmie pulled me to him again, kissing me and hugging me. When we finally let go of each other, Jimmie asked, "Why did you send me that letter?"

"Your visits are starting to become too regular, and Dixon is too small," I said. "I don't know your girlfriend or what she's capable of, but I don't want any trouble. Why did you suddenly start coming over here, anyway?" The moment filled with tension as reality descended upon me again. Jimmie wasn't mine anymore. Jimmie had someone else now.

But when he spoke, he was the same Jimmie I loved. "I came because I missed you," he said. "Shoot, I still have four tires in your garage. If I had to, I was gonna come get them one at a time."

We laughed together, and I basked in the joy I felt at realizing he still loved me—that he hadn't been able to abandon me so easily.

But things weren't so simple anymore, and after a few moments, our laughter faded. "You have someone else in your life now," I said. "I do still love you, but you can't have me and her too."

Jimmie slumped against the doorframe and pulled me into his arms. "I made a mistake," he said. "I made the wrong choice."

Electricity crackled between us—but I pulled away from him. Seeing him and feeling his arms around me again left me giddy, but I had no intention of being his other woman. I had decided a long time ago that I was worth having on my terms.

"That's not my problem," I said. "I've got to go get my hair done."

I locked up the house and got into my car. Jimmie leaned into the driver's side window and asked, "Can I see you tonight, just to talk?"

I could see he was genuinely troubled by his situation, but until he figured things out, I didn't want to see him. The temptation to fall into his arms was too great.

"No," I said. "I've already got plans for the evening. You need to go home and figure out your life and what you want. In the meantime, I'm seeing someone, and I plan to continue seeing him."

Of course my fling meant nothing to me, but Jimmie didn't need to know that. I felt a twinge of triumph when his face fell.

Every day when I went walking, Jimmie would show up somewhere along my route, following behind me in his car, hoping to talk to me. I didn't know the extent of what he was dealing with, but I knew he had to deal with it himself. I just kept on walking.

After a week or so of this, Sylvia called me early one morning before I'd gotten up for work to say, "Well, I don't know what happened, but Jimmie ended it!" I was confused. I asked what he'd ended. "He told her she had to move out!" That woke me up.

I was flooded with mixed emotions. I spent the rest of the day trying to figure out what would be next for me if Jimmie wanted to get back together. I had been trying to work him out of my system for three months and move far away from him, and now this had thrown everything into question. What did it all mean? I wished I still hated him so I could be protected from ever loving him again.

That night, Jimmie came to my house to tell me the news himself. I acted like I knew nothing. I wanted to hear things from his perspective.

He walked into the kitchen and sat on a stepstool across the room from where I sat at the table. Without preamble he said, "Well, it's over. She's gone. I told her I still loved you."

We sat in silence for a very long time. I was wondering what that meant. I felt the same way I always had: I wanted a relationship that was going somewhere. If Jimmie still wasn't ready for a commitment, then I wanted him to keep on moving. I didn't have any more time to waste on games or playing house.

I broke the silence. "So, what's next? Nothing has changed for me. I still want what I wanted when we broke up, so where does that leave us?"

He walked over to me and pulled me up from my chair. "All I know is

I'm in love with you," he said, "and I'm going to give you everything you want, if you'll let me."

"How do I know I can trust you?" I asked.

He gave the most heartfelt answer: "From this point on, it's just you and me, no one else. I promise."

When we talked about how things had unfolded between us, he said, "I thought when you told me to stay out of your life, that that was it."

When I asked about his behavior leading up to our big argument, the only explanation he ever gave was that he'd just wanted to come and go as he pleased, without a lot of yackety-yak.

I asked him why he'd moved in with another woman, then, instead of just remaining single, and he replied, "She didn't have the same hold on me that you did."

Jimmie told me, "If you'd just come to Jamaica with me, we would have gotten back together."

"That was a chance I wasn't willing to take," I said. "You could have gotten me over there for a great time and then gone right back to your girlfriend. I wasn't about to give you any more chances to make a fool out of me."

I wanted to hear, "I'm sorry I hurt you, can you forgive me?" What I got instead was, "I made a lot of mistakes." I decided that was the closest I would get to an apology.

Jimmie seemed to pick up where we'd left off, becoming the same caring, dependable man I had fallen in love with. He fell into his old routines with the boys, who were thrilled. Yet things were different for me. We came back together, but our love was no longer infallible. Instead of feeling confident, I was cautious. My head was telling me to run, but my heart gave me enough optimism to keep moving forward. A couple of weeks after we had reunited, while we were in bed, Jimmie kissed me softly and held my face in his hands. He said, "I love you so much. I'm so lucky to have you back in my life." I didn't say a word as we lay there holding each other, but I decided that nothing could change the past, and I wouldn't punish him *or* me for it. At that moment, I chose to love Jimmie. Whatever I was still trying to work through was between me and God.

Less than a month later—on September 12, 1995, the three-year anniversary of when we first met, danced, and talked long into the night—Jimmie asked me to marry him.

Jimmie never kept up with sentimental things, like the date we met, even though we each had a mug with the date printed on it. So I was surprised when he expressed regret that he had to work the overnight shift on our special day. He suggested, "Let's go to Al & Leda's for pizza, and then you can drop me off at the bowling alley." That was my favorite meal and the spot where I first told Jimmie I thought I was in love. For Jimmie, that was pretty romantic.

When I picked him up and took him home to get ready for work, I thought, *All this chauffeur service doesn't make sense.* He got out of the car and ran into his house to get his lunch pail and thermos. He came back out, sat on the side steps, and pulled me onto his lap. I remember the sky was dark—no moonlight or stars shining. I stayed sitting between his legs, his arms wrapped around me, and then he turned me around to face him.

He asked, "Do you know what today is?"

I laughed and said, "I do, but I'm surprised *you* do."

He stood up, reached into his pocket, and said, "Versie, will you marry me?"

Before he'd even pulled the ring out of his pocket, I screamed, "Yes!"

He finally got the ring out and put it on my finger. I was laughing like a schoolgirl, and then I ran into his kitchen and turned on the light so I could admire the ring. I ran back outside and kissed him over and over, saying yes over and over. We both just sat there laughing.

I knew Jimmie: He took life as it came, so for him to go out, pick a ring, and plan the day was in some ways as significant as actually asking me to marry him.

When Jimmie and I set about to planning the wedding, he said, "I want this all to be on me." I convinced him to narrow his list of groomsmen from eight men to three: his brother Jerry, his lifelong best friend Ulysses, and George. I asked Bonita, Candy, and Evelyn to stand with me as bridesmaids. I wanted a small, simple autumn ceremony, where I would wear a dressy off-white pantsuit. Jimmie vetoed all of that in favor of a more formal affair in July so his mother "could see her baby boy march down the aisle." He said, "Nobody's wearing a suit but me." I found a very elegant sheath gown and a veil I could afford on my limited budget.

I had always dreamed of an outdoor wedding. One day I saw an ad in the paper saying that White Pines State Park, just a twenty-minute drive from Dixon, offered outdoor weddings. We decided this was where we'd have our ceremony—amidst the natural beauty of the magnificent forest, lush white pine trees, and blue skies.

When my mother learned that Jimmie and I would be getting married, she asked in her usual dismissive way, "So this is what you want, huh?"

"Yes, Mom," I said, irritated. "This is what I want."

I was growing discontent at Kreider Human Services, bored and sick of the off-color racist comments I often heard from my direct supervisor. During the autumn of 1995, a new opportunity presented itself.

Jimmie and George coached a girls' softball team, and one of the team sponsors hosted a dinner for the coaches. Jimmie couldn't go, so I agreed to go in his place. While I was there I was talking about business with the owner of Dixon Autobody. I listened to his concerns and made a few recommendations for ways to start advertising and improve his business practices. He was intrigued by what I was sharing. "I'll write it out for you," I said. After that dinner, I went home, wrote a business plan, and sent it to him.

He liked it and asked, "Would you be interested in working for us?"

Here I was, creating another job for myself. "If I was the business manager, I would be," I said.

"Okay then," he said. "You'll be our business manager."

So I quit my job at Kreider Services on a Friday, and that Monday I went into my new job at Dixon Autobody, where I started evaluating their business practices. I designed a few marketing ideas, began a new process for collecting outstanding debts, and wrote HR policies.

That December, we moved into Jimmie's house. Around the same time, I was served with notice that a former MCI employee was suing me for wrongful termination, so that winter and spring I traveled to Minnesota for the deposition. This is what I used to do, so I knew how to handle myself, answering questions thoroughly but carefully. Once the deposition was over, MCI's attorneys told me they'd been very impressed with my responses. "Have you thought about coming back to the company?" they asked.

I explained what I was going through with Lester—my internal complaint had been resolved in my favor, but the EEO charge was still open—and one of the attorneys said he would look into it.

Our July wedding grew closer, and just a few weeks beforehand, I began having second thoughts. I couldn't kick my fear of being rejected and hurt again.

One day I packed a bag and took it with me to work. Instead of driving home at the end of the day, I drove to visit Bonita in Rockford, where she was living now. I didn't say anything to Jimmie, who was working the night shift. I needed to clear my head.

Bonita suggested that I postpone the wedding until I knew for certain I could trust Jimmie. Nothing was feeling like the right decision to me. I decided to drive home instead of spending the night with Bonita as I'd planned—I wanted to be by myself in my prayer chamber and seek an answer from God.

I got home late and woke up early, before Jimmie had come home from his shift. I decided to go for a drive.

I parked in front of the Dixon Memorial Pool. I cut the engine and just sat quietly in the early morning light. After a while I heard the Holy Spirit speaking to me, saying, "Move through the fear."

That was it. That was the answer I had been waiting to hear. I had to trust that what God had planned for me was on the other side of my fear.

I started the car and went home. Jimmie was sitting in the kitchen drinking a cup of coffee. He looked up at me and said simply, "Are you sure you want to marry me?"

I walked over to him. He stood up and folded me into his arms.

"Yes," I said. "I'm sure."

I couldn't keep looking to Jimmie for my peace and security. There was nothing he could do or say to wipe away my memories of the painful months we'd spent apart. This journey of love and true forgiveness was also one of faith, and I knew God would walk with me.

The day before the wedding, it rained without stopping. It poured from morning to night, all the way through our rehearsal. We had a tent set up in case of inclement weather—but if it kept raining, even that would be a mess. I was afraid my dream of an outdoor wedding would be ruined.

The morning we were to be married, rain fell lightly but steadily. Evelyn, who was my maid of honor, prayed with me for the skies to clear. By noon the rain had stopped, and the skies cleared from gray to blue. We were blessed with a beautifully warm, sun-filled day, with birds singing as though God had sent them to be our background music.

I had designed the entire day around God's promise: "The one I have for you will come to you as a man."

I set the wedding to begin at three p.m., three being symbolic of divine completion. I decided my three sons would be my dowry to share with Jimmie. I had them march into the ceremony in front of me single file—first Clinton, then Canthon, and finally Preston.

I marched in after them alone. I paused at the back row of guest seats, and Jimmie came down the aisle to bring me to the altar with him. The songs I chose were "He Looked Beyond My Faults and Saw My Need" and "I Owe You Me."

Remembering God's message about my true husband, I thought about how Jimmie had come to me as a man. He had given to me unselfishly, never expecting repayment. He never showed any signs of being intimidated by my career—in fact, he encouraged me. He had stood by me through the twists and turns of parenting and death in the family, never once shying away from responsibility or expressing frustration. He had come to me in all his human frailty, with all his imperfections, to accept me as I was, another flawed human being. We had almost nothing in common except our deep love for each other.

Jimmie and I didn't speak the usual wedding vows. Instead, we said vows I'd written, patterned from a book by Marianne Williamson. We asked our immediate family members to stand and speak words of acceptance to each of us. We pledged to call on God often and stay together always, even in death. The entire wedding was designed to speak to the miracle of love that God had given us.

It meant so much to us to have the love and support of our families. The boys had grown completely attached to Jimmie. Everyone saw how he made me laugh after being so serious most of my life. Since my mother's initial skeptical reaction to my engagement, she had been nothing but supportive. She helped me with the wedding plans, co-hosted my bridal shower with my friend Bonita, and on my wedding day even handed me a blue and white handkerchief to carry with me as my something borrowed, something blue. I saw Jimmie's daughter crying at the wedding, and because our relationship had been so strained, I assumed she was upset—but she told me she was crying because she had never seen her father so happy.

My heart had finally found a place to call home. I knew I had the husband God intended for me, and I accepted his imperfections, as he accepted mine.

At the reception, a friend of ours sang a rendition of "Wind Beneath My Wings," which I dedicated to Jimmie.

During the song Jimmie leaned over, saying, "I'm gonna see how high you can fly."

I gave him a wide smile. "Okay, watch me."

chapter 20

SHIFTING SANDS

On the way home from our honeymoon in Jamaica, Jimmie pulled me into his arms and said, "Listen, I know how much your career means to you, and I know you're not happy in Dixon, doing what you're doing. I want you to know anything you want to do is okay with me. I can retire—my check will follow me wherever you want to go."

This was what I needed to hear: I was growing frustrated with living in Dixon. I had begun to call it "the dead zone." It had nothing to offer me anymore. I was forty-four, ambitious, and eager to get back into a position where I felt like I was making a difference. Once again, I could see that God had taken me in a different direction than the plans I'd mapped out. I kept looking for HR positions in Kansas City.

Jimmie continued working his tough schedule at Northwestern Steel and Wire, with alternating shifts and just one long weekend a month. He sometimes fell asleep sitting at the dinner table. Our life revolved around his work schedule, and he was almost always ill-tempered. I was feeling restless. Dixon Autobody management had embraced and executed all my recommendations, and I was drafting an HR policy manual for them. Every day I prayed for a new assignment.

One day as I returned from my lunch break, I sat quietly in my car before I walked back into my office. The Holy Spirit gently spoke: "Complete all that you promised to deliver, and your assignment will be complete."

Then, as an answer to my prayers, in January of 1997 I received a call from the EEOC. The representative I spoke with wanted to know what it would take to close out my claim against MCI. My heart leaped—this could be the new assignment I'd been waiting for.

"I'd want to come back with my time bridged," I said, "and a salary at the level where I would be if I had never left."

"I can't make any promises," she said, "but I'll get back to you."

Two days later I got another call. Was I open to relocation? I assured the representative that I was, depending on where the job would take us.

Then things started moving quickly. MCI called to interview me, wanting to know if I'd continued to develop and grow my HR experience. I described the seminars I'd attended, the courses I'd taken, and the jobs I'd held since leaving the company.

A few days later, I heard from a man named Fred, who'd be my supervisor if I got this new position—which was based in Cleveland, Ohio. We arranged to have an interview at the Rockford airport.

Jimmie was sleeping after a shift when I got off the phone with Fred. I woke him up and said, "Want to move to Cleveland?" *Hell no*, I expected him to say.

"Yeah, if that's where the job is, it's okay with me," Jimmie said.

The day of the interview, I put on my dress-for-success navy power suit and drove to Rockford. I prayed the whole way there, and then I allowed peace and confidence to wash over me. I was confident that God was the author of this opportunity, and I gave him free reign to do His work.

I found Fred, a rather short white man maybe in his mid- to late thirties. Fred told me about the position, the clients, and the region I would be supporting. I liked Fred, and I felt like he was impressed with me.

On my way home, I called Northwestern Steel and Wire. Jimmie's foreman answered the phone. "Did you get the job?" he asked. I laughed and said I hoped so.

When Jimmie got on the line, I said, "I didn't get an official offer, but I think it's mine."

I got an offer the very next day.

When I told my mother, she shook her head and said, "Poor Jimmie. I hope he knows what he got himself into, because you'll move at the drop of a hat."

I'd never been to Cleveland, and Jimmie hadn't been there in thirty years, so I decided we needed to go see it before I officially accepted the job. Fred gave his approval for a three-day visit to see if our family would want to live in Cleveland.

By this time, Canthon had joined the Army. Preston was still living near Streamwood and working for Sony. Clinton was the only child I had to worry about moving this time.

Within the week, Jimmie, Clinton, and I flew into Cleveland Hopkins Airport. At the car rental agency, we asked about areas to explore. Cleveland is built around Lake Erie, so it's fairly circular—we kept driving around trying to figure out where the downtown was. We visited the Rock and Roll Hall of Fame and drove through suggested areas, trying to picture ourselves living there. By the end of our trip, we concluded that Cleveland offered more for us than life in Dixon.

I signed my offer package, and that was it. We were officially leaving Dixon. Clinton would need to stay to finish out the school year, and Jimmie would stay and continue working until Clinton's school was out at the end of May. I didn't expect Jimmie to care for Clinton while I was gone. My mom said she would take Clinton, but I disliked that idea. When I was explaining my dilemma to Jimmie, he put both hands on my shoulders.

"Listen here," he said, "when I married you, I married those boys. You go do what you have to do, and me and Clint will be fine right here for the next couple of months until he finishes school."

I'd never loved him more than I did in that moment. I'd never had someone share the responsibility for my sons that way. We figured that my mother could help out when Jimmie had overnight shifts, and I'd come back every other week to get the house ready to be sold. Everything was falling into place.

The first week of April 1997, nine months after our wedding, I headed to Ohio to begin my new job as HR Manager. I was energized and excited to be back in the field of work I loved. After living in a hotel for several weeks, I finally found a suburb about twenty-five miles from my office, called Aurora, which was an affluent, quiet bedroom community. I found a nice rental community called Lakes of Aurora, which offered condos and townhomes. Our townhouse offered more square footage than we'd had in Jimmie's house, plus a basketball court for Clint, a pool, and a beautiful pond that would freeze in winter, perfect for ice-skating.

In late April, Jimmie called me in a panic—after working at Northwestern Steel and Wire for thirty-one years, he was leaving ahead of schedule. He'd been planning to stay until May, so freedom was within sight. But when he'd been asked to unload a truck, and the request was outside the realm of his responsibilities, he refused. His supervisor insisted, so Jimmie had walked off the job, gone to HR, and said, "I'm done. You can stick a fork in me. Get my paperwork together, cause I'm retiring today!"

I was glad for him, because he was so excited finally to be free of his grueling schedule and working day in and day out with hot steel. Yet I knew it was going to be a challenge to live on my paycheck alone until Jimmie's pension kicked in—which wouldn't be until September—or the house sold. This was going to have to be a walk of faith.

On Memorial Day weekend, I went back to Dixon to get my husband and son and all our earthly possessions to begin our new life in Ohio. Moving at the beginning of summer made it difficult at first for twelve-year-old Clint to meet kids his age. After a few lonely weeks, though, he began shooting hoops at the recreation area basketball court, and he started to meet some of the guys he'd be going to school with in the fall.

With Jimmie it was harder. I was used to adjusting to new cities, and making friends had never been a priority for me. I also had my job to keep me busy. But moving and starting over was a different experience for Jimmie. He'd come to Dixon when he was twenty-five years old. Dixon was where he had married, built a home, raised a child, and buried his wife, and now, at fifty-six years old, he was leaving all that behind. I watched the light slip out of Jimmie's eyes in those early months, and it broke my heart. What had I done to him? There was nobody in our new community he felt any connection to. He'd gone from working constantly to doing nothing. For a person as outgoing as Jimmie, coming from a community as friendly as Dixon, this move took him completely out of his comfort zone.

He shut down on us—he simply didn't talk. Clint would call me at work and whisper, "Mom, what's wrong with Jimmie? He's just sitting on the front porch staring into space." Jimmie slept all the time. He could fall into a deep sleep while sitting at the kitchen table reading the newspaper. One day Clint called my office, very concerned, and said, "Mom, I think Jimmie's dead!" But he was just sleeping.

Jimmie was a lousy housekeeper and an even worse cook, so there wasn't much I could suggest for him to do. I knew he was dealing with some level of depression, but I couldn't get him to talk about it.

This adjustment wasn't easy for me either. I was working long hours, driving a fifty-minute commute, and having to come home to cook dinner. I often didn't get home until 7:30. Jimmie hated fast food, so I couldn't use that as a solution. He also let me know how much he disliked having breakfast for dinner, my other quick answer for a meal. I was growing resentful, but I tried to hide my frustration. Then I began condemning myself, believing his deceased wife had probably cooked him a good hot meal every night, so I tried to do the same. We were still newlyweds, and neither of us knew how to adjust to the shifted responsibilities in our lives. My resentment showed up in a passive-aggressive way, with me slamming cabinets and huffing around the kitchen. Jimmie stayed silent, watching TV.

Four months into our new life in Cleveland, we admitted that we had to make some compromises. It was a difficult conversation, but as my mother always said, "Nothing beats an understanding." I described how difficult it was trying to juggle everything and see him do nothing. I explained how exhausted I was with my schedule. Jimmie told me, "Listen, if you get home and I haven't tried to cook something, and you don't feel like cooking, just don't worry about it."

"What would we eat?" I asked with a laugh.

"If you and Clint order some pizza or go to McDonald's and I don't want to eat that, just go ahead. I'll be fine," he assured me. The next major hurdle we had to address was how to manage our finances. Jimmie had always been the breadwinner and responsible for paying the bills, but now the roles were reversed. We talked it through and worked out a budget plan that supported our household needs and didn't make Jimmie feel like a kid getting an allowance.

With this conversation and the resulting compromises, some of our unspoken angst was dissolved. We were making progress. After a while Jimmie even began to experiment with cooking. Most of his menus consisted of boiled meals, beans and neck bones or Glory Greens from a can and neck bones. But we soon learned he fried the best pork chops and made the best sour cream cornbread ever.

...

A year after moving to Ohio, on a visit to Dixon in March of 1998, I noticed that my mother had lost some weight. She'd never been a heavy woman, but she'd picked up a few pounds with age. Now it was noticeable that she had shed them. I pointed it out, and she scoffed and said it was just her outfit. "Well, you look good," I said.

A month later, we were all going to Kansas City for Easter to visit Candy for her and her husband's house blessing for their new home. Jimmie, Clint, and I drove from Cleveland to Dixon, picked up Mom, and headed to Kansas City.

On that drive, it was my general rule to limit bathroom stops to just one—but Mom demanded to stop several times, and once she stayed in the bathroom quite a while.

"Are you okay?" I asked when she finally came out.

"Just something I ate this morning," she said brusquely.

In Kansas City, I asked Candy, "Does Mom seem okay to you? Does she look okay?"

Candy shrugged and said she hadn't noticed anything.

When I asked Aunt Kathleen the same question, she said, "She just seems tired." She thought for a moment. "I did notice her taking a lot of aspirin, though."

On the ride back home to Dixon, Mom stopped frequently again. She and I went to lunch in Dixon before Jimmie, Clint, and I returned to Ohio. The slack outfit I'd bought for her made her weight loss even more evident, and she pushed the food around her plate, now and then lifting her fork to her mouth and then putting it down before taking a bite.

"Okay," I said firmly, "I don't know what's going on, but you need to get a doctor's appointment."

"I already have one," she said. "At the Monroe Clinic next week." The Monroe Clinic, about an hour away, was where Mom got her yearly checkups. She was very confident in their medical capabilities. I prodded her for more information, but that was all she would say. I would be in D.C. for training during her appointment, but I told her to call and update me.

A week later when she called, she said she had to have surgery—immediately.

She didn't explain further. I cancelled the rest of my training sessions and got a flight to Chicago, where I caught a bus to Rockford to meet Mom to drive to the Monroe Clinic.

During our drive, my mother talked about my life decisions. She rehashed my marriages and my career choices. "Versie, admit it," she said, "you've spent your whole life trying to prove to me you could make it without a college education. Isn't that what all these promotions and job moves have been about? I get it—when are you going to stop?"

I felt my frustration growing, but I tried to breathe and stay calm. I clenched my teeth.

"Mom," I said, "do you believe in God?"

"Yes, I believe in God," she said, sounding offended. "I had to, to raise *you*."

I gathered my thoughts and continued. "I loved a man, and I married him and had his children, and it didn't work out. When I knew I was going to have to leave him and make it on my own, I went to God and asked Him to make a way for me to be able to take care of my babies. God opened the doors, and I just took every opportunity He presented to me. I was more afraid of failure than I was of the risks I was taking. You, of all people, taught me how to overcome obstacles, and the rest has just been raw faith in God. I've just been trying to raise my boys and prove to *myself* I can survive. I don't have time to even think about proving to *you* I can make it without a degree. Now can you just let it *go*?" I finally took a breath. "Anyway, Melvin has an MBA, and he's still a sales rep. If I had an MBA, I'd be running a company somewhere."

Mom laughed, relenting. She said, "I'm sure you would. I just wish you'd settle down."

"Sometimes I do too," I told her, "but I'm not sure that will ever happen. I promised God I'd go wherever He needs to send me."

Looking back later on this exchange, I thought my mother was trying to justify God's favor in my life. She couldn't reconcile the difference between her own plan for me—a plan that centered on an education like the one she'd pursued herself—and God's, where He was my source.

We spent what was left of the ride talking about the boys. When we arrived at the Monroe Clinic, I got Mom checked in and comfortable in bed, and then we watched her favorite TV show, *Wheel of Fortune*. After that, I went to check into the clinic wing set up like dormitory rooms for patients' family members who stayed the night. I went and got something to eat, and then I returned to check on my mother, who was sleeping. I headed to my room to pray and write, trying to relieve my uneasiness.

The next morning, I went to her room early to speak to the doctor about the surgery, which was scheduled for the following morning. Mom sat in bed silently.

"Okay," the doctor said brightly, speaking to my mother. "It looks like we're all set. When we go in tomorrow, our hope is that the cancer—"

With that single, terrible word, I stopped hearing him. My stomach dropped. I looked at my mother, who stared straight ahead, not meeting my eyes.

"Wait, wait," I said to the doctor. "Wait a second. You're saying she has *cancer*?"

The doctor turned to Mom, confused, and then he understood. He changed his tone. "Yes," he said carefully, "we found some growths in her colon, and the biopsy told us they're cancerous. We're going to go in tomorrow and remove them and determine if the cancer has spread to her lymph nodes." He paused, and then he asked if we had any questions.

I had plenty of questions, but not for him. Once he'd left, I said to Mom. "How long have you known this? Why didn't you tell me?"

At last she looked at me. "What good would it have done?"

I thought furiously. "Why didn't you get the surgery earlier? When we went to Kansas City, you clearly were not well."

"I wanted to be there for the house blessing," she said simply. "I'm glad we went."

And with that, she was finished talking about it.

It fell upon me to deliver this news to everyone else. First Evelyn, because I needed to talk through my shock, and then Candy, Brenda, Melvin, and Aunt Kathleen. I spaced out the calls to center myself. I spent the rest of the evening praying the surgery would show the cancer had not spread.

The next morning, I waited with Mom, spoke with a doctor, and watched as attendants took Mom away on a gurney. The surgery lasted less than ninety minutes. A nurse came to the waiting area and told me the doctor would be down to speak with me soon. She assured me that Mom was okay.

The doctor came in and explained that they had removed the polyps and a portion of Mom's colon and affected lymph nodes. The cancer had entered her bloodstream. She would need chemotherapy. My head was swimming. I asked about a prognosis, and the doctor responded cautiously. "If she responds well to the therapy," he said, "I've seen patients in her situation live five years or more."

Mom stayed in the hospital about a week. Brenda and Melvin came, but Candy had childcare issues and had to stay in Kansas City. The night before Mom was discharged, Brenda, Melvin, and I stayed up all night talking, exchanging childhood memories. We reminisced about our long car trips to Mississippi when we all piled into the family station wagon with Aunt Tutta's kids and drove through the night. I always loved those car trips—the adventure of it and being together. Brenda had hated being so crowded, she said, and Melvin agreed. To this day, he can't stand car trips, whereas I always loved them. I thought about how people could be affected so differently by the same experiences.

Before we went to bed I told Brenda and Melvin, "Tomorrow, I'm going to take Mom back to Cleveland with me to recover. I also want to get her to Cleveland Clinic for a second opinion. If she needs anything, I will take care of it. If I need your assistance, I'll let you know!" I felt protective of my mother, determined to fulfill what I viewed as my responsibility.

So my mother came to live with us in Ohio for the next month. The woman I had feared and loved my whole life was different now, almost apathetic. When I tried to convince her to seek a second opinion at Cleveland Clinic, she showed no interest. I asked her several times to get me her medical records so I could set her up with a doctor, but she simply wouldn't—so I dropped it.

As she regained her strength, we took slow walks together around the complex in the evenings. I wanted to ask some probing questions about our early years, but it was a fragile time, and I didn't want to disturb it with questions that might cause her to withdraw from me. I hoped a better time would come.

My mother enjoyed being with Clinton, but she grew bored. The soft peace we'd had was hardening. I heard her on the phone with friends, saying, "I've got to get out of here." Before she left, she said, "I don't know how you live with that man—all he does is sleep."

On Memorial Day, marking a year that we'd lived in Ohio together, Jimmie and I drove Mom back to Dixon. She was scheduled to begin chemotherapy the first of June. Remembering the doctor's five-year prognosis, I felt confident that Mom could beat the odds. Cancer had never met an opponent like my mother.

While we were in Dixon, we learned that Jimmie's daughter was in some serious trouble, and she wouldn't be able to care for her twenty-two-month-old daughter. I learned that her mother's family was caring for the baby, but nobody was sure what would happen next or who would care for the baby long-term. I thought, *I have to go get her.*

I discussed the whole situation with Jimmie, and Jimmie agreed, but he left everything up to me. I proceeded to put a plan together. I felt I had to go and rescue our little granddaughter.

I went and talked with the family members who had Kecelyn, and they were more than agreeable to having me and Jimmie take our granddaughter to live with us. I bent down to Kecelyn and asked, "Do you want to go bye-bye with me?"

She didn't hesitate. She said good-bye to her cousins, grabbed my hand, and walked out without any tears or second looks. Before I brought her back to Mom's house, where we were staying, I went to the mall and bought her new clothes. I fed her, gave her a bath, and rocked her to sleep in her new pajamas. I had made her a palette next to our bed because I wanted her to feel safe. I stayed with her and watched her sleep a while.

That night, she never cried. But that was the last peaceful night we had, and from that point on our adorable diminutive charge wreaked complete havoc in our household and in our lives. Putting her to bed, either for a nap or for the night, was an ordeal every time. Even seeing her fall asleep was no assurance you were headed for a quiet evening. She had nightmares and woke up screaming. She clung to me, so I was always the one who got up and slept with her so we could get a sliver of rest.

Kecelyn would look us in the face and defy any directive we gave her, and the threat of a spanking provided only temporary relief. She had no impulse control. When we were unable to find disciplinary measures that had any impact on her behavior, I brought her to a child psychologist, who eventually diagnosed her with reactive attachment disorder. The psychologist, although not very hopeful about any relief, recommended some parenting classes to learn behavior modification so that we could provide as much structure as possible. I attended, but Jimmie refused.

The structure and behavior modification worked when I was home to enforce them, but I was the only one enforcing it, and I was often gone at work or on business trips. Jimmie did whatever was necessary to get some degree of relief from his granddaughter's chaotic behavior. Instead of disciplining her, which would cause her to begin screaming, Jimmie just allowed her to run around until she simply lay down on the floor and fell asleep.

Jimmie simply didn't have the patience or capacity to manage her, and I thought I would explode with the anger and frustration I was feeling toward him. Every time I woke up bleary-eyed in the dead of night to quiet her shrill screams, I felt my resentment toward Jimmie growing. I needed him to give me a break.

It was too much to deal with. I was juggling a lot of balls. My job was demanding, I was worried about my mother, I was worried about Kecelyn, and I was frustrated with my husband.

In November of 1998, Mom announced that her chemo had worked—she was in remission. At last, here was some good news, some relief from my worries. Mom took a cruise with a few of her friends, and I planned a big Williams family Thanksgiving dinner at her house to celebrate the news. I made sure all my boys would be there.

At Thanksgiving I noticed that Mom looked exhausted, and when I asked about her cruise, she mentioned that she'd spent a great deal of time seasick. She was on edge, snapping at everyone, which I took as a good sign—she was back to her usual fine form. I was relieved when it was time to return home to Aurora.

I was so tired, and I felt no power against the anger I was dealing with: I couldn't pray it out, talk it out, or write it out. I was angry that Jimmie's daughter had gotten herself into a mess. I was angry about the emotional problems our granddaughter was facing. I was angry with Jimmie for not trying to deal with the situation better or doing more to relieve my load.

One day on my drive to work, as I prayed, God sent me the memory of my wedding vows with Jimmie. The pastor had said, "I remind you that God, who brought you together and nurtured this relationship, is the key to your success as a married couple. Allow God into your marriage, and He will guide your thinking and your actions and bless your home. Call on Him often." Those vows became my promise to God.

There were days when I couldn't stand to look at Jimmie's face or listen to him when he opened his mouth. But day after day, I went straight to God and asked Him, "Please return the joy of my love for Jimmie and erase the anger that I'm feeling."

I called on God often during that time, and He guided me through the battle we were waging, allowing my love for my husband to be refreshed even when none of his behavior changed. Many times my prayer was simply, "Lord, change me." Some days Jimmie and I could laugh at our life or simply shake our heads, and other days we just got into bed and held each other, not saying a word. We were both exhausted, but we needed each other to get through.

Then in early February 1999, we got the news that MCI was being bought out by WorldCom. I got a letter telling me all HR functions would be managed from Chicago. My position at MCI was eliminated.

I didn't tell anyone. I couldn't—I couldn't bear to add another burden to the heap. I worked on my résumé at home on my laptop, and I let Jimmie and Clinton assume I was working from home, which I did often. I went on like this for about two weeks.

Finally I worked up the courage to tell Clinton. One Saturday before he went to basketball practice, he and I were out for breakfast together and I said, "Clint, I got laid off from my job, and I don't exactly know what that means for us. I want to stay here, but I just don't know."

Without missing a beat, Clinton said, "I'm not worried, Mom. You always make sure we're taken care of, so I'm sure whatever you say we have to do will be the answer. Don't worry about me—I'll be fine."

I laughed. It was just the response I'd needed.

I still dreaded telling Jimmie. He'd left his job of thirty-one years, sold his home, and followed me to support me in my dream, and now here I was without a job. After dropping Clinton off at practice, I came home and joined Jimmie at the kitchen table, where he was drinking coffee and reading the paper.

With no preamble, I said, "Jimmie, my position was eliminated and I was laid off."

Jimmie set down the paper. "Okay, what does that mean? Is there something you want me to do?"

"No," I said. "I just need you to have faith we'll be fine."

"Okay," he said. He picked up his paper and took a sip of his coffee. Once he was done, he took a shower. When he was out and dressed, he said, "I'm going to pick up Clint and go for haircuts."

I just looked back at him and nodded. He came over, pulled me to him, and held me. He said, "We'll get through this even if we have to live in a pup tent."

In that moment, my months of anger and resentment fell away. Here was the husband God had sent me.

I didn't have the energy to look for a job outside of Cleveland. The idea of job searching was daunting enough, but with all the other issues resting on my shoulders, I knew I didn't need to also be thinking about starting over in a new city. Every day I played Yolanda Adams's song "The Battle

Is The Lord's," and I prayed, "God, I'm standing still and thanking you for opening the door you want me to walk through."

Before I got too wrapped up in my job search, though, I went back to Dixon to go with Mom to her follow-up appointment at the Monroe Clinic.

This time I thought I knew what we would hear. I suspected the cancer had spread, and I was scared. After some tests and X-rays, the doctor confirmed my fears. The cancer had metastasized to Mom's liver. The new prognosis was that she had six months to a year.

I felt like some mistake must have been made. We were supposed to have three to five years, not one year. *One* year? How could her time left have shrunk so quickly? Everything seemed out of control and moving at such a fast pace. It was so hard to process. Still, hearing the doctor's words, I instantly reassured myself. If he said six months to a year, I was betting that she had at *least* a year.

"I'd like to start you on chemo again," the doctor said.

Mom got angry. "Where's all the research I've been paying for when I donate to the American Cancer Society?" she spewed. "My husband died of cancer twenty-eight years ago, and the treatment is no different today than it was then."

The doctor just looked back at her, his face sad and understanding. While Mom was dressing, he gave me a prescription for pain patches. He said quietly, "Get these for her and use them when she needs them. She's going to be in a lot of pain."

I took Mom to the hospital cafeteria to grab a bite to eat so I could get a little time to myself—I had to grapple with what I'd just learned. I walked around in circles outside, digging deep within myself for any kind of spiritual solace I could find. I refused to cry. I picked up the prescription and went to get my mother and take her home.

When we got into the car, she said, "You just wanted to be alone, didn't you?" It was the first time I ever thought she knew me.

I brought Mom back to her house, where we sat together in the dining room having a cup of tea. My hand shook as I brought my cup to my lips. I felt like I was drowning in disbelief, anger, and confusion. I asked my mother, "Why didn't you get a second opinion when we had a chance?"

She looked me in my face and snapped, "I—don't—know! I've never been sick before. I left that up to you."

I pounded my hand on the table. I yelled back at her, "Well I wish you had told me I could make those decisions for you, because I wouldn't have sat back and done nothing!" Then I jumped up, got my keys, and left. I had to get out. She was throwing some mean punches, and I couldn't fight back.

I was devastated. I kept screaming in my head, "I wish I had known she wanted me to take control—I would have responded so differently." How could she put her health in my hands and never open her mouth? Now I felt like it was my fault that her time on earth was dwindling.

I tried to pull myself together. If she was going to give me responsibility for her care, I was going to do everything within my power to help her. Once I have permission to run things, I run them. I drove to the cancer clinic just outside Dixon and asked if they could take on Mom as a patient, but they said they couldn't. They recommended an oncologist in Sterling, so I drove to see him. He agreed to be Mom's local doctor, which gave me a huge sense of relief—I knew she couldn't keep making the drive to Wisconsin.

When I got back to Mom's house, neither of us mentioned our heated exchange. I just told her I'd gotten her a local doctor, news she accepted with a nod.

For the next several days we stayed busy. As I watched, Mom began the daunting and sad process of getting her business in order. We met with her attorney. She wanted me to help her get her taxes done. I asked if she'd like to go see Aunt Tutta, who was in a nursing home. "Nope," she said sadly. "I've done all I can do for her." I believe Mom knew that if she went to see Aunt Tutta, she would know something was wrong. Mom wanted to spare her sister.

When I called Aunt Kathleen to tell her what was happening, she said, "Well, Versie, it sounds like Zee is getting her business in order. She knows better than the doctors that her time is short. Just do whatever she tells you to do."

"She has more time," I said. "The doctor said she has at least a year."

Mom and I reviewed her will. I noticed her Mercedes wasn't mentioned, and I asked her, "What do you want me to do with your car?"

She looked thoughtful and asked, "I don't know, what do you want to do with it?"

I shared my idea with her. "I want your name to live on in education, so I'd like to create a scholarship in your name. If you leave me the car, I'll sell it and use the proceeds to set up the scholarship." She liked the idea, so we brought it to the attorney.

Mom had me pull out certain boxes and all her investment papers and directed me from her place on the living room sofa as I sat on the floor with the boxes and papers surrounding me. Box by box, paper by paper, we went through everything, and I took notes on how she said she wanted everything handled. She seemed to have thought out every detail, and I took comfort in her usual matter-of-factness. It made me feel the end was still far off.

We laid out a fairly comprehensive plan of action for the next few days; she seemed to have mapped everything out. I wrote it all down so we wouldn't forget anything.

The following day I completed each task as she requested, confidently and robotically moving through the items on our list with her by my side. That evening Mom handed me a notebook and began to run down a list of her life accomplishments. I didn't know what was happening, but I dutifully took notes on what she said. Then I understood—we were working on her obituary.

It was then that the finality of what lay ahead truly hit me. I put down the pen and broke down crying. She didn't get up or try to console me. She didn't say a comforting word. All she said was, "If you can't do it without crying, leave it alone and let someone else do it!"

At that moment I collected my emotions and put them in a private place in my mind, not to be opened again until later. I completed my task.

Next we talked about her funeral service. She said, "I want you to sing, but if you can't do it without crying, don't do it."

"I'll do it," I said. I hesitated. "Do you want me to take you to the funeral home tomorrow to pick out a casket?"

"Nope," she returned. "That's where I draw the line. I'll leave that up to you."

When she was going to sleep that night, I sat at the foot of her bed while she crawled under the covers. We didn't say anything for a while. Before she fell asleep, she reminded me, "Anything that Melvin gave me, let him have it. I don't want y'all fighting over things." I nodded.

The next day, I packed up and prepared to head back home. I'd sent out some résumés and gotten a few bites, so I wanted to get back and start the interview process. Before I set off, Mom reminded me to call her when

I got home, like I always did, so she knew I'd made it back safely. On my way out of town, I went by George and Sylvia's and asked them to check on Mom once in a while to see if she needed anything.

I drove home to Aurora, walked into the house, and went straight to the phone to call my mother. She sounded good—George and Sylvia were visiting, so she was entertaining.

"Well, go ahead and get back to your guests," I said. "I love you."

When I hung up the phone, everything rose inside me. I rushed to our bathroom and allowed some of my sadness to pour out, overtaking me.

Little Keccie came in on my heels, pulling on me. "Nana, what's wrong, what's wrong?" she chirped. I kept crying, my tears flowing uncontrollably, releasing everything I'd held in while I was with my mother.

Keccie ran out to Jimmie. She said, "Papa, Nana's crying . . . tell Nana to stop crying."

Only then did Jimmie come into the bathroom. He asked, "What's the matter with you?" His voice held no sympathy, so I didn't want to bare my feelings to him—I just wanted him out of my space.

"Nothing," I said.

He went to leave, but Keccie kept tugging on him, begging him to comfort me. "Come on, pull yourself together," he said. "You got Kecelyn all upset."

I pushed him out of the bathroom. "This may be the last time I get to call my mother to tell her I made it home okay," I screamed, "and all you care about is me pulling myself together . . . just leave me alone!" I slammed the door. I sat on the edge of the tub, pulled Keccie into my lap, and rocked her. She grabbed a towel and used it to wipe my face.

In all this darkness, I saw glimmers of light when I got interviews at a couple of companies. One was Progressive Insurance. In my interview, I told them my mother was terminally ill and by late summer I may need a leave of absence to be with her. They called a week later and offered me a job.

My new director, Mary, reassured me she was glad to have me on the team, and she said I should just let her know what I needed—she would do her best to accommodate me. In a little less than two months, I'd gotten a job. I gave God all the glory. Now all I had to pray for was the strength to handle the other issues on my plate—Mom and Kecelyn.

Soon after I began working for Progressive, I started questioning my decision to work for the company. I was supposed to support the IT department, but they were facing Y2K concerns and didn't want HR support—they wanted to be left alone, so I was often bored. Plus, Mary had previously been a project manager, so as director of HR, she wanted to manage us like we were working on projects. I had to keep a project chart and show how much time I spent with each of my managers. I was used to more autonomy. I didn't like feeling like I was punching a time clock.

One Saturday afternoon, Sylvia called to tell me that Mom had been admitted to the Dixon KSB Hospital. Mom was as weak as a kitten, Sylvia said, and she'd had to be put on a stretcher at the doctor's office while she waited to be seen. "She seemed to be doing better once they got her to the hospital," she said, trying to reassure me.

Candy was finally able to make a visit and she planned to get there to be with Mom the next day. I'd just been on my job for just three weeks, I told myself—I shouldn't take off work. But I went to bed and tossed and turned. I got up at 1:30 a.m. and packed some clothes. I woke up Jimmie and told him I had to go and see for myself if Mom was okay. He tried to convince me to wait until daybreak, but I wouldn't listen.

I drove all night, stopping only for Mountain Dew and bathroom breaks. I pulled into Dixon around 10:30 a.m. and went straight to the hospital.

When I walked into my mother's room, her face lit up. "I knew you'd come," she said. "Isn't Candy coming, too?" I told her Candy would be there soon. I sat with her until I thought I'd collapse myself, and then I headed over to her house to get some sleep until Candy made it in.

The next morning, on Monday, I got up early and called Progressive to tell Mary where I was. "I expect to be home in a couple of days," I said. Candy and I went for breakfast and then headed to the hospital, where we would meet Mom's new oncologist so he could let us know what was happening.

His news was not good. The cancer was progressing, and he felt Mom was too weak to take anymore chemo, which meant the prognosis was now three to six months. I was devastated. This thing was real—it really was going to happen. The biggest force in my life besides God was moving toward her exit.

They moved Mom to the hospital's cancer floor two days later. I hadn't been at Progressive long enough to accrue time off or qualify for family medical leave. I called Mary and said, "I'll understand if you have to let me go, but I can't leave my mother right now."

Mary just asked me to keep her updated, and she wished us well. At the end of my first full week away from the job, Mary called me first thing in the morning on payday and said, "Carolynn, check your bank account. We don't want you to worry about anything here. We're not going to let you go, and we'll pay you until you can return."

I didn't know what to say. All I could manage was, "Thank you!" I knew what Mary was doing for me was a gift from God. He was taking care of me.

For the three weeks my mother was in the hospital, I never left her side. I had a routine: I'd get there by nine a.m. and stay with Mom until after lunch. I brought her lots of reading material, but she never even looked at any of it, so I read to her or helped her into a recliner while I put lotion on her legs and massaged her feet. After lunch, which she barely ate, I got her into bed for some rest and ran some errands. I never stayed away for more than a couple of hours before returning to spend the rest of the afternoon and evening with her. I took comfort in this routine.

One day while Mom and I were watching *The Price Is Right*, she said weakly, "It's time."

I cut the volume and said, "Time for what?"

She looked at me and calmly said, "You need to go on over and make the funeral arrangements."

I knew I couldn't show any emotion. I asked, "Are you sure?"

She nodded and added, "And I think I'm going to need the pain patches from the house."

"I'll take care of everything," I promised.

We kept on watching TV. When the program ended, Mom turned to me and said, "You were always so much stronger than me."

"What do you mean, Mom?" I asked.

All she would say was, "You just always were."

I went back to the house while she took her afternoon nap. Jimmie had brought Clint to town to see his grandmother, and I told Jimmie what Mom had asked of me.

"She must know she's reaching the end," he said.

I began to cry. "No, that's not possible," I said. "The doctor said three to six months. It's only been two weeks."

Jimmie held me and asked me, "Do you want me to go with you?" Brenda was supposed to come, but she was having car trouble, so Jimmie and I went and made my mother's funeral arrangements.

When I returned to the hospital with the pain patches, I asked a nurse how to apply them. She was the most honest and straightforward woman I met at the hospital. She sat down with me outside Mom's room and gave me her honest evaluation of Mom's situation. She said, "Your mother is a beautiful and proud woman, and she must have been in a lot of pain for quite some time. The fact that she's finally requesting pain medication tells me it's unbearable. I don't think she has months—I believe she has days. I think she would prefer to be taken home to die. Let me get the doctor to set you up for hospice care so you can take her home."

I agreed, but I still didn't accept what she was saying. It was all so surreal.

After that conversation I went for a walk around the hospital. It's hard to explain how painful that conversation felt. It truly registered in my mind that her death was imminent. I could not imagine my life without my mother in it. As tough as our relationship had always been, she was still my mother. I processed everything, pushed my emotions again into a box I could open later, and walked back to Mom's room to watch *Wheel of Fortune* with her.

When I saw my mother she asked, "Did you get everything done?"

"Everything except the burial site," I said. "I'll go with Brenda when she gets into town tomorrow." I thought of how Uncle Narvell had asked to be buried under a shade tree. "Do you have any preferences about the site?"

"No," she said, closing her eyes. "Just get me as close to Cle as you can." After all these years, she still wanted to be with her sister.

Then Mom opened her eyes and looked at me. "I don't want you hanging around here taking care of me," she said. "What about your new job? I don't want you to lose your job watching over me all day."

"Everything's under control," I said. "I've set up a family schedule where we'll rotate weeks staying with you."

"When do you have to leave?" she asked.

I felt the tears gathering, threatening to fall. I turned to the window. I wasn't going to sugarcoat it. I said, "I'm not going anywhere. I'm staying with you until the end."

chapter 21

VALEDICTION

That night I left Mom's room and went back to the house. When I told Jimmie how she'd been talking, he sat down beside me on the sofa and took my hand. "Listen, kid," he said, "I think we should go back up there tonight and spend some time with your mother. It doesn't sound good."

I resisted at first, but I finally agreed. We drove back to the hospital and just sat in Mom's room in the dark. She was sleeping, but it was a restless sleep. She woke up and sensed that I was in the room. "What are you doing back up here?" she asked.

"I just wanted to spend some more time with you," I said.

"I was dreaming about Candy," she said, her voice little more than a whisper. "We did good when we got Candy, didn't we?" I agreed. Then she said sleepily, "She's my baby, too . . . take care of my baby."

I promised her I would and kissed her goodnight.

Driving to the cemetery the next day, I thought about how God had answered my prayer and allowed me to be with my mother during these last days. Taking my mother's care into my own hands was for me the most important assignment of my existence. I needed to do this as my one way of reclaiming my mother. I had spent my entire lifetime sharing her with everyone else. I needed this final time to be just about us. I'm not sure if anyone could understand how important that was for me.

Jimmie met me at the cemetery. I didn't know where Brenda was, so we continued without her: I could get Mom a place down the hill from Aunt Cleretha and Daddy. I didn't want her to be alone, so Jimmie and I bought two plots beside her.

Once we were finished, I went looking for Brenda. When we finally connected, she was upset—she'd already been in town for a couple of hours. She wondered why I hadn't come back to the house and picked her up, and I wondered why she hadn't just come to the hospital, where she should have assumed I would be.

It was only the first of many misunderstandings that would begin to fray the patchwork quilt family. I admit that during that time, I was operating from a different place, one where it was Mom and me against the world, just as I had always thought it should be. Isolating myself this way would end up playing a part in weaving this web of misunderstandings—but I was thinking only of my mother and me.

When Brenda and I brought Mom home, hospice care was set up. They had already briefed us on what they'd be doing in the next few weeks. We were ready.

Brenda was much better at preparing Mom's food than I was, so I was grateful for her to stay a couple more days. I slept in the back bedroom, which had once been her and Daddy's bedroom. I gave Mom a bell to ring to signal me, the same one Daddy had used when cancer stole his voice. She rang it whenever she needed something. I never fully slept. I hovered at the edge of sleep, always ready to respond when she rang the bell.

Taking care of my mother was not easy—she was even angrier at cancer's hold over her than I was. She was often nasty, especially to me. The hospice workers explained that she was lashing out at me because I was the one closest to her. One day when my cousin Roger was visiting, just quietly sitting in her room, she said, "What are you sitting there staring at me for?" Then she snapped, "I don't need you to sit there and watch me die." He got up and left.

The hospice nurse talked to me about the stages of dying Mom would go through. She left me a book to read that clearly laid out the information. One day the nurse asked me, "Has she spoken of seeing dead relatives?" I said she hadn't, and the nurse said, "You might ask if she's seen anybody she was close to who died."

One day after I'd given my mother a sponge bath, I asked, "Mom, have you seen Uncle Narvell or Aunt Cleretha?"

Mom shot back, "*No*, fool, what are you talking about? I haven't seen any dead folks!"

I left the room laughing to myself.

Yet there were also good moments, ones I'm glad we got to share. One afternoon she seemed to be picturing our lives once she was gone. She said, "Well, I'm glad you've got Jimmie. You finally seem happy, and I can see you really love each other. Use the money I'm leaving you to get your life straight. I'm so glad Candy and Gerald finally got settled. There should be enough money for her to send my babies to college."

One of the hospice workers told me that the pain patches I was giving Mom would be insufficient to manage the kind of pain she must be in. Her liver was full of cancer, and it had metastasized into other organs. The nurse explained that Mom was so focused on her pain that she couldn't relax and release herself, so she asked me to begin giving her morphine by mouth.

She added, "It's also important for you to tell her it's okay to let go."

I told her, "One thing I know is my mother does not need my permission to die. If anything, she'll resist just because I told her." We laughed.

When I started giving my mother the morphine, she resisted, saying, "What is this you're making me take?"

"It's for your bowels," I said. She relented and placed the pill on her tongue.

On Sunday morning, April 11, 1999, my mother rang her bell and I ran to see what she wanted. By now Candy had left, and Melvin had come for his shift helping out. Mom began barking out orders: "Get me out of this bed. I need to eat so I can get my strength back. I want some rice, poached eggs, and toast, and I want to eat it at the dining room table! Versie, you make the rice. Melvin, you fix my poached eggs!"

Our efforts would have been comical to watch. Neither Melvin nor I knew how to make poached eggs. The only rice I knew how to prepare was instant rice, and all she had was the real stuff that took forever to cook to the consistency she could eat. We made a valiant effort.

Once Melvin and I had completed our cooking assignments, we got Mom into a wheelchair and brought her to the dining room table to eat her overcooked poached eggs and hard rice.

Mom began to eat the eggs and rice. She complained, "Y'all sho don't know how to cook." Then she immediately vomited it all up.

She refused to go back to bed, so Melvin and I cleaned her up and took her to the sofa, where she collapsed. She was exhausted. She looked uncomfortable, but we didn't want to disturb her.

Around noon, when city churches had let out, people began coming over to visit. We got Mom back into her hospital bed, and for the next five hours, she greeted guests and talked with them. She seemed to come alive for each new visitor. She laughed and joked with everyone and seemed to savor each moment.

My mother had been asking after her good friend James, but he had yet to arrive. Around six p.m., the doorbell rang, and I was relieved to see James standing on the porch when I opened the door. She so badly wanted to see him.

I heard them talking and laughing for a while, and then she called for me to come back. Her bed, I saw, was badly soiled. I asked James to step out so I could clean Mom up, but he was tired from his journey from Louisiana, so Melvin offered to take him to where he was staying. As James was leaving, my mother said to me, "Take care of him. Get him some place to stay."

I cleaned my mother up. Her bed was soiled all the way down to the mattress, so I got her up and into the wheelchair so that I could strip the bed. In a conversation we had many years before, I told Mom that if she ever got sick, I would do anything it took to care for her except wipe her butt. Now here we were.

She had assisted me as I got her into the wheelchair, but when I tried to get her back into the bed, she was unresponsive—dead weight. It took all my strength to get her back into bed, and I grew afraid I'd pulled out her catheter in my effort to move her. I called the hospice and asked them to send someone over to check on her. A nurse arrived within a half-hour, she adjusted the catheter, and she told me to increase the morphine to every four hours.

Mom had found new strength that day and acted like her old self, so I was hopeful. I called Jimmie before I went to bed and told him, "I think I need to come home. Mom is mean as she can be, and I don't need my final memories of her to be her yelling at me, calling me a fool. I can't take anymore! Her friend from Chicago is due in tomorrow, and as soon as she gets to the house, I'm coming home."

I was up by six a.m. and prepared Mom something to eat, but she didn't wake up to ask for it. I figured she was worn out from the previous day's activities—she'd probably be awake soon, yelling for breakfast, I thought.

A hospice worker arrived at ten a.m. to check on her.

"I'm leaving later this afternoon, as soon as she wakes up," I told her.

"I wouldn't leave if I were you," she said. "This is the end. You need to call the family."

I pulled away from her. "You're wrong," I said. "She's just tired! She had a lot of company yesterday, and it wore her out. I shouldn't have let so many people come in. Watch, she'll get her rest and wake up and be just fine."

The nurse said, "Take a look at the urine in her bag. When I came by last night, I emptied it. There should be more in here. Her system is shutting down."

"She's been asleep," I protested. "She hasn't had anything to drink."

"Keep an eye on it," she said. "I doubt much more fluid will accumulate. That will be your sign."

I wouldn't let the hospice worker touch my mother. I wanted her to get her sleep.

After the hospice worker left, Melvin took me by my shoulders and tried to reason with me. "You need to call Candy and Brenda," he said. I refused. I was certain she was going to wake up, and I hated Melvin for being so negative.

The hours slipped away, and I kept watching that bag. I thought I saw urine in it. I couldn't give up—I wouldn't. I went for a walk, trying to see my life without my mother in it. I couldn't create an image that helped me accept losing her.

When I got back from my walk, Reverend Darby from Second Baptist was getting out of his car. Mom wasn't a member of Second Baptist.

"What are you doing here?" I asked.

Reverend Darby kindly explained that he was the chaplain on duty for hospice care, and he'd been told he needed to come by.

At that moment it all became real, crumbling down around me. I collapsed into Reverend Darby's arms and cried.

I went back in the house and called Brenda and Candy. "I guess it's time for you to come home," I told them. I called Preston and all the cousins. I couldn't reach Canthon, who was in Killeen, Texas. I asked Reverend

Darby to find him for me and tell him to come to Dixon. "I can't do this without my sons," I said.

Then I went back into her room and sat with her. I played Della Reese's "Walk With You," the theme song for *Touched by an Angel*, over and over again. Mom loved that show and that song. I stayed by her bed and watched and waited for some sign she would wake up. I talked to her, but I did not cry.

When Preston came, he locked himself in her room so he could have some time alone with her. He asked me if she could hear him, and I said I'd been told she could. Preston had been her first grandchild, and she loved him dearly.

One by one, everyone went in and said goodbye.

By midnight the entire family had gathered. I asked for all of us to gather in her room to hold hands and pray. I asked my brother-in-law, Candy's husband, to lead us in prayer, and I sang one of the songs Mom wanted to be sung at her funeral, "Swing Low, Sweet Chariot."

After all that, I simply said, "Mom, we're all here now. It's okay for you to go."

We quietly filed out of her room, and all of us found spots where we could sit in quiet vigil, waiting for Mom to complete her transition.

A few hours later Candy went to the linen closet looking for a blanket. She came back into the living room and announced, "Well, at least she's not making that funny breathing sound anymore."

We all leaped to our feet and ran into the bedroom, knowing what the end of the death rattle meant.

• • •

Even in dying, my mother had shown no evidence of the pain she was experiencing. She took her life in her hands and managed her exit much as she had tried to manage her life. She was silent and in control. Mom hadn't called out anyone's name or looked into the mid-distance like she was seeing something invisible, like you see on TV. Instead she waited until we'd all arrived and quietly slipped away. I'm sure that when her heavenly escorts came for her, she told them, "Okay, I've done all I can do for them—let's go."

I moved into action. I knew just what I was supposed to do. I went to the phone to begin making the necessary calls, and Candy followed me, crying. "Vers, she's gone," she said. "What are we going to do now?" I put my arms around my little sister and said, "We're going to rejoice, because she doesn't have to suffer anymore. She's finally free." I never dropped a tear.

I noted the time of death, or at least the time when we discovered she had passed: 3:45 a.m. I called the hospice. They came and confiscated the drugs and told me to call the funeral home. When the funeral director arrived, I went with him back to Mom's room to kiss her goodbye one last time. I was surprised she was still warm. I asked them not to zip her up in the black bag. I didn't want to see her looking like she was being rolled out in a garbage bag being carried to the garbage dump.

The day before the wake, we went to the funeral home to preview her body. They had the sign-in book open for us to see. Melvin read her obituary, and when he read the part that stated she was survived by two children and two stepchildren, he voiced his disapproval for being called a stepchild. Brenda was quick to remind him, "Well, that's what you are. We did have a mother, you know."

Before the funeral, Jimmie gave me a pep talk before we went into the sanctuary to remind me Mom did not want me crying. Throughout the ceremony, I lived up to my promise, even when I heard my oldest son crying, completely torn apart in his grief. I wanted to hold him in my lap and rock him when I heard him crying so hard. When I sang the song my mother had requested—"If I Can Help Somebody"—I sang with my eyes shut so I could hold it together.

After the funeral, when we went to First Methodist Church for the funeral repast, my mind kept taking me back to the cemetery. I was sorry I'd dressed my mother in that flimsy peignoir; I should have given her warmer clothing. I wanted to return to the cemetery to see if she was okay.

From that point on, I completely retreated into my circle of one. I didn't do it on purpose, it just happened—I shut everyone else out. I felt as though a part of me had died with my mother. I gathered up my clothes to leave the house, which was no longer Mom's home or mine. Upon her death it had become the property of Melvin and Brenda. We all agreed we would come back in June to put her things in order.

When I returned to Aurora, I felt like I was falling apart, like I was dead inside. It was a devastating, gut-wrenching time. I was trying to process the pain and all the emotions I had pent up for years. I had a difficult time working or being around people. I retreated into my own thoughts and grief while still trying to appear okay.

Then, when my pain was still so raw, things got even worse. When we returned to the house in June, we discovered that Melvin had secretly packed up all the possessions he wanted or felt he deserved, without allowing any of us to choose. He chose not to return to the house with the rest of us, as we had agreed. Instead he gave Brenda instructions to get him more things. Mom had raised four children, yet so soon after her death, the family she had given up her life for was being torn apart through greed, lies, and misunderstandings.

What we found in my mother's house only deepened my grief and confusion. First I found items of mine that I had thought were lost, but that Mom obviously pilfered from my home. There were personal photos of me and Greg and the wooden carved sign Mom apparently stole from our porch. Why would she want these things?

And then I found the box, the secret box in the basement that it seemed my mother had left there just so I could find it, a trove of secrets she had kept. The contents of this box shook me to my core. My three birth certificates, each bearing different variations of my and my mother's names. All my life, I'd been telling people they would know my name, and I hadn't even known it myself. Aunt Tutta's and Regina's letters: Your daughter needs you. Come and take care of your daughter. The realization that my mother, always so quick to rescue other children, had not rescued me.

The contents of the box brought up so many questions—about my past, and about the decisions my mother had made that had shaped both of our lives.

As I began uncovering more information and putting together the pieces of the puzzle, I was amazed at the lies my mother had told, the duplicitous life she'd led. I was shocked. These discoveries, especially when I was already wracked with grief, completely devastated me.

Just before we left Dixon to return to our respective homes, Brenda, Candy, and I went to Dixon Monument to choose Mom's headstone. I knew I wanted Mom's face etched on the headstone, along with a scripture—Proverbs 31:10–31—that idealized her and gave her the image I wished for. The proprietor said, "With the base you've selected, you'll have room to have all her children's names inscribed on it." I put off making that decision.

As we said goodbye, Candy hugged me and said, "Whatever it costs, I'll pay my part." Brenda hugged me but didn't mention making a contribution. She may have assumed Mom had left money to cover it, but because everyone had been left some portion of her estate, I had hoped her headstone might be a collaboration, a symbol of the family she had brought together.

During the months that followed, Brenda and I would speak on the phone and exchange frequent emails, but neither of us ever brought up the headstone or paying for it.

I told Jimmie, "I like the idea of having our names on the base of the headstone, but I will speak the truth—I'll just put mine and Candy's names on it!" Jimmie strongly discouraged me for fear of the backlash this decision would draw. He urged me to put no names on the headstone. He could see the road this decision would take me down.

But the crisis I was dealing with was about me. I was the only one who knew what I was feeling. It was *my* truth, and nothing mattered to me except setting the record straight. I had tried to live the life my mother designed for me, even when it felt like a straightjacket restricting the truth from flowing. I wanted to be free of the lies. It was time to shed the ugliness from my spirit, like a butterfly breaks free of its ugly cocoon, spreads its wings, and flies away, free of the past.

I told myself I was reclaiming my mother. I felt that a wrong had been inflicted on me my entire life, and now I had to right it. *She was MY mother.* That is all I felt. I wanted to reclaim her. After all, I told Jimmie, Brenda had said it herself—she and Melvin had their own mother.

So when I received the call from Dixon Monument asking what to put on the base of the headstone, I made my final decision. I instructed them to chisel the words on my mother's headstone: *Mother of Carolynn and Candace.*

That put the final tear in the patchwork quilt family. Brenda sent me a scathing email telling me she never wanted anything more to do with me. Then she and Melvin cut off all communication with me. For years there was only silence between us. Now I felt not just alone, but also betrayed, and I didn't know which was worse.

My spirit shut down on me. It was like I was disconnected from everything. I would get into my car and just drive around Aurora, not wanting my husband or my son to know the depth of my despair. I would drive and scream, yelling and crying at Mom and at God, trying to scream out the pain, hoping to erase the words that still played in my head. I would have vivid flashbacks to when she died. Whenever I settled a piece of her estate, I would have a dream where she was still alive. Seeing her in these dreams was so vivid. I would tell her, confused, "I knew you weren't really dead."

She was gone, but I still needed answers. I desperately wanted some final words from her. I needed to hear her validate me in some way. The child in me wanted to be held and hear her say, "I always loved you."

More than a year passed this way. Then, little by little, I started feeling better. I began feeling like I'd gone through a cleansing. There started being longer stretches of time when I wasn't sad.

In June of 2003, four years after Mom's passing, Clinton graduated from high school, and I held a graduation celebration for him. I sent invitations to all the family members who had touched Clinton's life, and I decided to invite Brenda. I didn't expect a response, but I decided I wouldn't leave her out. I was surprised when she called and said, in a Brenda-like blunt tone, "I'll be there!" I was elated. I had missed having her in my life.

A few days later I got a call from Melvin. "I hear you're having a party and didn't invite me. If you don't mind, we're coming too." I didn't mind at all. I would have invited him too, but I didn't think he'd come from California for a high school graduation party.

Candy and her family were there, and so were all of Aunt Tutta's kids. I was ready for the healing to begin. They came to the party, and we never discussed the past. We simply picked up where we'd left off.

The threads of the patchwork quilt had not been completely torn, and the family bond created through Mom and Aunt Cleretha still had life. We started out as cousins, we became siblings, and now we are just family. And now, when we talk about Mom, we all agree that we have no idea what would have become of us if she hadn't made the sacrifices she did.

・・・

Everything has a meaning, and everything has a purpose. Sometimes you just have to keep on living to understand it all. Now I understand that I was meant to know my mother. She had to play her role in my life. I miss her, but I don't miss how she made me feel. I'll never know what it took to be her, but I no longer judge her. I see that her death released me, and what remains is love and respect.

I like how my mother shows up in me. She taught me so much. She waged the battles that life presented and overcame the obstacles that threatened to block her dreams, and on her journey she touched and empowered so many. I love her for her fight, her passion, and her determination, and I believe she passed these on to me, giving me the strength and resilience I would need to push through my perceived limitations.

Now I dream of my mother often, and the dreams are always so peaceful. Most often I dream the two of us are walking quietly through a park, stopping to sit on a bench in a garden. Her face always looks so soft and kind. We talk, although I never remember the conversation. We laugh together and she lovingly pats my hand, and then she gets up and walks away alone. I believe God sends me these dreams to let me know my mother is finally at peace.

God's sovereign hand made no mistake. I was born into His perfect design for my life. I sincerely believe He purposely chose me for the assignment of my birth. He knew who my earthly parents would be. He knew all the challenges I would face being the daughter of Zelodious Williams-Ashford, and He equipped me with what I would need to thrive in an environment filled with so much change and uncertainty, rejection and disdain. Through it all He was preparing me for kingdom work.

In my life, I've learned many lessons of empowerment through spoken words. My mother's lesson to hold my head erect, commanding all men's respect, gave me stature beyond my 5'4" frame. The restlessness and tugging I felt as a young child was God speaking into my spirit, reminding me that before I was in my mother's womb, He knew who I was, and there was nothing anyone could do to destroy the destiny He had designed for me. He taught me He had orchestrated the events in my life—not to destroy me, but instead to prepare me for the future only He could see, to accomplish His purpose for me.

God proved to me He was always my source, my only source. The betrayals and the adversities, the abandonment and the rejection taught me how to push through my perceived limitations to discover the unlimited power and authority God had placed within me.

I will teach others the same.

EPILOGUE

A year after Mom's passing, I wished she could have been here to see the start of the fourth generation when my first granddaughter, Imani-Grace, was born. I imagined calling Mom and planning a road trip to see her first great-grandchild. She would have been so proud.

In 2002 when I was promoted to vice president of Human Resources, Mom was the first person I wanted to call. And what would she have said when, in 2006, I moved into the C-Suite of a Fortune 500 company as the only female and the only African American to become the companies first chief diversity officer?

Before I understood that life and death are in the power of the tongue, I used my words as a spade, trying furiously to uproot the images of myself that the world was trying to plant within me. My words gave me a sense of empowerment and strengthened my image. My words were all I could stand on to protect my spirit.

I spent my whole life saying, "One of these days you're going to know my name." I finally came to understand that was what God was saying to me. It was His name I would know.

God has shown me that there truly was a battle I had to fight. It was the battle of faith. He struck preemptively to protect me when forces of evil—abortion and rejection—came against me to utterly destroy me, and then He kept fighting for me throughout my life. He strategically placed people into my life to speak up for me and speak strength into me. Satan knows an inferior spirit can't accomplish great things, so Satan tried to use people's words to destroy my identity, kill my spirit, and strip me of my destiny. But greater was the God in me.

I spoke words aloud when I was thirteen, trying desperately to establish my independence and gain control of my life. Those words were the seeds that took root in my heart and shaped the way I lived. In the end, this was my most difficult dependence to break—my self-reliance, the way I leaned on my own wit and personal strength, my own words.

I had to relinquish all this and realize that God was the one in control. I had to conquer my fear and my pride. I am still working to grow in these areas. There are always more lessons to be learned.

Isaiah 61:3 (KJV) says, "To appoint unto them that mourn in Zion, to give unto them beauty for ashes, the oil of joy for mourning, the garment of praise for the spirit of heaviness; that they might be called trees of righteousness, the planting of the Lord, that he might be glorified." After my years of ashes, God gave me so much beauty and planted me in places to display His glory. Challenges never stopped rising up before me, but every time I pushed through them, I saw the power of God within me showing me the way.

I was stretched to discover my own resiliency, challenged to build new levels of faith, and broken to learn where my strength comes from. I don't stand in anybody's shadow anymore. I am the bold and bodacious woman God says I am.

It is my prayer that this book helps to strengthen your spirit, forging it like tempered steel. I hope it inspires you to PUSH—persevere until something happens. The limitations and struggles you perceive are the battles being fought in the heavenly spheres, with the forces of evil working to prevent you from completing your assignment and fulfilling your destiny. Don't cower—instead, step out on faith and PUSH!

I hope this book inspires you to embrace the person God created you to be. We are all God's handiwork, gifts to this world. I've learned that God can use not only our greatest accomplishments, but also our greatest failures to accomplish His will. He knew who we were before we entered our mothers' wombs, and He designed long before we were here the good works He needed us to do. To move forward on our path, we must choose between fear and faith and then be prepared to PUSH.

God taught me in my youth, and now that I am grey-headed, I will use my experiences to declare the strength and power of God to this generation and the ones to come. Aunt Tutta was right—God did have something for me to do, and I do it every day by trusting Him and being obedient to whatever He commands me to do.

Every day I will listen with great expectation and excitement for what is yet to come.

www.ingramcontent.com/pod-product-compliance
Lightning Source LLC
Chambersburg PA
CBHW030818090426
42737CB00009B/783